STRUTTING AND FRETTING

Strutting and Fretting

STANDARDS FOR SELF-ESTEEM

Jann Benson and Dan Lyons

University Press of Colorado

The University Press of Colorado is a cooperative publishing enterprise supported, in part, by Adams State College, Colorado State University, Fort Lewis College, Mesa State College, Metropolitan State College, University of Colorado, University of Northern Colorado, University of Southern Colorado, and Western State College.

The paper used in this publication meets the minimum requirements of the American National Standard for Information Sciences—Permanence of Paper for Printed Library Materials. ANSI Z39.48–1984

Library of Congress Cataloging-in-Publication Data

Benson, Jann, 1936–
    Strutting and fretting: standards for self-esteem / Jann Benson and Dan Lyons.
— 1st ed.
      p.   cm.
    Includes bibliographical references and index.
    ISBN 0-87081-192-4 (cloth). — ISBN 0-87081-193-2 (paper)
    1. Self-respect. 2. Honor. 3. Shame. 4. Ethics—Psychological aspects.
5. Values—Psychological aspects. I. Lyons, Dan, 1930– . II. Title.
BJ1533.S3B48 1990
170'.44—dc20   90-13120
                                                            CIP

Cover illustration by Kristin Geishecker.

Contents

Preface

By what standards do individuals develop, heighten, or diminish their self-esteem? How should they decide what values to strive to uphold? A partial answer to such questions gets much attention from parents, teachers, religious leaders, and philosophers. They speak in detail of moral standards, and people feel at ease talking about that subject. Two uncomfortable emotions, guilt and shame, serve to reinforce behavior that follows the moral standard. People are supposed to be decent to each other and to do things for each other.

But morality is only a partial answer to questions about self-esteem. Not all standards people wish to uphold are strictly moral. Of the two sanctioning emotions, shame is far more feared than guilt, and it often occurs over a failure that has nothing to do with morality. Individuals find it important to accomplish feats that others admire — to be promoted in their jobs, to create, to discover, to feel that something got done in their lives. People often plan an action with a desire to achieve, not because it is required by morality. What's more, people naturally have the desire to avoid being laughed at or cast aside or disgraced. They want to avoid humiliated shame. Again, humiliation doesn't always mean that a person has been immoral. Sometimes it just happens because of a weakness or deformity that signifies no moral fault.

In this book we examine the standards of self-esteem under four categories. Two of them are moral: decency and beneficence. The other two are quite separate from morality: honor and achievement. Our concern is that the neglect of these latter two has skewed social dialogue about values in a dangerous way. Since the latter two don't get a hearing in discussions (and training) about morality, they escape coming under the same weight of examination. Yet honor and achievement still play an important role in determining what people do and how they feel about themselves.

Our purpose here is to expand social dialogue about self-esteem to include nonmoral values. The common belief that shame is only a childish way of feeling guilty neglects the power of shame to direct people into destructive or noble ways. Humiliation is an emotion so fearsomely painful that one may be tempted to violate morality in order to avoid it. This happens at all levels of humanity: Nations vie for dominance on the world scene, and the child on the playground violently strikes out at a fellow who has insulted him.

We discuss the four categories of standards in three stages. Chapters 1 through 4 are introductory. There we distinguish between guilt and shame, and we show why all four categories need attention if one is really to understand standards of self-esteem. Chapters 5 through 7 discuss minimal standards for avoiding guilt and shame, standards we call limit norms. Chapter 5 examines decency on a commonsense level and gives an overview of everyday intuitive morality. Chapter 6 takes up the subject of honor; a subject that may not seem as close to common sense because it is rarely discussed in our country. We expect, however, that the ideas will strike a familiar chord for readers once they reflect on them. Chapter 7 presents some complex relations that norms of decency and honor bring about between the individual and community. The remaining chapters add the concept of a goal to our discussion. This requires thinking about all four types of norm at once. The relations among these types can become quite complex. Readers will find some shifts in the level of reading difficulty as they progress through these three stages.

We make some absolute-sounding points here without qualification. We do this not in order to pontificate but for the opposite reason. Before careful, technical discussion of these themes is possible, a general airing must first take place. Our broad claims, we hope, will provoke vigorous objections and thus start a lively dialogue.

For simplicity we have referred to ourselves in the first person singular and have not distinguished between us as voices. The reader may wish to keep in mind that one of us is a man and one a woman.

What many may notice as unusual for current style is that much of our language is sexist. This is not because we are sexists. Rather, the conventions we speak of are often themselves sexist, and that forces us to use examples that mention men as main participants more often than women. Avoiding sexist language in every case would therefore make the examples distractingly artificial. Until recently our society has not seemed collectively aware of the plain fact that women as well as men are committed to accomplishing goals. Even now, we find many people surprised at the notion that a woman's honor might be more than chastity or pride. It is a little comical, because odd, to speak of a woman upholding her nonsexual honor. But it ought not to be comical. After all, women as much as men want to avoid shame. And women as well as men wish to achieve things recognized as worthwhile. That they have been left out of the mainstream of achievement and honor is a symptom of sexism we hope this book will throw light on. Woman's honor is a subject large enough to require another book. We have covered it here only enough to indicate directions for deeper treatment.

We have addressed ourselves to the general, thoughtful reader. No sources elsewhere discuss the uncomfortable but universal notion of *warrants* for self-esteem. We think this discussion will illuminate literature, social philosophy, psychology, and women's studies, when those fields touch on self-esteem.

A note on our way of handling text citations for quoted passages — we've kept footnotes out of the text. In the back of the book, a Notes section has all the references; page numbers in the text are listed, each with a note identifying the passage on that respective page.

Last, we'd like to acknowledge the help of Mary Lyons and Pat Shade, who read the whole manuscript and made spirited and useful suggestions. (In the end, though, we rejected Mary's suggested subtitle: *The Jann/Dan Way to Emotional Fitness*.) The following people offered us great assistance: Bill and Ginny Slauson, Diane Van Loo, Bob Harker, and Mike McCullough, as well as the students in Benson's class in Philosophy and Literature. We also want to thank Jody Berman, Alice Colwell, Carol Humphrey, and the other staff members at the University Press of Colorado for their patient help in shaping the book.

STRUTTING AND FRETTING

Chapter 1

Judging Ourselves and Others

Look back to a time when you were talking before a group of people and you forgot what you wanted to say next. You paused and said "uh" several times. The people waited patiently, though they were uncomfortable. In fact, it seemed to everyone like an eternity, when it was really only a few seconds. Then the "uhs" gave way to the words you wanted. The listeners shared your relief and became even more interested. The rest of your talk went well enough.

But afterwards you relived those eternal few seconds, wondering why there was that flaw in your speech. Maybe you vowed never to give another speech. Maybe you resolved next time to memorize better. Or maybe you talked yourself into ignoring your lapse, reminded yourself that everyone knew the right words would finally come.

What was so uncomfortable, so anxious, about those seconds filled with "uhs"? Why do we regret such moments later, try hard to forget them? Why are they all the more painful if the listeners are especially patient, waiting quietly with tense heads and mouths partly open, encouraging your words to come?

We know the answer: Those few seconds are embarrassing. Worse, they are humiliating.

Someone who analyzes his feelings might say that what was uncomfortable in those seconds was the hot blush in his cheeks. He might recall the anger he felt when, during his eternity of "uhs," he saw one woman move her jaws just a little — as if to remind him of his next sentence. He hated her then, and he hated her afterwards. He can't help it — only with great self-control can he be civil to her even now.

But why should he hate her? How did she enrage him? After all, she showed no hatred or ill will toward him; in fact, she showed a helpful feeling.

And why did the anger relieve somewhat the unbearable hot blush? For that matter, why was the blush so unbearable? The answer is the same again. The "uh" time was humiliating. It was even more humiliating that someone else noticed how humiliating it was and wanted to help. The anger felt better than the humiliation.

Almost *any* emotion feels better than humiliation. This is a feeling so painful that we're humiliated even to talk about it. Most people would rather talk about how angry they were or how guilty they felt. It's easier to say, "Her sugary sympathy enraged me" than to say, "She witnessed my humiliation." It's easier to say, "By my bad preparation I let that audience down, made them wait and squirm" than to say, "I just forgot what to say next; I was mortified!" (We *can* say this last thing and even laugh at ourselves — much later.) In this book I want to talk about humiliation — which is so very difficult to talk about — and other emotions related to humiliation. I think these emotions are important in people's lives; if people only understood them better, they'd lead happier lives.

Norms and Normative Judgments

Why did our cool, rational speaker feel such painful humiliation that it felt good to cover it with anger? He had expected to perform perfectly, and he didn't do quite that well. But this answer seems too simple. If he were alone, practicing the speech, he'd just look at his notes when he faltered or forgot. Then he would simply try again without the notes; eventually he'd get it right. So it was not just that he failed temporarily at what he was trying to do. It was that woman watching him that hurt so much, and her disgusting attempt to help — her humiliating attempt to help. The discomfort comes from two sources; not living up to his own expectations and someone's noticing that failure.

Let's call the idea behind his self-expectation a norm. A norm is a kind of rule or standard for judging actions and people. We might say that he set a standard for himself but did not live up to it. He made a *normative* judgment about what he should accomplish, then he failed to measure up. The woman who angered him, who saw him fall below his own standard, sympathized and tried to help. This made things worse. The very sympathy she displayed made his standards public. (He couldn't pretend that he found the difficulty merely amusing; he knew that she knew better.) That's why she enraged him. It's not just having a standard we don't live up to that marks humiliating failure. It's the social aspect that marks it: Maybe someone else also accepts that same criterion and then notices that, by that standard, we have failed. We set standards for ourselves every day. Any time we try to do something, we need some idea of what will count as having done it. When we judge about how we ought to act or how we ought to do something, we are making normative judgments.

Suppose you set out to paint the house. First you decide what supplies you need. You must already have a norm in mind to settle that, from knowing how much area needs painting, what areas need tape-shielding, and so forth. Your list is the record of the things you think you ought to buy for the job; it is a normative guide. Driving to the hardware store, you decide which road to take, which way to turn, from a normative idea of "the best way" to get there. In the store you mark off each item as purchased. There is a pleasant sense of accomplishment as you scratch off the last item. You feel an even greater sense of accomplishment when you've finished painting the house, especially if it is well done. The fact that you can judge whether the job was well or poorly done shows that you made some normative judgments about how it should be done. When you decided what you ought to buy and whether your job was well done, you were making normative judgments. These are judgments that guide action.

Normative judgments are involved even in the simplest parts of our lives, even though we may not notice what those judgments are. We become more conscious of these judgments when other people know we've made them, because then others will know when we succeed by our own standards. And if we fail to measure up according to our own norms, then those other people — the observers — will know we failed. That makes failure much worse! That's why the man who faltered in his speech was so humiliated when he saw the woman sympathize with him.

The normative judgments I have been talking about are personal in the sense that some one person has been setting norms for himself or herself alone. But society sets norms, too. That just means that many people agree on what norms they should try to live up to, and they will tend to judge themselves and each other according to these norms. We may call these *social norms*. A social norm holds wherever most (but not necessarily all) people agree about some guide to action.

Some of these norms have to do with morals. People usually feel guilty when they cause someone else distress or pain. Even if they don't feel guilt at the time, they may feel it later. For instance, think of someone who double-crossed a friend, or stole a boyfriend or girlfriend, or laughed cruelly at another person. We expect that person, or someone with normal kindly feelings, to be a little "queasy" about it. Normal decent people feel guilty when they hurt others. They know that if someone tramples them after they do something mean, they have no complaint. It's not because we all have guilt complexes or are eager to judge each other. It's because we have generally accepted the moral norm that people should be kind rather than cruel to each other. So even though a young woman stole a friend's boyfriend when he liked her better, most people would think she was hardhearted if she didn't feel a little bad about it. We expect her to feel guilty because she is normally a goodhearted and friendly person.

Nonmoral (Aesthetic) Norms

Not *all* our social norms are related to morality. We have norms about how houses are supposed to look, about what sort of job we can be proud of, about personal good looks and ugliness. These we can call aesthetic norms.

For instance, it has been a normative judgment in our society for several decades that women and girls are ugly if they are overweight. This is different from many other cultures where storing extra weight is considered a mark of beauty in a woman. But in our society (for the last sixty years or so) plumpness has been considered a mark of failure as far as looks are concerned. Consider the following letter to Abigail Van Buren:

DEAR ABBY: I am a 9-year-old girl who has juvenile rheumatoid arthritis. To treat my symptoms I take a heavy daily dose of cortisone. Until my illness I was a normal kid in size and appearance, but the medicine I take has made me "moonfaced" and very heavy. Abby, many of the kids at school call me names and tease me because of my weight, and lately it's been hurting me.

What's the best way to make my classmates understand that I can't help the way I look, and it's not from eating too much sweets?

— FAITHFULLY YOURS, WAITING IN MASS

DEAR WAITING: You need not be ashamed to tell your classmates exactly what you have told me. Please do. When they learn the truth, I bet they'll stop the teasing and name-calling. Please write again and give me a progress report. I care.

Abby answers this letter with a great deal of sympathy because the girl can't help being overweight. She knows she can't help it, and maybe even her classmates know that, too. But the normative rule against obesity is so strong that they think of that first. They have perhaps not thought through how much it hurts her feelings when they apply that rule to her. They have not thought through how humiliated they would be if they were in her place. The mean little children may not have thought about Abby's moral norm, but they have not made a mistake about the norm against being overweight. There are two social norms involved here, and they conflict. One is against causing pain; the other, against being ugly. Abby clearly does not want to break it to the little girl that this is so.

Knowingly or not, people hold standards of esteem. In an episode of a well-known cartoon, Frank and Ernest have come, with broad smiles, from their therapist. Frank says, "Isn't it wonderful? He's convinced me that I'm not fat, and you that you're not short!" Just then a cop yells, "Move it, Fat Stuff! And your buddy too — is he standing in a hole?" It's no favor for a therapist to tell people that they can *will* their self-esteem increased when current public aesthetic standards still warrant little esteem for their type of person.

Here is another example of how social norms can play a part in our daily lives. This one is from the Andy Capp comic strip.

Reprinted with special permission of North America Syndicate, Inc.

This example is more complicated than the one about the little girl. The word "gentleman" is certainly a normative word. It conveys the idea that people are supposed to act according to certain norms. Again we have not just one norm but two, but in this case they are collapsed into only one word. Think about it this way: On the one hand "gentleman" means a man who is decent and gentle. He is not rough or unfair with other men; he is gentle with children and polite with women. On the other hand "gentleman" means a man of honor, someone who is true to himself, never tells a lie, cares about honor, and always lives up to his commitments. Andy is taking advantage here of that double meaning of "gentleman." That way he gets to hit his opponent but still can live up to the norm. But he is deliberately misinterpreting the referee's injunction.

Now consider this example where The Born Loser is jealous because Frank Sinatra has surpassed normal men in his singing. Sinatra has not just lived up to average expectations; he has gone beyond them to achieve fame. The Born Loser is trying to reduce Sinatra's achievement to a chance affair. If he could do that, he could discredit Sinatra's achievement, and then he wouldn't have to feel inferior to Sinatra. But even if a good voice *is* only a chance affair, Sinatra is the man who

THE BORN LOSER

Reprinted by permission of NEA, Inc.

happens to have the voice. We don't praise a great talent less just because great talents are born, not earned. And so, as usual, The Born Loser ends up looking ridiculous.

One more illustration: A heavyweight champion was asked to comment on the snide remark that he had won his last fight "by a lucky punch." He thought for a moment, and then said quietly, "Well, I think I'm lucky to have that punch." If an untalented boxer makes a good hit by chance, that sort of "lucky punch" does lessen our praise. But even if having boxing talent is a matter of luck, we admire it no less for that.

Norms and Action

The point is that norms play a big role in our lives. That is why we can understand the cartoons and the little girl's sad letter to Abby. We have norms to live up to, norms to achieve by, norms about how to treat other people, norms about what is beautiful and what is ugly. Whenever we *do* anything we are using norms because we care about doing it well or poorly. And we do things all the time. Sometimes we may not care much about driving a car carefully, or about cooking a good dinner, or about walking with our shoulders straight, or about singing in tune. At those times either we have decided to ignore the norm for the time being, or we are too busy thinking about something else. Abby, in her letter above, is expecting the other children to act on a norm of kindness. They have forgotten about that norm; they're more concerned about the norm against being overweight. Abby expects them, when they think about it, to emphasize that beauty norm less and to remember instead the moral duty to be kind. Then they might act more kindly. But notice that when the children go back to a moral norm, they will have to make a decision about which norm is better — which norm is correctly preferred. In children it is simple and direct, but it still is a normative decision.

Any decision about what is good, about what we ought to do, is normative. We make decisions like that all the time. We care about whether our clothes look sharp or in fashion or in character with ourselves. We care about being honest and worthy of respect. We care about marrying someone whom others will admire and about raising children who will succeed. We care about making right decisions. We

7

are humiliated at having made wrong decisions. We are humiliated when our children or parents fail, and we want to hide when a sty deforms our eyelid. We feel guilty when we don't finish a job we promised would be done.

The last three paragraphs above are riddled with phrases that indicate normative judgments have taken place. Here are a few of them: "carefully," "shoulders straight," "others will admire," "fail," "feel guilty." There are many others. Did you spot them?

There is much talk these days about how we ought to be ourselves and not worry about justice and being moral or good. But that, too, is a normative judgment just as much as any judgment about justice or morals or beauty. It says something about what we ought to do or be. Let us hope there is no conflict between being fair to others and being ourselves. But even if there is, we still have to decide which road to take, and that will be a *normative* decision.

Thus norms play a big role in our lives. They are important to us in all our activities, from the most trivial short-term ones, like what to eat for breakfast, to the most significant long-term ones, like what career to choose.

This book is about norms and the emotions we have about them. It is not only about moral standards that make us feel guilty when we fall short of them but also the norms that provoke us to be humiliated or embarrassed at times. There are even norms that make us feel triumphant. I will talk about how different rules can become mixed up with each other and the problems people feel when that happens. We will see how many different kinds of standards there are: It is no wonder they get mixed up. I do not want in this book to say much about which rules *ought* to be dominant in each situation. The reader will have to decide about that. But I do hope to encourage clear thinking about norms. People go by standards in deciding what is important and what is not, what matters and what does not. So what could be more important than clear thinking about norms? To understand our own feelings and actions, what can matter more?

Chapter 2

Overlapping Norms

Actions Guided By Norms

Let us begin by looking at some fairly complicated situations where two or more norms are at work directing action. That way we will have the examples ready to hand as we go along. William Shakespeare's plays are full of clear examples of that sort. He wrote in another country and at another time, but his characters were as concerned about norms as people are today. Besides, Shakespeare was especially skilled at letting his characters talk frankly about their concerns.

In *Henry V* is a scene in which King Henry, for various reasons, plays a little practical joke. He disguises himself as an ordinary gentleman soldier, then deliberately picks a quarrel with a common soldier named Williams. Williams is a respectable and decent fellow who wants to do what is right and honorable and what is expected of him. He would never agree to fight with the king or "box him on the ear." But as luck would have it, he falls for King Henry's disguise. He and Henry quarrel. Williams, innocently eager to maintain his manly status, promises to "box his ear" after the battle, when there is time.

When they meet in a later scene, King Henry is not disguised, so Williams doesn't know he is confronting the very man with whom he had quarreled. To make his joke more fun, Henry asks one of his officers, Fluellen, if a man should fight another of higher rank if he has sworn he would. Fluellen says definitely yes, that a man should keep his word. According to Fluellen, it makes no difference that the fellow didn't know he was challenging a noble. Williams hears all this and of course agrees with it.

9

Finally the king reveals himself as Williams's earlier opponent. This means that Williams could be accused of treason because he has threatened to do bodily harm to the king. Williams protests that he is innocent: He had no way of knowing he had quarreled with the king. With good common sense he says, "Take it for your own fault and not mine: for had you been as I took you for, I made no offense; therefore, I beseech your highness, pardon me." King Henry has now enjoyed his joke, so he does pardon Williams and even gives him extra money.

What happens in these scenes is that Henry plays two norms against each other. He knows that Williams is a man of his word, and he knows Williams would not commit treason knowingly. His joke — which after all is not so very funny — works by putting Williams in a situation where he must either back down or commit treason. This is a little like the Andy Capp case in the previous chapter, except that Andy Capp was cheating. Williams is not cheating at all; he is the one who gets tricked.

Notice that the conflicting norms are of different types. One of them, "Do not attack the king," has to do with a person's duty. Especially since Williams is a soldier in the King's army, he is highly aware of the duty to obey his commander. That would be enough by itself to keep him from fighting as long as he knew who his opponent was. But in addition, there is something special about the king in monarchical societies. To challenge him is to attack the very roots of the society; it threatens the whole society, not just the king personally. That is why they call it treason, and that is why treason is so great a crime in many people's eyes. In a sense, treason is a threat to almost everyone in the society. It is no wonder that there is a powerful social norm against it.

The other norm, "Live up to your word," sounds somewhat like the norm of honesty or keeping promises until we remember that in the heat of a quarrel people don't make promises — they make threats. Williams threatened to fight King Henry. Someone who fails to act on a threat hurts no one but himself. It is humiliating to back down from a threat, but backing down does not usually harm other people the way treason harms them, or the way a broken promise or a lie might harm them. So a person eager to keep his word after making a threat is trying to avoid feeling weak and humiliated. He is not trying to avoid being immoral. And so Williams wants to carry out his threat, to preserve his own self-respect. He uses a self-regarding norm, not a moral norm.

However, there is also a moral norm working in this situation, and

Williams does care about being decent. Once Williams finds out that he has threatened the king rather than just another soldier, he has no trouble deciding on which norm to act. Clearly, treason is worse than backing down from his word. After all, at the time of the quarrel, he didn't really know what he was doing. In this case the dominance of one norm over the other is so clear that Williams does not even need to feel humiliated about not living up to his word. On the other hand, it is humiliating to be the butt of a joke.

Let us leave Williams for a while now and talk about some other Shakespearean characters. In a gruesomely comic scene in *Richard III*, two professional murderers are discussing an "assignment" they have taken on. (Shakespeare did not give them names; he just called them "First Murderer" and "Second Murderer.") Second Murderer expresses some pangs of conscience about killing the victim. He is mildly embarrassed about having the qualms. First Murderer talks him out of worrying about conscience by reminding him of all the pay they will receive. But then First Murderer himself begins to feel the pangs, and so it is his turn to be embarrassed. Second Murderer, now encouraged, says that the devil is only playing pranks on him. First Murderer rallies, and all is well. They are both in the spirit to finish their job, which is to kill a particular man who is now asleep.

This business of being embarrassed about socially decent norms is fairly common. If you search your memory you will probably find some time, very likely when you were a child, when it was humiliating for you to admit that you cared about being decent, that you cared about caring about others. You can probably also find some time when you coaxed another person away from his or her moral cares. Such awful moments often happen in childhood. Children are particularly open to the conflict between being decent and being "brave" because they are not sure of their values and it is easy to persuade them. Cowardice appears obviously wrong to them, but sympathy is a strong feeling, too. Sometimes sympathy and bravery conflict. Fortunately, most of us do not face the extreme decisions that First Murderer and Second Murderer were facing.

Shakespeare's characters often show contempt for common decency. Iago, the well-respected employee in *Othello*, makes fun of a conscientious servant for acting like a "slave." Iago implies that sincerity and honesty are slavelike traits. He apparently thinks that normal,

11

decent behavior is a foolish waste of time. That tells us what Iago's norms are. And then there is Hamlet, the Prince of Denmark, who feels ashamed because he can't muster up the courage to commit murder.

This is a good time to take a closer look at the young prince. His uncle, Claudius, has apparently murdered his own brother, Hamlet's father. At least that is what the father's ghost contends one misty night. The ghost-father tells Hamlet to go take revenge for that murder. So Hamlet is stuck with the "duty" of killing Uncle Claudius. It is a demand of honor, and it is also a matter of obeying one's dead father.

As plays go, this hardly seems like a great chore, but in fact Hamlet has a terrible time trying to decide how to go about it. He has some kind of normative problem about it. The problem must be a subtle one, for on the face of it, all of Hamlet's norms seem to bear the same message: kill Claudius. His ghost-father told him to do it, and you are supposed to obey your father (especially when he is a ghost). The manly call for revenge directs him to do it because Claudius has not only killed his father but married his mother as well. Even morality seems to call for the same thing. After all, Hamlet is the prince, and it is his duty to bring justice and order to the realm he is responsible for:

> I, the son of a dear father murder'd,
> Prompted to my revenge by heaven and hell,
> Must, like a whore, unpack my heart with words,
> And fall a-cursing.

No one else is available to punish the murderer-uncle. But even with all that agreement among norms, Hamlet becomes confused and muddled. We wonder: Why doesn't he just kill Claudius and get it over with?

Apparently, Hamlet's confusion lies in *how* he is supposed to kill Claudius. Think about it this way: When we say "Hamlet killed Claudius" we are telling about something that happened. But we are not saying anything about how it specifically happened. Did Hamlet attack Claudius at the head of a rebel army? Did Hamlet run over Claudius with a horse and carriage? Did Hamlet torture Claudius to death? Did Hamlet give Claudius fatal pneumonia? Any of these could count as killing Claudius.

Hamlet's problem is how — specifically — to kill Claudius, not whether to kill Claudius. The problem comes about because all those different norms direct him to kill his uncle in a different way, even though they agree he should kill him somehow. The moral duty norm (be just and serve your country, but never seek revenge as such) directs him to kill Claudius in some quick, efficient way, to get it over with and set the state of Denmark straight. Hamlet almost does that quietly one night when he comes upon the guilt-stricken Claudius praying for forgiveness. Just as Hamlet is about to thrust his dagger into the repentant man, Hamlet's norm of revenge stops him. It says something like, "Claudius is praying for forgiveness. You'll only send him to heaven if you kill him now. Wait until he is busy with something sinful. That way you'll send him to hell instead. That is what you ought to do. After all, he killed your father before he had a chance to repent *his* sins."

Hamlet cannot decide between the several norms about how to kill Claudius, and so he has mixed feelings about a job that clearly needs doing. He is so ambivalent, distracted, and confused about it that in one scene he suddenly kills an innocent but bumbling fellow named Polonius. The murder is swift and unpremeditated. Hamlet seems a little baffled by his own action. And now on top of his other problem he must deal with Laertes, the son of Polonius. Laertes seeks revenge for his father's murder. Hamlet understands perfectly — the same revenge norm that directs Hamlet to kill Claudius also directs Laertes to kill Hamlet.

Claudius and Laertes gang up against Hamlet. They invite him to have a gentlemanly play-duel with Laertes. Claudius dishonestly arms Laertes with a poisoned sword. At the duel Laertes pricks Hamlet's skin with the sword point. But before the poison takes effect, Hamlet figures out the dirty trick that has been played on him. With desperate violence he stabs both Laertes and Claudius.

The scene is disorganized, and Shakespeare was wise to write it like that. He let Hamlet finally do his duty without having to decide how to do it. Hamlet kills Claudius impulsively and so has done with all his confusion and troubles. He probably doesn't even think about how he is finally killing his uncle. He just does it without really solving his problem about how to do it. The audience is left to chew over these normative puzzles.

Different Types of Norms

We can observe several different types of norms in the examples we have just talked about. Williams, First Murderer, Second Murderer, Hamlet, and Laertes all have norms guiding their actions. It will be helpful to look at the various norms more closely and try to make some sense out of them.

Williams clearly wants to do the honorable, manly thing when he takes up the disguised Henry's offer to fight. He just as obviously wants to do the decent thing when he refuses to fight King Henry truly revealed. He does not want to take the money the king has offered him because it is humiliating. What different types of norms are involved? We may list them this way:

Type of Norm	Action Linked to the Norm	Sanctions
1. Honor or manliness	Taking an offer to fight	He would be shamefaced if he didn't.
2. Patriotism	Refusing to be violent to the king	He would be immoral if he did.
3. Pride	Not wanting to take money when the joke had been at his expense	He was humiliated to have been laughed at.

Notice that the name of the norm (the first column) in each case is an abstract word: honor, patriotism, pride. It is hard to define or say exactly what these words mean. People disagree a good deal about their meanings.

But the action in each case is concrete and definite. As we said before, norms guide action; and actions are always concrete. Therefore, there is no reason to think of norms as abstract and irrelevant. When people do that, they are just thinking about words. We should instead think about norms concretely by considering what sort of action they guide people to. Then, when as a shortcut we want to use an abstract word like "honor" or "patriotism," we will know what we are talking about.

In the third column we find a mixture of considerations that may have worried Williams. In the first and third cases he fears being humiliated, and in the second case he probably fears being guilty. It is hard to understand precisely what these fears mean, but most people have felt them on some occasion in their lives. Let us call these various fears *sanctions*, because they sanction against falling short of some norm. So Williams's fear of being humiliated is a sanction against backing out of a fight and a sanction against taking the money. (Actually, he did both and, we may suppose, felt humiliated about it.) His fear of harming the king was a sanction against doing anything violent toward Henry.

First Murderer and Second Murderer are pretty much alike; they just trade parts. We can list their norms in this way:

Type of Norm	Action Linked to the Norm	Sanctions
4. Ruggedness or coolheadedness	Calmly killing a victim	They didn't want to appear "soft" in front of each other.
5. Humanity	Refraining from killing a human being	They cared about the victim, even though they didn't know him personally.
6. Piety	Refraining from killing a human being	They feared the judgment of God.
7. Self-interest	Efficiently killing the victim they were hired to kill	They wanted to be paid.

In the column listing sanctions, several different motives are mentioned, and some of these conflict with each other. For instance, wanting to be paid conflicts with caring about the victim. These murderers share what we can call a self-conflict or internal conflict.

15

That is what makes the little scene a drama rather than just a conversation. Each is going through a struggle with himself. It's as if, in each man, one part of the self were addressing another part. Maybe Shakespeare used two murderers instead of only one in conflict with himself just so that he could have the conversation going on in the play.

Now back to Hamlet. His norms might go like this:

Type of Norm	Action Linked to the Norm	Sanctions
8. Filial duty	Obeying his father-ghost by killing Claudius	He would be guilty if he disobeyed.
9. Being conscientious	Killing Claudius, the usurper, to get rid of political strife	He would fail in his princely duty if he allowed this rottenness to remain in Denmark.
10. Revenge (retribution)	Killing Claudius, who murdered his father	It is not honorable to let a family member's murder go unavenged.

As pointed out before, Hamlet's conflict is not simply about the action. It is about how to carry out the action because different reasons dictate different ways to do it. We thus end up with slightly different ways of describing the action in each case. This reminds us again that action is indeed concrete. Killing Claudius in a way that will send him to heaven is a concretely different thing from killing him so that he will go to hell. That difference lies not so much in Hamlet's use of the sword as opposed to a dagger as it lies in his timing of the act. It makes a difference what Claudius himself is doing when he dies.

The norm and sanction columns explain this difference, and that raises an interesting question about the relation between these two columns. I said a while ago that actions are concrete whereas norms are abstract. When something is abstract that means it is related to many things at once. For instance, "heat" is abstract in the sense that it refers to all hot things at once. "Beauty" is abstract in that it refers to all beautiful things at once. When we talk about the beauty of a sunset or the beauty of a bridge, we mean that each one is beautiful; each has something in common with all other beautiful things. That is an abstract way of talking.

When people talk about honor, they are again using an abstract term, talking in an abstract way. To understand it clearly we need to know what sorts of things the word "honor" refers to. Just as when we talk (abstractly) about beauty, we understand what that means by thinking of a beautiful sunset, a beautiful bridge, a beautiful woman, so it is with honor. We can better understand what honor is if we keep in mind specific examples. We will know what we are talking about when we speak of honor if we can think of different concrete, honorable acts.

This works the other way, too. By knowing what beauty is, we also know about ugly things or at least things that are unbeautiful. Likewise, by knowing what honor means, we also know about things that are dishonorable.

Notice that in the case of honor we use different standards to decide what is honorable and what is not. Look again at the tables above. Notice all the different concrete acts that could be called honorable:

1. Taking an offer to fight
3. Not wanting to take money offered
4. Calmly killing a victim
10. Killing a murderer for revenge

What a strange list of acts to call honorable! Offhand, would anyone call all of these honorable? And yet each seemed clearly to name an honorable act when it was first listed. What was clear then seems odd now. What can explain that?

To understand the oddness, we need to look at the situation where we expected each act to be carried out. Each act was accompanied by a sanction, as listed, and the sanction makes us suspect that honor is involved.

In Williams's case, a social norm made it honorable to accept an invitation to fight. In his society he would have been shamefaced and humiliated if he had not accepted the offer. Other people might have made fun of him; he would have been disgraced.

17

We can think of many times when declining to fight would not invite disgrace. In our own society, many people wouldn't dream of fighting in that situation. After all, maybe the quarrel was trivial anyway. Why waste time fighting over that issue, especially during a war? Many people would consider it foolish to fight because of a minor quarrel. They might even be embarrassed to think it worth fighting over. These people would think Williams was silly to accept the offer to fight.

Still, even if you think the quarrel was too minor to fight over, you might be thinking something like this: Even if it was silly, as long as Williams thought it was important, then it is honorable to accept the fight and dishonorable to decline it. If a person thinks some act is dishonorable, then there is a sort of sanction against doing that act. There would be an emotional penalty if he did it.

But there is another complication besides. Let us suppose Williams doesn't personally care about the quarrel one way or another but that other people would feel contempt for him if he failed to accept the offer. Suppose he knows that his fellow soldiers will make jokes about him and laugh if he refuses to fight. And suppose that women will not respect him and may even ignore him when word gets around that he didn't fight when most men would have. If that's how people would react to Williams's refusal to fight, then we can understand the strong pressure on Williams to accept the challenge. No matter what Williams thinks, there is then a strong social norm saying that Williams ought to accept the offer. A person who would decline to fight in a society that held that norm would have to have one of two traits: Either he would really be a coward and so deserve the way men laugh at him and women don't notice him, or he would have to be willing to look like a coward in front of other people. If he is willing to face the way people treat cowards, then he is unusual: He is either indifferent to other people's opinions or courageous enough to face their contempt. It takes a great deal of courage for a sensitive person to go against social norms. In Chapter 7 I will discuss those callous people who are not deterred by dishonor.

We can sympathize with the way Williams acted even if we in our society would not do exactly what he did. Different concrete acts count as honorable or dishonorable in different societies, but the sanction about honor has much the same logical "shape" from one society to another. No one in any society can feel all right about being laughed at by his fellows. Any normal person in any society feels some pain when other people ignore him. Everyone wants to be counted as a person. Humiliation, embarrassment, being shamefaced — all of these are sanctions. They all indicate that some norm is operating, telling people what they ought to do.

Consider now the situation of First and Second Murderer. Probably most of my readers have little sympathy with them. These murderers feel ashamed about hesitating to kill an innocent sleeping man. To normal, decent people that seems horrible. But we find in this example the same sort of sanctions as in Williams's case. First Murderer is afraid of appearing soft or unmanly in front of Second Murderer, and it turns out that Second Murderer has the same sort of fear. So just the two of them form a small community. In that "mini-community" the ideal of ruggedness and the painful emotion of embarrassment or shame play out their action-guiding roles. In order to understand them, you have to imagine what it would be like to live among hired murderers. Most people can easily imagine how it would be, even though they would never dream of entering that sort of community. Of course, Shakespeare knew that. He represented these deviant characters as being a little ridiculous because he knew his audience would feel contempt for them.

Hamlet's case is more complex. He seeks revenge, and the norm of revenge brings special humiliation or shame on a person who falls short of its demands. I will deal with this subject in detail in Chapter 9.

Let us look back at the examples again and examine some of the norms besides those of honor. For instance, morality or decency is a type of norm common to several of the concrete situations in these examples.

2. Not offering violence against the king
5. Not killing a sleeping man
6. Not killing a human being
8. Hamlet's obeying his father-ghost by killing Claudius
9. Killing Claudius, the usurper, to get rid of political strife

Just as with the list of acts that related to honor, we again have a varied assortment of acts. The list includes both killing a man and not killing a man! Once more it looks odd to see these grouped together. But when we reflect back on each concrete situation, we can see why each of these acts fits under a decency norm. To be more specific, most decent people in our society disapprove of murder of any kind, but especially when the murder is premeditated, callous, and cold. It is also easy to understand disapproval of violence against the king, who is a political leader. Most people are especially shocked by assassination attempts, whether or not they happen to like the politician attacked. Further, most people feel regret or distress about disobeying a parent, even when that seems necessary. Last, most people keep hoping (though perhaps no longer expecting) that our political leaders will be conscientious in their service to us. These are the sorts of moral rules that guide Shakespeare's characters. Even though there are great differences of detail, self-respecting, decent people generally agree about them in our own society. While we as individuals disagree about many issues (think of all the arguing we do at election time), we sometimes forget how much agreement there actually is.

One of the acts in the examples fits under neither decency nor honor. That is number 7, the one where the murderers just want to do their job efficiently so that they can be paid for it. I have called that self-interest. In our society self-interest norms may seem rather obvious and easy to understand. Actually, self-interest is much more complicated than it appears because it becomes so mixed up with other norm types. I have therefore decided to discuss it in a later chapter in order to examine honor and decency first. That will make self-interest easier to understand.

Another of the example acts really fits under both decency and honor: Norm number 5 makes the two murderers hesitate to kill a sleeping man. Cold, premeditated murder is always wrong — people widely agree about that. But probably most people would say it is cowardly as well when the victim is weak or helpless or sleeping. Notice that this killing can count both as wrong and as disgraceful. It is not disgraceful just because it is wrong (any murder would be disgraceful in that sense), but also because there is the air of the "big bully" about it. Picking on a weak or disadvantaged victim makes the bully look ridiculous because he seems to have too little confidence to face a victim equal to him. No expert chess player would brag about defeating an amateur. No ninth-grader should gloat that she can do long division better than her little third-grade brother. It is not a matter of morality or just being honest and decent. It is a matter of pride and self-respect.

These many examples show that there are at least two different types of norms, honor and decency. There are other types of norms also.

I will discuss some other types later, like self-interest, love of achieve-ment, love of kindness or beneficence. For now, consider only decency and honor. They are the simplest, and yet even so they are complex enough to require some careful self-reflection.

The Repressed Idea of Honor

I have been suggesting in the last section that honor norms and decency norms are different, even though in one case they clearly overlapped. I have used the idea of honor to talk about people's eagerness to avoid appearing to others as cowardly, weak, inept, or clumsy. The issue here is that common feeling in human beings, the fear of failure. At the time Shakespeare was writing, people often referred to honor, but the word is no longer much in use. Everyone is familiar with fear of failure and humiliation at being bettered or one-upped by someone else. Why, then, do we seldom talk about dishonor? Everyone knows the unpleasant feeling of being embarrassed or humiliated or laughed at. We all know what it is like to imagine that others would laugh at us if they knew certain things about us. We think that is ample reason to hide certain facts about ourselves. So honor norms play a significant role in our lives. They frequently guide our actions and decisions, and yet we have no good single word to use these days to talk about that kind of norm. "Integrity" comes close but isn't quite right. Why should such an important type of norm be so difficult to discuss?

Here is a possible answer: The idea of honor in our society, though active in the way it influences us, is nonetheless repressed. The psy-chologist Erik Erikson noted that "shame is an emotion insufficiently studied, because in our civilization it is so early and easily absorbed by guilt." But that answer will not quite satisfy; immediately we ask, "*Why* has it been repressed?" There are three main reasons for this: (1) The fear of failing or being laughed at is so great that it is painful even to talk about it, and we easily take that very fear to be a sign of weakness. (2) We live in a democracy and so have a kind of "social myth" that nobody is supposed to be better than anybody else. Hardly anyone fully believes this myth, but few challenge it for fear of sounding antisocial. (3) Much of our moral training (that civilizing process our parents put us through to make us decent) is done by means of our fears of humiliation and embarrassment. In other words, our parents used honor norms to plant, deep inside us, the norms of decency. After a long process like that, it becomes a habit to think that both norms are the same.

Now I will discuss these points one by one.

Fear of Exposing Fear

A recent example of this "fear of fear" is given throughout Tom Wolfe's novel *The Right Stuff*. This is the story of men involved in flight-testing new fighter planes. These pilots make careers of facing death, but they do not center their lives around the thought of death (their wives tend to think about that). Rather, they orient their actions toward having "the right stuff," which comes as near to "honor" as any term we have in English these days. Wolfe makes rather a big point of not being able to say quite what the right stuff is. He suggests it is manly courage, but any reader of his book recognizes that he is not satisfied with that. What best captures the idea is Wolfe's description of the men's "code of honor" (or "code of the right stuff," if you like): Their main rule in life is "flying, drinking; drinking, driving." This means they are supposed to spend the day calmly risking their lives in flight testing. Afterward they must go to a bar to drink and meet women. Then they drive home drunk. The next day they are supposed to return to work, smooth and cool, to risk their lives again. To behave this way a man must obviously have "the right stuff." This ideal guides their actions and shapes their whole lives. But they must never *talk* about the right stuff. Each is supposed to *show* that he has it. The minimal way to demonstrate it is to carry out that daily regimen calmly and reliably. Someone especially confident about drinking half the night and making an exacting flight the next day might comment to other people, "I don't advise it; but it *can* be done." That shows for sure that he has the right stuff. It is necessary for each of these men, from time to time, to make remarks of that sort or otherwise advertise that he has the right stuff. They are not afraid of death, either in their flights or in their risky driving. They are afraid of only one thing: being caught without the right stuff.

Why aren't these men able to talk about a matter of such overriding importance to them — something more important than their lives, their families, their incomes? One guess is that it is just *too* important, too sacred, to mention. It is something shown in action, too subtle for mere words to capture. Chatting about it might destroy the spell, an evil too great to risk. The precious guiding star might go out. For you may have noticed that telling about that star in so many words, as Wolfe has done for us, dims it a bit, because it goes against what people commonly think of as self-interest. Having these men care about the guiding star, their ideal of how to be men, is a good cheap way to get fighter planes tested from the country's point of view (for the pilots were rather poorly paid), but it doesn't clearly benefit the men themselves. Most of them — those who do not make it as far as being the seven astronauts of our country's initial space flights — do not even get to be public heroes. So they are not only underpaid but also underappreciated for their heroism. If the men talked about these things among themselves, they might develop some doubts about the very ideal that makes their lives meaningful to them, and that is a terrible thing to happen to a human being.

In other words, although I have said above that they fear nothing but lacking the right stuff, another fear lies behind that one: namely, losing their idealism about the right stuff. It is a fearsome thing to lose an ideal, to stop valuing whatever it is that makes life meaningful. No one can take that calmly.

There may have been still another fear. The men may have been afraid to show any sign of fear, regardless of how appropriate the fear might be. This point is rather complicated. I am supposing that, paradoxically, the men are afraid to show their fear of not having the right stuff. Why are they afraid? Because if you have the right stuff, then you are not supposed to be afraid of anything! Theirs is a demanding code of honor. It's clear, then, why the men are not able to talk about it, why they repress it from their talk and live out the ideal only in action and by subtle, unspoken messages to each other. This example shows one way in our society that the idea of honor is frequently repressed.

Avoiding the Undemocratic

Debbie, a sixteen-year-old student, was having a conference with her teacher about an exceptionally fine paper she had written. Her teacher told her that she had unusual talent, that she could aim high in life and take on more responsibility than other people because she was more talented than most. "No I'm not," said Debbie modestly (she was proud of her modesty). "But Debbie, you really are," the teacher told her gently. "I'm not, I'm not, I'm not!" cried Debbie, and with a tense jaw and thinly compressed lips, she respectfully left the interview.

This kind of case is not at all unusual. It's a situation where a person's moral code forbade her to shine out among others. We will later distinguish the desire to shine, which Debbie repressed, as holding an achievement norm. Achievement norms are enough like those of honor to show the sort of repression we are talking about. Debbie was concerned with the moral rule that she must not put anyone else down. She was not afraid of failure because with her talent she had little chance of actually failing. For her, guilt about being better than others was a much greater concern, and she actually hoped that she would fall below what in fact she could accomplish.

Here is another example. A sign on a college campus says:

MEET THIS AFTERNOON IF YOU WANT TO
JOIN OTHER CHRISTIANS IN PLAYING
BASKETBALL FOR THE GLORY OF JESUS

Here we have some glory-loving athletes who, in Christian modesty, are going to assign all their renown to Jesus. One of the points of games like basketball is to excel in the competition. Yet these people would rather not admit that they want to excel.

Drawing by D. Reilly;
© 1981 The New Yorker Magazine, Inc.

Being excellent seems undemocratic; to be accepted by others, people do sometimes hide traits that would distinguish them.

Honor Norms Harnessed to Moral Norms

In most people the fear of being laughed at or humiliated is much greater than their fear of feeling guilty. Imagine a man overhearing two women talk about him. One woman says, "I admit that he's bold, clever, and fascinating, but I don't approve of his ruthless conduct." Now suppose she says instead, "He's a wimp and a loser — a silly ass!" Which of these criticisms do you think he would prefer to overhear?

In a sense, humiliation also seems more natural than guilt. Fearsome pain is first felt in a child's infantile experiences. The mother who, in spite of all her tenderness and love, shows disgust at a dirty diaper, can unwittingly make a baby feel ashamed and rejected.

Parents often teach decency norms to their children by using the honor norms that children tend to have naturally. When a child screams out for a bigger portion of cake than other children are getting, the mother will say, "You ought to be ashamed! You must learn to share!" This is effective training. The child then feels humiliated and is afraid of being shunned. A preschool teacher once commented, "Nothing humiliates a three-year-old like standing in the corner — especially in front of other three-year-olds."

Using people's fear of humiliation and fear of being abandoned is, as we all know, not limited to controlling children. Most adults have gone through the rather simple humiliating experience of being stopped by a traffic cop for speeding or driving wrong on a one-way street. It is a time of feeling ridiculous, of dreading the stares of other motorists freely going by, trying not to notice them. If only the cop will just hurry up and write the stupid ticket, turn off his flashing lights, and go away! We sometimes relieve the humiliation by getting angry or indignant. That may feel painful, too, but not as much as the humiliation it covers over. It matters little whether the driver has actually violated a traffic rule. The incident itself is what embarrasses, having to sit there while a cop leans above you on your car door and talks officially to you through the window, while flashing lights draw everyone's attention. Any normal, decent, and competent driver knows well that it is useful to himself and everybody else that we should have reasonable rules of the road. But unless there has been an accident, it is not usual to feel guilty about speeding. It is just humiliating to get caught. It can also be costly, but notice that even a "warning," where the police officer gives no ticket, is a humiliating, unpleasant experience.

For a long time different societies, including ours, have used the fear of humiliation to keep people minimally decent. Criminals must bear not only the discomfort of their punishment but also the humiliation of it. Long ago (four centuries before Christ) the philosopher Plato made a key point of trying to harness to decency norms that common fear of humiliation and being shunned. He wanted to talk people into being moral and decent. If he could show that a person who behaves indecently is automatically incompetent, Plato reasoned, that would do the trick. People would then try hard to avoid indecent and antisocial conduct. By and large he was right. The method works well. In fact, it works *so* well that many people today are slow to notice any difference between feeling guilty and feeling ashamed.

"Shame," an Embarrassing Word

In the last chapter I began by pointing out that norms are an important factor in whatever we do. For the most part, norms guide our actions, and so it is important for each of us to understand what our norms are and to think about them seriously. In this chapter I have talked about how different types of norms can be active in some one situation and about how they sometimes conflict with each other. So far, two types, honor and decency, have been singled out. We can tell from the examples of this chapter that certain feelings go with each of the two types of norm. These feelings serve as sanctions, feelings that enforce respect for the norms. When people think they have violated a decency norm, they feel guilty. When they think they have violated an honor norm, they feel humiliated, embarrassed, ridiculous, or ashamed.

I have avoided using the word "shame" because to many people there is something embarrassing about it. Just as the word "honor" is repressed from our conversation, so the word "shame" is often hard to utter. The very sound of it seems to make people uncomfortable sometimes, almost as if they were undergoing shame itself when someone mentions it. So in this chapter I have spoken of humiliation and embarrassment instead. They serve well enough for talking about many cases where honor norms guide action, but they do not quite capture the full meaning of shame. People seem to find it easier to talk about being embarrassed or humiliated than to talk about being ashamed. But even those emotions are more often repressed from conversation than is the idea of guilt. People mention guilt frequently, often even trivially.

To see what I mean, try this little experiment: Think back over your last two weeks or so about how many times you have heard someone say something like, "I felt guilty about forgetting to call you." You've probably heard that kind of talk or used it yourself. People often show little distress in saying they feel guilty. Guilt-talk is not repressed at all in our society. Now ask yourself how often in the same two weeks you have heard something like, "I am ashamed that I forgot to call you." Doesn't that sound strange? Try saying it to yourself and notice that it does not even feel the same as talking about feeling guilty.

Of course, different people have different feelings about words. We vary in our habits and manners of speaking. But if we varied much, we would not understand each other even as well as we do. For most people, shame and guilt have a different "feel" about them. They call forth different emotions. But that should not be surprising, for the examples of this chapter make it evident that honor and decency are two different types of norm. It is not surprising, then, that we have different emotions about each one. Also, since the idea of honor is largely repressed, you would expect shame-talk to be quite rare among adults.

I began this book saying that I would write about norms because they are so important in our lives. I want to do what Tom Wolfe's astronauts seemed afraid to do. They were afraid to discuss their code of honor. Yet it would be shameful not to get clear on standards that guide our actions and shape our lives.

Chapter 3

Humiliation and Guilt:
Sanctions of Honor and Decency

In the last chapter we saw several examples of people strongly motivated by their fear of humiliation, embarrassment, or shame. Other
people were described who feared mainly the feeling or reality of guilt.
Guilt and shame turned out to be quite different, though they often
overlapped. When persons fear humiliation, as does Shakespeare's
soldier Williams when he becomes the butt of a joke, they are concerned for their honor. But when they fear guilt, as Hamlet does when
he shrinks from murdering his uncle, their concern is for decency or
morality. Thus, honor and decency are two different types of norm.

Guilt and shame and their related emotions are sanctions support-
ing and enforcing these norms. I use the word "sanction" to mean a kind
of "motivator" that gets people to act in some desired way. We could
call shame and guilt *negative* sanctions in that they persuade people to
avoid certain "bad" ways of acting.

Go carefully, now — a certain action or character could be both
decent and honorable, or it could be both wicked and base. These
standards often overlap; but they may also clash. We saw how the
murderers in *Richard III* feel embarrassed about their pangs of conscience. And there is a modern jingle that goes like this:

The rain it raineth every day
Upon the just and unjust fella —
But more upon the just, because
The unjust has the just's umbrella.

The jingle sounds contemptuous of "fair-minded" people, who might be called suckers. In our society it is humiliating, dishonorable, to be a sucker. You may sometimes have heard the saying, "Don't get mad, get even," which expresses this attitude. Adolescents especially hate to be seen by their peers as weak or docile or naive.

Again, there is conflict between the honor requirement to take revenge against someone who has insulted you and the decency requirement not to harm others. Decency and honor, then, are distinct ideas, though they may overlap in some cases, just like the notions of "tall" and "Lutheran." Consider these parallel tables:

Many decent actions are also honorable.	Many tall people are Lutherans.
Some wrong actions, violations of decency, also involve humiliating dishonor.	Some short people are non-Lutheran.

But

Some decent actions could be humiliating (for example, backing off from an unjustified fight).	Some tall people are not Lutherans.
Sometimes the fight required by honor may be an immoral violation of decency.	Some Lutherans are not tall.

Pervasiveness of Sanctions

And just as the two distinct kinds of standard can overlap, so can the corresponding sanction-emotions. One can feel rational guilt and warranted humiliation at the same time, over the same action — yet these emotions are also in themselves distinct.

A Chapter in Dick Gregory's Life

Dick Gregory tells of two shaming incidents in his childhood: One involved no wrongdoing on his part (illustrating the distinctness of honor from decency), whereas the other incident illustrates the way the two sets of norms-with-emotions can blend together.

As a child Gregory earned money delivering papers. He offered some money for a classroom fund drive to help the poor (partly hoping to impress a special little girl). The teacher refused the money scornfully: "We're raising this money for families just like yours!" Without any decency violation on his part, the boy was mortally insulted. He felt shame deeply.

But another time he was shamed because he hesitated to pay for a wino's food in a tough restaurant. As the enraged owner pounded on the feckless wino, the boy finally offered the money, but the bum said, "Hell, no, I've taken my beating already — you waited too long!" Gregory felt guilt over letting the wino get beaten. He also felt humiliated over his sluggish generosity.

People talk piously as if we can always avoid shame by not doing wrong, as if in guarding our honor we need not fear guilt. But things may not be this simple: Different people may feel each emotion more or less intensely, may weigh the importance of each norm differently.

Different Codes Yet Same Norm Type

The words "honor" and "decency" name two *types* of norm, not the particular rules a given set of people may accept about what counts as honorable or decent. Wolfe's test pilots think they show the "right stuff" by driving at breakneck speed while drunk. To someone else, such driving might seem foolhardy and disgraceful, even if no one else is endangered. People may disagree over what is dishonorable, but they all care about honor. They have a common basis for debating their particular norms.

Another example: The most intellectual of American males are usually proud of their knowledge of cars and engines. If they are at a loss when the car breaks down, they'd rather not discuss it. An Oriental intellectual, on the other hand, might be humiliated to show too much proficiency at car repair. He might see such skills as appropriate to workers of more lowly station. Both intellectuals care about honor, but they disagree about what is honorable. (This example also helps to distinguish the general care for honor from the more narrow concern for "machismo.")

To elaborate this distinction, consider how we refer to differing "codes of honor." We expect one code of honor for the Mafia, a different code for old-fashioned cowboys, another code for the Spanish nobility, another for astronauts, and so on. (A local blacksmith reports that he *must* light his cigar with a glowing-hot iron; the code of the blacksmith forbids using a lighter.) In saying that each group has a code of honor, I don't mean they value exactly the same sorts of action. They might disagree vigorously about how the "honorable" person should behave. Rather, to say that each has some code of honor means simply that they all respect the same norm type.

Likewise, different cultures can accept quite different norms of decency. Many Americans see no guilt in housing their elders in nursing homes where they can be cared for specially, away from the family. But in Saudi Arabia people see such practices as horribly immoral. Both cultures have a code of decency, but the specific values expressed in each code differ, sometimes clashing.

I will talk later about specific codes in some detail. For now, remember that whenever someone acts on a given type of norm, it is relative to some specific code. (Analogously, "law-abiding people" abide by some specific laws, such as the laws of England; they don't live by law-in-general. But it's still useful to think of contrasting local legal rules as included in one general type of norm. That's like the consideration going on here.)

Norm Types and Sanctions Across Cultures

Here's another way to put the same point. Honor, as a norm type, is cross-cultural; it is found in many different communities. In fact, whatever humans are doing, they are sometimes proud and sometimes humiliated. Each honor norm guides us about what to be proud of, what to be ashamed of. But the specific code expressing that norm type in each community may differ vividly from the rules of the next community.

The same holds true for decency as a norm type. All peoples seem to have *some* idea of right and wrong, but they might disagree over what acts are wrong. Hindus may not eat beef, Muslims may not eat pork, but each would recognize the feeling of guilt the other displays after an illicit meal.

We'd also expect some groups to put more emphasis on decency, others on honor. Neither kind of norm is ever totally lacking but different communities weigh them differently. For instance, Chicago street-gang members are gung-ho for their honor, whereas Quakers are more concerned about morality. Anthropologists might say that the street gang is a "shame culture" and the Quaker community a "guilt culture." The gang members are more fearful of shame; the Quakers see avoiding guilt as more important.

One reason we know that decency and honor are cross-cultural is that their sanctions, guilt and shame, are felt as similar emotions in diverse cultures. The Nigerian farmer will feel ashamed of growing corn too short, while the Chicago gang member will be ashamed of his ugly motorcycle. Again, an American woman would now be ashamed to be fat, whereas seventy years ago American women were ashamed to be skinny. The shame in each case is *about* something quite different, but the emotion itself is much the same. (We've already noted cross-cultural similarities in guilt feelings.)

Uneasiness in Talking About Shame

A word of caution before proceeding: Remember, "shame" is an embarrassing word in our culture. People feel uneasy discussing it; shame is so much more fearful than guilt. But practically everyone feels shame or humiliation now and then. It serves as a powerful warning against certain kinds of behavior, just because it is so fearful. So we will better understand our values if we come right out and talk about the sanction-emotion. To feel embarrassed, humiliated, or disgraced is to have emotions similar to shame. The word "shame" covers all these more specific feelings, so I will usually use it for convenience.

I noted in Chapter 2 that people are often ashamed to be ashamed. That's why they don't like to talk about it. But why this reaction? For one thing, shame is so hard to get rid of. If we feel guilty we can apologize, confess, make up for our wrong. But shame is not so easy to escape — if my performance was really pathetic or ridiculous, that's that. What's more, the very experience of even mild embarrassment may suddenly isolate me from my fellows.

A student said to his teacher, "I feel guilty about doing so poorly on your test." Well, our code of decency certainly doesn't require people to do well on tests, but our codes of honor and achievement do require

this. The student felt isolated and abandoned for a failure he took seriously. To admit this feeling in so many words would make him feel even more isolated, so he changed to guilt-and-decency talk instead. Punishment or apology can end an incident where guilt is involved, but it's hard to change people's minds once they decide you're dumb or ineffectual. (A devastating cartoon showed a nasty teacher saying smoothly to outraged parents: "Actually, your Johnnie works very hard; he's just stupid." Suddenly you realize why so many parents are convinced their children are "underachievers.")

Another reason people avoid honor/shame language is that it makes them feel childish. That creates a particularly difficult trap: One mark of shame is to feel childish — alienated, helpless, confused, abandoned. So to admit that you feel ashamed is to admit that you feel childish, which is in itself another source of shame. Small wonder this experience is almost impossible to talk about calmly.

Closely connected with the trap of feeling childish is the surprise element typical of many shame experiences. Embarrassment and humiliation tend to hit suddenly. The victim has seen his place in the world in a certain way; suddenly his proper level seems lower — the ground caves in beneath his feet.

Finally, being ashamed makes you feel out of control, even of your own body. Hot blood flushes into the cheeks. The shoulders and neck muscles slump involuntarily, as if hoping to hide but sluggish for movement. It's a weakness not to have control of your body, and weakness is shaming. Once again, it is shaming to feel ashamed.

All these features of shame are illustrated in a simple, everyday scene: A businesslike man buying garden seeds in a drug store lays the packets on the counter along with a money-off coupon cut out from a newspaper. "This coupon is no good," says the amused clerk. "Oh, am

I too late with it?" "No, it's for Walgreen's, and this is Skagg's!" "Oh, that is dumb of me!" laughs the man, his face and shoulders already turned away for escape.

Such normal, human vulnerability seems grim, but there is also some good news. Some students have learned to discuss shame openly. These people report that they no longer find shame experiences so unbearably intense, that they understand certain blind alleys in their past life much better. If we could weaken the hold shame has on us by facing it openly, then we might think more clearly about which of our "local" honor standards need revising. For instance, a needless highway quarrel led to murder in England recently, because one man thought the "code of the road" required him to give an obscene hand signal to a driver who was crowding him. Obviously, this man's version of the code needs revising.

Shame and Guilt Contrasted

Our discussion has brought out some general features of shame. Further light is cast by comparing this emotion with guilt feelings. Though our habits of language often confuse these two emotions, a careful look reveals important differences. Below is a chart comparing guilt and shame. It might help to read it over twice. First read across, to get each special contrast between shame and guilt. Then read down each side, to get a fuller description separately of each emotion.

Guilt	Humiliation (Shame)
One feels guilty for voluntary wrongdoing (wrongs of omission or commission).	One is humiliated over weakness or ugliness or failure.
Guilt expects deserved pain. (One who feels guilty might be proud of the power and cleverness displayed in the wrongdoing.)	Shame wants to hide, fears being seen and ridiculed, even if no punishment is feared.

35

Guilt

The opposite of guilt is moral self-respect, the feeling that one deserves reward and happiness, and the feeling of resentment at undeserved suffering.

We react to wrongs by others with resentment and indignation.

The guilty person pictures others leaning toward him, threatening him.

Guilt may originate in the child's fear of being punished.

"I couldn't help it — I'm weak" typically mitigates the guilt seen as appropriate.

If the wrongdoer repents, and tries to repair the injury, he can be forgiven by victims or onlookers.

The person feeling guilty is not much aware of his own body, is even distant from it.

Guilt is typically expressed in auditory images.

Humiliation (Shame)

The opposite of humiliation is self-esteem, pride, glory; the desire to shine and be seen, to manifest one's beauty or splendid achievement (whether or not that achievement will be rewarded).

We react to others' weak or ugly behavior with contempt, ridicule, or pity.

The shamed person may picture others leaning away from him in revulsion, or laughing at him.

Shame may originate in the child's fear of abandonment. (It could be brought on by seeing in mother's face distaste at soiled diapers.)

Shame allows no excuses of internal incapacity. "I couldn't help it — I'm weak" increases humiliation.

Shameful failure can't be forgiven — if a person is pathetic or absurd, he just is. He can earn esteem only by ridding himself of his weakness or other flaws.

Shame creates high body awareness via reactions like blushing, sweating, cramped muscles.

Shame is typically expressed in visual images.

Guilt	Humiliation(Shame)
Guilt comes about in a predictable and accountable way.	Shame often strikes a person by surprise, from sudden exposure.
Guilt can be readily communicated if the person so chooses. (Confession may ease the soul.)	Shame isolates a person, puts him out of communication.
Any guilt feeling out of proportion to the incident is considered abnormal and mistaken.	Feeling shame out of proportion to the provoking incident is frequent and normal.

Consider now some individual features of shame. Keep in mind that both shame and guilt feelings are negative sanctions for the norm types honor and decency. They are not themselves the norms, but we must understand them before we can talk easily about the norms.

Shame Wanting to Hide

Both shame and guilt require that we be involved with other persons in our community. That is, both presuppose an audience, but in different ways. To feel guilty, I must believe typically that there is someone I have wronged, someone who has a valid complaint against me. It's something like a creditor-debtor relationship: I can't owe money unless there's someone I owe it to. But I need no audience for my *feeling* of guilt. Just as I can think about the money I owe when my creditor is absent, so also I can feel guilty in the absence of the person wronged.

With shame, the dependence on audience is much more intimate: The feeling itself is one of being stared at contemptuously or pityingly by some real or imagined observer. The shamed one identifies with the people she imagines looking at her; she suddenly sees herself as others see her, and is almost torn apart from herself. That's why the French philosopher Jean-Paul Sartre described shame as a painful awareness of "The Look," or "The Stare." One is exposed to The Stare from others. It's even worse when they suddenly see her "exposed."

Suppose I gave a great belch, thinking I was alone, and then realized a society leader was on the other side of the bush. I would quail before her imagined cold stare. Most descriptions of shame speak somehow of eyes, of looks, and of the consequent desire to hide.

Feeling guilty, I can imagine being resented if found out. If I had some bad luck, I'd expect people to say I deserved it. Others looking at me is not central here. But feeling shame just *is* imagining my fellows laughing at me. Anything to conceal a defect that provokes such scorn! If it does get exposed, I'll want to hide myself. "I felt about two feet tall. I wanted to sink through the floor!" These are the words of a humiliated person wanting to hide, wiching, "If only the world could be blind!" "Shame dwells in the eyes," said Aristotle. He retold the story of some men who were sentenced to death by cudgelling, a punishment that would leave their corpses ugly and disfigured. The doomed men hid their faces from the crowd, unable to look back into eyes that would later see their degradation.

A modern play, *Equus*, is based on the true story of an English youth who put out the eyes of horses. As the playwright tells the story, the boy saw a kind of pagan divinity in the horses, splendid and scornful of weakness. When he thought they witnessed his sexual failure with a local girl, he blinded them to escape their scornful looks.

And we may remember *King Lear*, another Shakespeare play. In that play, when a decent fellow named Gloucester predicts that he will see the king's wicked daughter punished and confounded, her ruthless husband promptly puts out Gloucester's eyes, "lest they see more." It would be humiliating for them to have Gloucester see and gloat over their comeuppance.

In an old Western ballad, Sam Hall is a hardened criminal about to be hanged. He defies society in his last words but suddenly falters from shame: "They can kiss my ruddy bum, damn their eyes! damn their eyes!"

Shame wants to hide, whereas guilt involves fear of deserved pain. A child who fears punishment also has reason to hide. What really makes shame different from guilt is wanting to hide even when there is no danger of punishment: The shamed one fears just the stare of ridicule or contempt or disgust or pity. Wanting to cover up is central to the very idea of shame, but not of guilt. The guilty person may even ease her pain by confessing.

Excuses for Guilt but not for Shame

What a person is ashamed of might not be something he could avoid. Someone could be ashamed of his retarded child or of having a clubfoot since birth or of speaking with a foreign accent or of falling down on the dance floor. Others wouldn't blame him, perhaps, for such defects. But they might find him amusing or pathetic, or nice people might say he needs help. Dick Gregory knew his teacher didn't blame him for his poor family, but he was humiliated to be treated as one of those needing help when he wanted the splendid role of helping others. My relatives, my body shape, my stammer — these things are not of my choosing, but they may be sources of humiliation.

It is otherwise with guilt. It wouldn't make sense to say I'm guilty of causing a death that I simply could not avoid. Suppose I'm driving carefully, and a suicide leaps out from between two cars to be killed. I'd feel terrible, of course. I might even feel vaguely "polluted" by this brush with horror. But if one of the suicide's relatives told me she forgave me for the killing, I'd bristle at her implication that I was guilty. I might even feel that the suicide wronged me, used me as his death instrument.

Some cases seem ambiguous, though. The chart contrasting guilt and shame claims that the feeling appropriate for weakness or failure is shame, not guilt. But if a person neglects to secure his car brakes after parking on a hill, causing someone's death, we might hold him responsible for culpable negligence. Yet the trouble came from his weakness or failure, not from any conscious choice to be negligent. We presume that the negligent person didn't care enough about the welfare of others to take due care. For this lack of benevolence he is guilty, though less guilty than the malicious or deliberately reckless killer. (Insofar as his neglect can be shown to stem from some mental disturbance, we find him even less guilty, because now the external failure doesn't show such a lack of care for others.) Once again, guilt and shame overlap; the fellow is partly guilty for not caring enough for the safety of others; he's deeply shamed that he was careless. (He'd be shamed — mortified — even if the only damage resulting was to his own car; but he wouldn't then be guilty at all if there were no chance all along that others could be hurt.)

This helps to explain more carefully the point that shame allows no excuses. It would, in fact, be oversimple to say there's *never* an excuse. Suppose some vicious spectator flashes a mirror in the eyes of a baseball fielder. The fielder could cite this incident to excuse his missing the catch, so an error would not be charged to him. In this case, his not catching the ball doesn't count as a personal failure, is no indicator of any personal weakness. So shame may allow excuses of a certain sort, like external bad luck, which somewhat weakens the connection between external failing and internal weaknesses. But, "I couldn't help it; I'm weak" — this kind of excuse *increases* humiliation.

In a similar way, guilt norms allow excuses that weaken the inference from "he harmed others" to "he didn't care enough for others' welfare." The crucial difference, then, comes with excuses appealing to personal weakness. The alcoholic who worries his wife can protest that he really does love her, only he can't help drinking. We may accept this as partly true and partly excuse him from guilt. But it is mortally shaming to be so enslaved to drink that this swamps the real love of one's wife.

Shame allows no excuses for ugliness. It may be true that a person can't help contracting a disfiguring disease, yet he is not irrational to feel humiliation. A Denver newspaper told of an athlete suffering from a slow degenerative disease of nerves and muscles. He was surprised to find that he felt ashamed, as if he were responsible. His surprise came from confusing the logic of guilt with the logic of humiliation. Of course it is humiliating when one's superb body is turning ugly and useless.

A classic case of ugly deformity in literature is Philip in W. Somerset Maugham's novel *Of Human Bondage*. Philip is born with a clubfoot. The other schoolboys, at one point, physically force him to let them stare at his foot. It is an excruciating scene. Later in his life, his girlfriend, Mildred, knows that at any time she can crush him by calling him a cripple. That gives her an unfair power over him.

Shame allows no excuses for weakness. If a schoolboy is defeated by a peer, he's not likely to say, "I'm not ashamed; I couldn't help being beaten; he's just stronger than I am." After all, that's what he's ashamed of — not being stronger and tougher.

There is a good example of this in Jack London's novel *The Sea Wolf*. A delicately raised youth, Hump is kidnapped by brutal sailors and must live among them. Hump recalls how he fled at first from the bullying cook. He tries to excuse his flight by asking what else a man of his soft background could do in such circumstances. But this response doesn't satisfy him:

> There was no more reason that I should stand and face these human beasts than that I should stand and face an infuriated bull. . . . but this vindication did not satisfy. Nor to this day can I permit my manhood to look back upon those events and feel entirely exonerated. The situation was something that really exceeded rational formulas for conduct and demanded more than the cold conclusions of reason. When viewed in the light of formal logic, there is not one thing of which to be ashamed; but nevertheless a shame rises within me at the recollection, and in the pride of my manhood I feel that my manhood has in unaccountable ways been smirched and sullied.

A Positive Aspect of Shame

All this begins to sound rather harsh, so let me remark here that shame has a positive force in life as well as a painful one. It has the good-news aspect mentioned earlier: The emotion of shame stems from the basically positive desire for self-esteem. Humans need to aspire to full active development, to have a high self-ideal. We feel shame because we have such high aspirations, and surely that is a good thing.

Helen Lynd has argued that the experience of shame has a certain ironic positive effect. It does isolate the victim at the time, but no one escapes such experiences. This very fact helps humans to form deep relationships with one another, sympathizing with the human vulnerability they find in each other. Consider, for instance, the loving mother whose one moment of carelessness allows her child to drown. Sensitive friends will offer her support, not scorn. And while tactless sympathy can deepen shame, tactful sympathy can help enormously.

Again, think of Maugham's character Philip, with his clubfoot. He is fully into his medical career before he gets over feeling humiliated about his deformity. Here is how that happens. One day Philip casually hurts the pride of a senior doctor, his employer, by presuming to take over the elderly employer's duty to make a house call. To strike back, the crusty old doctor quips about Philip's foot: "This is a job for a man with two legs." As usual, Philip's whole body jolts from the attack of shame, but he silently recovers and goes on. Afterward, the older doctor says to him in a matter-of-fact way, "It stung you up a bit when I spoke of your game leg, young fellow?" Philip matter-of-factly answers, "People always do, directly or indirectly, when they get angry with me." From then on, the two are son-and-father friends. When Philip's vulnerability comes out into the open, is expressed in straightforward words, it ceases to be shadowy and "infinite," becomes definite and manageable. After all, his is just a human defect like the doctor's elderly feebleness — such defects are part of the human condition, and we can learn to live with them. (As noted before, the very discussion of the logic of humiliation might help us to handle our own shames better.)

More will be said later about this positive aspect of shame. I mention it here just to assure the reader that studying about honor norms is not entirely grim. Feeling abandoned and excluded is central to the experience of shame. Yet for that very reason it can be a bond between people. We hear someone say, "I felt embarrassed for her," in a kindly and sincere way, and we appreciate a profound generosity.

The philosopher Gregory Vlastos proposes a minimum of respect due to the human dignity of every person. A criminal may be punished *within* the community, but no one is to be expelled from the human caste, no matter what he has done. Even the condemned criminal may have a clergyman accompany him to the death chamber, signifying his continued membership in some human parish. This is also the idea behind the poignant line in Arthur Miller's *Death of a Salesman:* "He's not the finest character that ever lived. But he's a human being. . . . So attention must be paid. He's not to be allowed to fall into his grave like an old dog." That latter fate would be the ultimate, unbearable shame.

Similarities Between Shame and Guilt

It was important to point out the contrasts between shame and guilt in order to avoid confusing the norms of honor and decency that each emotion enforces. But here are also some similarities to be noted:

1. Both are painful emotions, feelings people will take care to avoid. That's why these feelings work to enforce society's norms. Occasionally we'll find someone who doesn't bother to avoid wrong or weak conduct. That's usually because that person simply doesn't feel these emotions intensely. If he feels no guilt when we think he should, we say he has

no conscience and call him ruthless; if he does not feel "warranted" shame, we call him *shameless*.

Note, incidentally, that rarely is anyone literally without shame. Though some people display little feeling of guilt, most "shameless" people would in fact feel quite ashamed of defeat or failure. What bothers us is that these people don't feel the normal shame at wrongdoing. "You ought to be ashamed!" scolds the concerned mother at a bold and naughty child. Later I'll discuss this special shame over wrongdoing that many people say is required for decency. For now, let's keep it simple by concentrating on normal humiliation over *nonmoral* shortcomings.

2. Both shame and guilt can arise over some specific incident. I can feel humiliated at falling down on the dance floor or at gullibly believing the line a sharp salesman has fed me. I can feel guilty about callously revealing a child's secret or about bullying a subordinate.

3. Both shame and guilt can involve a person's sense of who he or she is, what his or her identity is. The very style and manner of Philip's life is shaped by the shame he feels over his ugly, clumsy foot. He sees himself as inferior, as a person others could push around.

A person's self-image can also be profoundly affected by the guilt he feels. St. Augustine recalls, in his *Confessions*, an incident when he was a teenager that left him with a permanent self-image as a guilty person. One night he joined other boys in stealing some pears. Augustine felt only mild guilt about the actual theft (and perhaps a mild humiliation — the pears weren't that good). But he saw his profound wickedness in realizing that he had enjoyed the very *wrongness* of the stealing. This marked his later identity.

4. Feelings of both shame and guilt can be private, hidden from any outside audience. Although it is central to shame that I want to hide, I might have reason to hide guilt also (for fear of punishment). Again, both can be public. Guilt is easier to confess and perhaps easier for others to investigate, since it typically involves wrong done to others. That's the subject of detective stories. But being shamed necessarily involves at least the agent as his own audience. And the physical marks of shame, like blushing and sweating, are often all too easy for others to see.

5. Both emotions can be "unconscious." Psychiatric treatment for unconscious guilt is a familiar story in our culture. But persons repress

shaming experiences also. Treatment of a troubled young woman revealed that her father had repeatedly used her sexually, in front of her mother and without any affection, when she was four years old. She had forgotten that. And the psychologist Helen Lewis says that patients who are obviously feeling shame will seldom admit it. They prefer to say they are "depressed." Thinking of the current epidemic of "depression," one wonders how much shame is being misdescribed.

6. Both emotions can be warranted or unwarranted, justified or irrational. People nowadays tend to see a certain conventional aspect of moral rules, realizing that the diet forbidden to Hindus is not the one forbidden to Muslims. But they tend to think that the norms of honor binding themselves are just natural and obvious and universal. As I have mentioned, however, our society tells male intellectuals to be proud of mechanical skills, while Oriental society may tell the intellectual to be ashamed of such skills. Our society tells us which acts are guilty, what we should feel vain about, and when we should feel humiliated. But *wait* a minute. About any of these matters, our society might be *wrong!*

Philosophic ethics is the inquiry into which *social* norms of decency are "really" valid. What violations would really warrant guilt feelings? Sadly, recent philosophers have not often looked into which of our actual norms of honor are valid, would really warrant humiliation. This book is an attempt to get such a dialogue under way. And the time has come to move the discussion from the emotional sanctions to the types of norms that these emotions enforce.

Four Types of Norm

The Limit Norms of Honor and Decency

Fear of guilt or humiliation can strongly motivate people to control their behavior and frame their personal characters. When people actively fear shame they are trying to live according to something like a code of honor. When they fear guilt they are trying to live a moral life. Most people have both of these fears, though in varying degrees. Normal people don't want to fall below the minimal thresholds demanded by the norms of honor and decency. We may thus describe these as *limit* norms, because they set definite limits to what is acceptable conduct or character.

The spirit and content of honor and decency are, in different communities, expressed in different sets of specific rules. We call these special sets of social rules codes. So each community can be said to have its own code of honor and decency, a set of quite definite rules directing behavior. Often the rules are negative, in the form of "don't do such-and-such." That "don't-do-it" negativity is a typical characteristic of limit norms.

Below is a partial list of rules we take as fairly typical of the code of decency in the United States. Each reader might set up a different list because individual perceptions differ about which standards the whole community or culture accepts. But with all our differences, there is much agreement also. I may not accept all of these myself, but I'd expect most Americans to accept most of these limit norms. The list should serve at least to give a concrete example of what I mean by a social moral code.

The American Code of Decency

Don't steal or damage the private property of others.
Don't steal or damage public property.
Obey the laws of the land.
Don't act as if you are better (or significantly less) than others. Don't even harbor such thoughts.
Don't do bodily harm to others; don't injure people's pride by negative remarks.
Don't lie or cheat; be faithful to wife or husband.
Respect the majority vote in elections as decisive, even if you disagree.
Be cooperative with neighbors and colleagues.
Don't interfere with the right of others to express their honest opinions.
Don't interfere with the religious preferences of others.

. . . and so on. You can probably think of many other rules to add to the list.

Below is a partial list of rules in the American code of honor. This list is more difficult to agree upon because Americans don't talk comfortably about honor. But there is evidence for honor norms at work in people's behavior. Judith Viorst wrote a tongue-in-cheek poem speaking out as a wife frustrated by her husband's honor-bound refusal to ask for road directions. The frustration peaks in this last verse:

And even if I, in a tone I concede is called
    screaming,
Enumerated his countless imperfections,
I still would be incapable of persuading my
    husband, when lost,
To stop the goddamn car, and ask for
    directions.

Like Viorst, we can observe which incidents and actions people in the United States avoid from fear of shame. Since honor consists in avoiding shame, this can tip us off to our culture's code of honor.

Remember that I am not *endorsing* these normative rules but merely reporting them. You may find that some of them are a little silly, that our culture should "outgrow" them. Many of us may not feel bound at all by certain ones. A few are immoral, conflicting with decency. But some also overlap with the code of decency.

The American Code of Honor

If you start something — even something illegal and immoral — be sure to finish it.

Be male if possible. Barring that, don't admit to liking sissy things. (If you like pink flowers, don't admit it.) Don't show you can identify colors like mauve and puce.

Keep your promises; be trustworthy, predictable, reliable. Also, back up your threats.

Be able-bodied, but don't let the pursuit of bodily fitness weaken you in the mental competition, say, in business or government.

Don't be a sucker.

Don't let others take advantage of you.

Be cautiously generous but not overly sympathetic.

Don't be quick to share your troubles with others or to expect sympathy from them.

(For males): Don't be dependent on a woman, except for womanly things.

Be cool: Never let them see you sweat.

Don't take welfare. If you're poor, don't admit it. Never try to blame the system for your personal failures.

(For urban males): Never ask directions unless you're desperate. Better: Don't get lost or desperate.

(For males): Don't display ignorance of machines or computers or sports.

Don't be a coward; don't back down.

Don't bluster or brag beyond the point you plan to fight.

Don't bungle so you must cheat or lie when cornered by necessity. (It's OK to cheat to beat the system, but be sure to be cool and clever about it.)

Demand full payment for any job you have done.

(For females): Don't accept money from a man unless you're willing to repay with sexual favors.

Be slow to admit you are wrong.

Be decisive, practical, realistic.

Don't be intellectual — but don't be dumb or stupid either.

(For males): Don't draw attention to your dress or appearance; seek admiration for your accomplishments, not your appearance.

Don't be naive or too innocent or trusting.
Don't be a bully, a wife-beater, a rapist, or a child abuser.
Don't get mad, get even.
Don't flatter the boss.

Goal Norms

In following definite rules like those in the two lists above, a person shows respect for the limit norms, the minimal standards, of honor and decency. To avoid shame and guilt, one must attend to some such rules. But even strict obedience to minimal codes like these does not guarantee escape from guilt or shame — because there are other standards that do not just specify limits, as the examples above do. These other standards specify mandated *goals*, without mentioning the definite means to reach these goals. For instance, most people would feel guilty if they fell short of these goals:

Do your utmost to promote your children's education and health.
Help out friends in a jam.
Support your parents if they are old and needy.
Give at least something to charity.

Notice that these standards don't tell the agent what means to take. That is, they don't say how a person should go about doing the task. They mandate an earnest attempt to attain the goal *somehow*. Just get the job done. Persons of good will feel guilt if they fail to work toward these goals. These standards specify goals, whereas the code of decency sets limits on conduct.

Likewise, many active, talented persons may feel inglorious if they fall short of standards like these:

Play to win — compete seriously with those well matched with you.
Get the closest parking place possible, even if you must wait awhile.
Promote the success of those subordinates who are loyal to your
    working team.
(For crude males): Have intercourse with many women.
Promote the sexual satisfaction of your partner.

Now look back in Chapter 3 at the chart distinguishing guilt from shame. It says that the polar opposite of guilt is not innocence, as one might expect, but rather moral self-satisfaction, the feeling that one deserves reward and happiness. This feeling of deserved reward, oddly enough, is not accepted as legitimate by mainstream Christians (more on this in a moment) but it is accepted by some other religions.

Similarly, the polar opposite of shame is called not honor but rather glory — pride, high self-esteem, or satisfaction at achievement. The desire to shine is not simply the avoiding of shame any more than moral self-satisfaction is the same as mere innocence from avoiding wrongdoing. The soldier Williams (in *Henry V*) maintains his honor, but he is not thereby glorious. And you are not a moral hero just because you never robbed or cheated anyone.

These thoughts suggest that the shame-guilt distinction points not to just two types of norm, honor and decency, but to two other types as well — achievement and beneficence. A person goes beyond avoiding dishonor by successful, splendid achievement. While some people are content just to maintain their honor, others are urgently concerned to rise above this level. They bind themselves by norms of achievement. Again, one person may rest at ease having fulfilled his definite moral duties, whereas another will see a need to "walk a second mile." If a soldier incurs terrible injury to save his friends, we say his action was "above and beyond the call of duty," deserving special reward and praise.

Peter, for instance, may be satisfied to play a respectable game of basketball, whereas Paul will not be satisfied unless he is hailed as a notable athlete. Both youths want to avoid disgraceful blunders on the court, but Paul is also eager to shine there. He will feel a sense of failure if he doesn't shine. Perhaps Peter wants to shine in some other way, say in computer science. So he will devote only enough athletic effort to avoid humiliation in basketball.

Let us say, then, that Paul is committed to a norm of achievement in regard to basketball. He demands of himself not just competence but outstanding excellence in that field. This throws him into fierce competition with other players having the same ambition — others who have also accepted that achievement norm. Not everyone can excel because excelling means being better, and everyone can't be better than everyone: "If everyone is Somebody, then no one's Anybody!" Thus, to accept an achievement norm is to commit yourself to competition, and to the reality that very few contenders can win first prize.

I said before that the decency norm can also be transcended. It sets limits on what is morally acceptable, and people who observe those limits are counted as decent and morally innocent. But some people feel a moral concern that carries them beyond the call of duty. They care intensely for the welfare of others. They are "good-willing" (that is, benevolent); they *do* good for others (that is, they are beneficent). They set out to help others in ways not required of them by decency norms. It seems to follow that the people they help should return them gratitude, whereas no gratitude is due to someone simply for not wronging another. But when a person goes beyond moral constraints and does benevolent things for others, moral praise and perhaps also reward seem appropriate from onlookers. When Mother Theresa received the Nobel Peace Prize and gave it to charity, an admiring world looked on.

Without some special explanation or story, we'd feel that a just God should reward benevolent people as well as punish the malevolent. It would then follow that the benevolent people themselves must realize that they do deserve reward and happiness for their strenuous concern for others. This realization would warrant their feelings of self-satisfaction.

Several paragraphs above, I mentioned that mainstream Christians do not seem to regard moral goal norms as legitimate. Now that odd point about Christianity can be explained. These Christians *have* a special story to explain their rejection of moral self-satisfaction. They say that every one of us, born in sin, will do wrong, not good, unless helped by the free gift of God's grace. So, although the wages of sin are death, eternal life is not the reward for virtue but is instead a free gift of God. Thus Christians don't reject the *logic* of moral goal norms. They simply hold that moral rewards are never in fact due to innately sinful humans.

Decency sets a lower moral threshold below which we cannot sink without losing innocence and deserving blame. Beneficence — the following of moral goal norms — invites us to promote the welfare of others and thus deserve moral credit. Beneficence and decency are each moral norms. One is goal-oriented (beneficence) and the other attends to limits. Specific codes reflecting these norm types vary from culture to culture, group to group, even from one person to another. But the structure of each of these codes will be similar. Each specific code of beneficence will set particular goals. Each code of decency will set particular limits on conduct and character.

The Ten Commandments are a well-known code of decency, an explicit code forbidding its followers even to covet the goods or mates of others. But the sayings of Jesus display in addition a code of beneficence. Jesus emphasized the active, helping love of all other people as a basic commandment. He focused on beneficence, beyond the demands of mere decency. He saw that minimal observance of moral limits was not enough for a full and wholesome life and for a healthy community.

The actual Ten Commandments don't explicitly mandate helping others. Later Judaism, of course, did see God as demanding mutual help. Jesus was not offering a startling new doctrine. But his *intensity* was startling. He laid his grimmest curse, not on murderers or idolaters or traitors but upon people who refused to help the needy:

> Depart from me, ye cursed, into everlasting fire, prepared for the devil and his angels: for I was an hungered, and ye gave me no meat. . . . I was a stranger, and ye took me not in. . . . Inasmuch as ye did it not to one of the least of these, ye did it not to me.

The Four Norms Compared

To classify the norm types we will hereafter be examining, I will use these four main ideas:

1. A *moral norm* has guilt as its negative enforcer.
2. A *nonmoral norm* has shame as its negative enforcer.
3. A *limit norm* tells you that certain types of actions are prohibited, even if they are necessary to promote certain goals. A limit norm tells you what to do.
4. A *goal norm* tells you to pursue a certain goal by the most effective means, whatever the means may be. A goal norm tells you what to get done somehow.

Thus we have four different types of norm. Two of these types are goal oriented (beneficence and achievement), two types set limits (decency and honor), two types give moral norms (beneficence and decency), and two are nonmoral (achievement and honor). Note that the nonmoral types have to do essentially with self-esteem. They are self-regarding but not necessarily selfish. Because they mandate splendid deeds and bar ugly conduct, we sometimes describe them as *aesthetic* norms. The scheme I've laid out will be easier to remember from a diagram:

	MORAL NORMS	AESTHETIC NORMS
	Decency Code	**Honor Code**
LIMIT NORMS	Avoid wicked acts, or else face guilt.	Avoid base, weak, or ugly conduct (like cowardice, vacillation, treachery), or else face shame (loss of honor).
	Beneficence Code	**Achievement Code**
GOAL NORMS	Work to improve the situation of others, thus deserving happiness and avoiding guilt of omission.	Accomplish shining deeds, thus earning glory and avoiding shame of failure.

Relations among these types of norms are complicated and interesting; we will want to explore them. For example, does the negative sanction of shame relate to the norm of achievement? If so, then how? And how does guilt relate to beneficence? How do each of the four norms relate and compare with the other three? We need to ask questions like these in order to understand better the norms and values that guide human action.

The next three chapters will concentrate on decency and honor. Then, later, we will consider the goal norms of achievement and beneficence.

Chapter 5

The Limit Norms of Decency

In the last chapter we distinguished the limit norms, decency and honor, from the goal norms, beneficence and glory (or achievement). When people act according to limit norms they concern themselves with staying within certain definite boundaries. Acting under goal norms, they are concerned to achieve certain ends, even before they worry about how to accomplish those ends. Action according to norms of honor or glory is *self-regarding* in the sense that the agent is concerned with what kind of person he or she is. The question is asked, "How do my actions reflect on me as a person?" Action according to norms of decency or beneficence is other-regarding, or moral, in that the agent is primarily concerned with the welfare of others and what he or she is doing to or for others. This gives us the four types of norm found in diagram form in Chapter 4.

This chapter and the next will discuss the two limit norms, decency and honor. To be clear about our concepts, we need to discuss each norm type separately, but this doesn't mean that in normal life they occur separately. People typically guide their action according to more than one type of norm at once. For instance, Caroline, responding to a beneficence norm, may believe she ought to do volunteer work at the hospital because she is especially capable of that kind of work and the hospital administrators have sent out an appeal for volunteers. Caroline will do what she can to help, perhaps giving up her normal routine of playing tennis two afternoons a week. But she also cares about the decency norm, and so she won't neglect her children for the sake of the hospital. She is acting, then, according to both a goal and a limit norm. Beneficence guides her to volunteer, however she can. Decency restricts her ways of volunteering. Notice that if there is no way she can volunteer without neglecting her family duties, then she must face a conflict between beneficence and decency. She can do one or the other but not both. These conflicts often arise, but they do not always arise.

Another important point from the last chapter needs repeating: The norm types we speak of have a fairly universal structure across different societies and cultures, even though specific codes under those norms may vary widely. That is, specific codes are typically relative to a given society, but every society responds in some degree to each of the four kinds of norm. Evidence for this is that the emotions of shame and guilt both appear in every culture. What people are ashamed or guilty about will typically vary from one culture to another. But the four types of norm behind those concerns have a similar structure.

As we discuss those universal structures, bear in mind the points of the last two paragraphs. Here they are in summary:

1. People are often guided by more than one type of norm in the same action.
2. Specific codes (sets of local norms of a given type) are relative to different communities, but the norm types themselves have structures universal enough to be described in general terms.

The Structure of Decency

There are two main requirements in the various codes of decency. A conscientious person who fails in either of them will feel guilt. One requirement is that we should avoid harming persons. The other consists in that cluster of definite duties that people take for granted, like honoring parents and being trustworthy. Both of these imply restraints, limits.

The first of these is normally expressed in some negative version of the Golden Rule: Do not do to another what you would not want another to do to you. Notice that the Golden Rule doesn't say, "Don't do harm," though doubtless it means that. Rather, the way it is stated gives a quick and ready criterion for *what harm is.* Generally speaking, I call an action harmful if it would harm me when done to me. I can quickly check out what that is with a little reflection about my own feelings and a little imagination about what a certain experience would be like. Here are some brief examples:

- It would hurt my feelings if someone told me that I look pregnant, so I won't say to the fat woman whom I've just met: "I'm so glad to meet you! Are you pregnant?"
- I have known disappointment when friends have broken promises to me, so I will keep my promise to you now if I possibly can.
- The woman who mows my lawn is in business by herself and doesn't have much leeway in paying the bills. That feels uncomfortable, so I don't put off paying her when she sends a bill to me.
- While saying goodbye to a friend at her car, I close the car door for her and, in doing so, accidentally catch the floppy ear of her dog in the door. The dog cries pitifully. I don't happen to have floppy ears, nor have I ever had floppy ears. But I can imagine what it would be like to have them and get one caught in a car door. So I make haste to open the door and free the dog's ear.

Any normal person can imagine himself in another's place in ways like these. It is part of what we mean by "normal person." There are certain experiences that almost everyone wants to avoid. They all involve pain of various kinds. I know what is — or would be — painful to me. Therefore I know generally what would be painful to others. "Pain" here includes any damage or harm, even subtle harms like frustration, humiliation, degradation, grief, disappointment. Pain, then, is what I am to avoid causing in others. So we can roughly restate the negative Golden Rule as "Don't cause pain to others any more than to myself," or even more simply, "Don't cause pain."

This is not to say that physical pain is *always* bad. It has an important positive function for all sentient life, for humans and all the other animals. It warns us when we are in trouble, as when we humans endure pain at the dentist's office or tweeze out a splinter. Again, sometimes pain is for the sake of another's good, as when the mother animal gives birth or endures pain to protect the young.

But *unnecessary* and *undeserved* physical or mental pain is bad. It is universally bad. It should be avoided, and the negative Golden Rule says that. That is a universal and first principle of the decency norm.

All specific codes of decency express it in one way or another. Here are examples from various cultures:

> What is hateful to you, do not to your fellow man. That is the entire law; all the rest is commentary. (Judaism)

> Let none of you treat a brother in a way he himself would dislike to be treated. (Islam)

> Do nothing to others which you would not have done to you. (Brahminism)

> The true Lord is in all men. Distress no one's heart; every heart is a priceless jewel. (Sikhism)

> Hurt not others in ways that you yourself would find hurtful. (Buddhism)

> Is there one maxim which ought to be acted upon throughout one's whole life? Surely it is the maxim of loving-kindness: Do not do to others what you would not have others do to you. (Confucianism)

> That person alone is good who refrains from doing to another whatever is not good for himself. (Zoroastrianism)

From this principle, however one presents it, many specific rules follow. They tend to be stated — not always but usually — in negative terms, such as "Don't assault other persons without reason," "Don't abandon a person who is in distress," "Don't stare curiously at cripples," "Don't lie."

The second main idea about decency centers on those definite and specific duties that people, just by common sense, know they ought to carry out. (This isn't to say that they always *do* carry them out. Almost everyone is guilty of omission now and then.) Here is a list of examples familiar in our own society:

Pay your debts.
Honor your parents.
Don't drink to excess.
Don't abuse your children.
Get to your work on time.
Be reliable.
If you are a doctor, care for your patients.

Keep your promises.
Don't undermine your health.

These specific rules have something in common. They all tend to help keep a community stable and healthy. Probably they evolved that way, but we do not think about that when common sense directs us to follow them. Typically, we just think of the rule itself, and it is self-evident to us that each describes an obligation. Many of them mention a specific role. That is, since they have to do with specific needs of the community, they are often connected with specific functions or roles of different persons in a community.

Thus, in our society, someone in the role of a father has definite duties that the name "father" implies. He is supposed to provide food every day, secure the home against intruders, and so on. He is supposed to be a model whom his sons can identify with and whom his daughters will learn to admire (so he shouldn't wear a dress or fluffy apron in front of the children). People who aren't fathers do not generally have those duties; they will have other duties instead, depending on the role they find themselves in. The father will likely be in some other role as well. Suppose he is a businessman. Then the businessman's role gives him duties in addition to the father's role. He should be honest about the product, be loyal to the company, show up to appointments on time, and so on.

Communities vary a good deal in the way they assign roles, and that variation accounts for the relativity of different codes from one society to another. Also, functions and roles evolve within a given community according to changing needs and circumstances. In our country, for example, it was most unusual a few decades ago for mothers of young children to work outside the home. Generally they did so only if necessity forced them; otherwise people tended to disapprove. But in the last few decades things have changed. Not only has the economy evolved new forms and needs but also some women have decided that they ought to have careers even while raising young children. The needs of these career mothers and their children have given rise to new roles for other people besides the mothers themselves. We now have daycare centers where people fulfill the function of taking care of the children of working mothers. We have, then, a new role — daycare tenders of children — that we didn't have before.

These differences and fluctuations are understandable in light of the general structure of decency. They are the details in answer to the question, "What does a given community need for stability and survival?" But people don't ask that question and then figure out the rules. Rather, the rules evolve in each situation as needs arise, and it feels as if they just come from common sense.

Conflicts of Decency Duties

Between the Golden Rule and duties following from specific roles, a good many moral duties are generated, and, unfortunately, they sometimes conflict. Sometimes one rule tells you to do one thing and another something else that can't be done at the same time. Almost everyone has been in this painful sort of conflict, conscientiously wanting to do the right thing but having to "do wrong" in one way or another just because the demands are incompatible.

Ten-year-old Judy found herself in conflict when her parents told her not to play anymore with Alphea, the little girl down the street. Alphea's house was poor and shabby, and it didn't smell good inside. Alphea's parents had rather strange habits, and her older sister was known to "run around." But Judy loved Alphea and felt responsible for her because Alphea admired Judy and gratefully imitated her cleanliness, good speech, and delicate manners. So Judy was torn between obeying her parents (which is the proper role of a ten-year-old) and being loyal to Alphea (which is proper as a friend). After a time Judy felt she must obey her parents, but she was always miserable when she heard through third parties about how sad and lonely Alphea was. And two years later, when someone told her that twelve-year-old Alphea had run off with a man over thirty, Judy felt guilty indeed. She felt it was her fault because her continued loyalty might have prevented that misfortune.

Here is a grislier example: In Henry Carlisle's novel *The Jonah Man*, George Pollard is captain of a whaling vessel. When they are sailing miles from any land, a furious whale attacks their ship several times and knocks it to pieces. The men disperse onto three small whaleboats with as many provisions as they can manage to bring with them. Though careful, the men use up the provisions and are left with neither water nor food. Days pass, and still the men don't see land. One day Pollard's cousin Owen, who is in the same whaleboat with him, notices in horror that the men in one of the other whaleboats are sharing in the eating of the lower half of a human leg. More hungry, thirsty days go by. The men's suffering is nearly unbearable. And an unthinkable idea — cannibalism — has been presented to their thoughts.

Captain Pollard is in this position: As a human being living under the negative Golden Rule it is obvious that he may not take another human life, especially that of a suffering comrade. But as captain of a ship it is his responsibility to see that as much of the community survives as possible. He opts for the cannibalism, with the full agreement of the other men on the boat. They draw straws — it is done fairly, with the consent of all, and without rancor. Owen draws the fatal straw and calmly holds still so that Pollard can shoot him.

Captain Pollard and the other survivors are finally rescued. Once back in his native Nantucket, he is tried for the murder of Owen, and the court exonerates him. Why? Because the court agrees that the cannibalism was necessary for there to be any survivors, and he has carried out the ugly deed as fairly and justly as he could. Not surprisingly, many people in the story think the court is much too lenient. That is, there are varying opinions on whether Pollard and the court have made the right decision about justice. That brings us to another structural feature of decency.

Justice

Think about the Golden Rule again for a moment. It calls on us not to treat others in a way that we wouldn't want them to treat us. But who are these others? Well, they are just all other human beings. (Perhaps they are animals also, but I won't discuss that issue here.) The point is that the Golden Rule reminds us that there are others like us: Others who can feel pain and sorrow and resentment and disappointment.

I must recognize, then, that I am not alone in the world. Unless there is some particular quality that makes me superior, I am not especially special. Every person is in one sense "special," like every snowflake. I may be special because of something wonderful I have done. Or I may be special to someone who loves me dearly or depends on me. But I am not special just because I am myself. After all, *everyone* is himself or herself.

Another way of putting this is that we ought not to make exceptions of ourselves. That certainly seems reasonable. Why would anyone ever *not* recognize the simple bit of logic that just because I am me doesn't mean I should count for more than anyone else? Well, most people do recognize that they are not special merely because they are themselves. But often people act as if they were special in that way. Often they act in a way that makes an exception of themselves. The reason for this is self-involvement. I live intimately close to myself, and it is hard not to take a special interest in how I'm getting along. If I'm applying for a job, and someone else is competing with me, I may have a hard time swallowing the idea that (given that my competitor is similarly qualified) she has as much right to the job as I do. Suppose Captain Pollard had said, "One of us must die in order for any of us to survive, but I ought not to be the one that dies because I am me and all the rest of you are only *you*." Imagine the outcry of his comrades and their intolerance of such crass selfishness!

Thus the negative Golden Rule provides the basis of a certain minimal kind of fairness or justice, the kind that says that everyone should be treated as a center of interest, of possible pleasure and joy and pain and sorrow. No one is a center of interest more than anyone else.

But now let's look at another aspect of justice, another kind of fairness. It is the kind that follows closely with that second main rule of decency, namely, that persons acquire duties because of a particular role they find themselves in.

Doing one's duty often comes to giving others their due. The father has a special duty to do certain things for his children, and we say that these things are the children's due. There are other familiar ways of putting it. We often say that children are *entitled* to certain things from their father or that they have a *right* to those certain things. As father I am obligated to do so-and-so for my children; as child I have it coming to me to have these things done for me. A certain type of treatment is a child's due. Another type is a father's due.

Of course, it isn't merely one's role that determines what one is entitled to. Sometimes we speak of entitlement apart from any particular role. Consider these familiar beliefs:

A soprano who sings high C clearly and in tune deserves her
audience's applause.

The employee who usually produces less than another doesn't deserve
to be paid as much as the other.

The soldier who risks his life for his comrades deserves a reward.

A soldier who lets others take the chances of being killed deserves
contempt.

Every human being deserves adequate food and shelter for survival.

A murderer deserves a sentence equal to the crime.

A neighbor who takes time to visit the lonely woman across the street
deserves to be admired.

The rich man who chooses not to provide his city with an extra park
doesn't always deserve to be blamed.

Each of these cases is a remark about a kind of justice, about what
someone deserves. And I've been describing the structure of decency
as having two main parts, both of them concerned with justice. We
should treat all persons as centers of interest, and we should give others
their due. So people acting on decency norms would want to examine
and think carefully about the above judgments.

Notice now that the judgments themselves are not all made with
regard to decency. The first two have to do with achievement. The
second two are concerned with honor. The third pair are decency
considerations, and the fourth pair refer to beneficence. This means
that a decent-minded person cannot always avoid thinking about
norms other than decency. Justice often requires considering the other
norm types as well. And there is something more to note here. What a
person deserves depends not merely on what that person *does*. It has,
to decent common sense, much to do with what sort of person he *is*.
One would not admire the soldier's brave act if it were just an accident,
or something he couldn't help doing because of, say, an outside threat,
or if he were just tired of fighting in the war and wanted to end it all
for himself. If he had any of these ulterior motives, people wouldn't say
he was courageous, and certainly it is the courage within him, not just
a single act, that deserves admiration. Likewise, we wouldn't be contemptuous of a man who avoided a dangerous act in order to save his
platoon later. The evasion might *look* cowardly, but it would not be
cowardly if it were done with courageous or decent intention.

61

Now take an example from the glory pair above, about the soprano reaching her high note. Suppose she had no sense of pitch but just happened to be able to sing high notes. Then the mere reaching of a high note, although remarkable, wouldn't be admirable, because no one would say she was an accomplished singer. What she is matters as well as what she does.

This point about what sort of person one is, what one's character is like, raises the question of virtue. Philosophers neglected virtue for a long time. Recently they have become much more interested in it because decency, as well as the other three types of norm, requires that we think about what people are as well as about what they do. Recognizing justice often requires an examination of a person's character.

Virtue

The word "virtue" in our society has fallen somewhat into disrepute in our daily talk, but reflection on the idea behind it will help in our examination of limit norms. It offers a bridge from decency to honor.

First, consider how we use the word at present. Here are some ideas about virtue that people have shared with me: In the 1970s when Jimmy Carter was president, one sometimes heard people say that he was "virtuous." They seem to have been referring not to his administrative abilities or to how he fulfilled duties associated with being president but rather to his careful following of moral instructions related to his church. He would not touch strong drink, for instance. He was honest and upstanding. He presented himself as an ordinary, unadorned fellow like you and me (that is, as a peanut farmer, in his case). He was seen as careful not to cross boundaries regarding marital fidelity. All this made him "virtuous." Of course, he felt lust in his heart, as he once said, but any normal, healthy male is expected to do that. If *that* was his only moral fault, then we had a pretty decent fellow for president.

The people giving me this example admitted that they were half serious and half jesting. They were serious in that they sincerely could find no fault with Carter as a decent fellow. They were jesting, however, in that they had no intention themselves of imitating such a style of conduct. This doesn't mean my friends ignore decency norms. It means rather that they take seriously Carter's decency but do not take seriously his code of decency. They consider it a rather antiquated code. The word "virtuous" seemed appropriate to describe a man who followed an old-fashioned code because (we surmised) "virtuous" is a rather old-fashioned word.

Here is another example my friends gave me: The word "virtuous" is often used with a slight irony or sarcasm, as in "Janie is *so* virtuous," when the speaker means that Janie follows all the rules precisely to the letter and is disgustingly self-righteous about it. The point of the irony in this remark is that Janie isn't really virtuous at all. Whatever virtue she might have had is tainted by her self-righteousness. In other words, Janie lacks a virtue that is particularly important to the speaker — namely, humility. She has the *vice* of self-righteousness.

Both of these examples indicate that in our modern culture we haven't forgotten virtue as an elemental part of normative thinking. Both examples above put the idea at a sort of distance but still take it seriously. The Carter example puts virtue at a distance by setting it back in time (it is a little old-fashioned). The Janie example envelops virtue in irony. But in both cases the speakers admitted that behind their use of the word lay quite a serious idea. Somehow there is embarrassment about using the word straightforwardly, even though it names something important.

To get at the serious idea, consider these straightforward uses. By "straightforward" I mean that they are said without irony. Try not to worry that some of them sound old-fashioned.

Statement	Meaning of Statement
Margaret is a virtuous mother.	Margaret does well and does consistently the things mothers are supposed to do.
Bathsheba is a virtuous wife.	Bathsheba is faithful to her husband and she does what wives are expected to do.
The virtue of the sap engenders the flower.	The sap of the plant is what enables the plant to bloom.
Herbert is a virtuoso at the piano.	Herbert plays the piano with dexterity and skill.

Statement	Meaning of Statement
The Christian virtues are faith, hope, and charity.	Christians are supposed to live with the inner qualities of faith, hope, and charity.
The pistons move by virtue of the combustion.	Combustion makes the pistons move.
Caesar Borgia had virtù.	Caesar Borgia displayed resolute courage, high ambition, and cleverness.
You can depend on John to act virtuously.	You can expect John to do things properly and to respect his duty.
This herbal will tell you about the virtues of tarragon.	This herbal will tell you what uses you can make of tarragon.

These examples indicate that "virtue" and related words have something to do with norms generally, something to do with evaluating how good a person or thing is. The uses show virtue as a *trait* of a person in a given role. Or it is a trait of a thing that one expects to function in a given way. And that trait is connected with the idea of power or strength. It has to do with the person's (or thing's) *ability* to function well in a given role. A virtuous person, then, is someone *able* to do well what he or she is supposed to do. The kind of ability referred to is relative to the role or function of the person. But the trait is not *mere* ability. It is also the tendency to use that ability. We thus may call it a disposition. It has to do with a person's character. So virtue is a state of character. To be virtuous is to be the sort of person you are supposed to be.

Admittedly, this doesn't tell us much, until we answer the question of what one is supposed to be. One's code of decency partly answers that question. Our decency code tells us what we are supposed to do and not do. But a person could follow all decency rules to the letter and still not be virtuous if he doesn't have the appropriate state of character. That is why Janie in the example above is not virtuous. Her state of character is to be self-righteous, and that is inappropriate, no matter how right her actions might be. The state of character that makes a person decently virtuous is this attitude: I should follow the decency rules because it is the right thing to do, not because it makes me "holier than thou."

But doing the right thing because it is right is not easy, for that means much more than just following rules. It means obeying the spirit of the rules rather than merely the letter. There is a story about one of the first ladies in the nineteenth century who was hostessing an elaborate dinner at the White House. It was extremely formal, and all the formal silver and china were laid out just so, the way they were supposed to be. One of the guests was an uneducated fellow from the backcountry who had never learned the niceties of formal table manners. He began pushing food onto the blade of his knife and sticking the knife into his mouth to eat the food off of it. Other guests inconspicuously cocked their eyebrows. Some of them no doubt felt shocked; some felt superior; some felt embarrassed for the boorish fellow. In this uncomfortable situation the hostess began eating with her knife also. Since a hostess dictates manners, the guests were obliged to follow her lead. Thus the evening was saved.

This example comes from rules of etiquette, not from moral rules directly. The spirit behind etiquette, however, is a moral concern. One should act in a way that keeps people comfortable and at ease so that social interchange can go on smoothly. Manners were made for people, not people for manners.

Following rules, then, doesn't make a person virtuous. One needs to follow the rules in the right way. The philosopher Aristotle attempted to give guidelines about "the right way" in order to characterize virtue a little more definitely. He decided that virtue is a state of character that steers a middle way between two excessive character traits. That is, he thought virtue lay in *moderation*. Don't act with too much of a given characteristic, and don't act with too little of it either.

The first lady in the example was abiding by this guideline. If she had continued with her fork (when it was her privilege to dictate propriety) she would have been too formal, placing too much importance on customary social graces. If she had imitated her ungraceful guest in *all* his manners (say, spitting on the floor, belching, smoking a rank cigar), that would have shown too little regard for sensible, important rules.

Aristotle gives us a number of examples of what he means by saying that virtue is moderation. And even though he lived in a different culture from ours, his ideas sound like fairly good common sense. You have courage, he says, if your character would keep you from shrinking from danger where you really need to face it, and also keep you from doing some sort of daredevil, foolhardy thing that doesn't matter. Thus, if you need to save a child from drowning, then you ought to brave the river's heavy current, and it would be cowardly not to. But if you can't swim, and no one is drowning anyway, then it is quite dumb to jump in.

Here are some other examples he gives:

• In handling money, you ought to be somewhere between a spendthrift and a miser.

• In enjoying yourself, you ought to find a moderate point between constantly indulging yourself and never having any fun at all.

• Thinking about your honor — how other people view you — you ought to have the proper amount of personal pride, but don't run yourself down and don't go all out trying to impress people.

• As for disposition or good temper, don't repress your anger: Get mad when you need to, yet don't blow up at every little thing.

• Regarding how friendly to be, don't be too shy. Approach people openly, but don't fall all over them with attention.

Aristotle lists a number of other virtues and then adds, with good common sense, that it is hard to find that middle ground that is just right. He gives the example of trying to find the center of a circle: It is easy to find *almost* the center, but getting the exact spot is hard. Not everybody can do it. Thus goodness, he says, "is both rare and laudable and noble."

Nonmoral Virtues

What pleasures to choose and how much to spend money are matters that our morality usually deals with, but notice that several of the virtues Aristotle mentions have little to do with morality. In some cases friendliness and good temper might be assets in following decency or beneficence norms, but they are not always necessary for those norms. Many of the virtues he lists have not so much to do with decency and beneficence as with the aesthetic, self-regarding norms. Aristotle spoke to an audience that wanted to be worthy of admiration. His list, then, covered both kinds of limit norms, the aesthetic as well as the moral.

Chapter 6

The Limit Norms of Honor

One famous passage in Aristotle's writings offers us a picturesque description of a man who excels in honor. Both self-regard and attention to honor limits reach an ideal in this picture. Aristotle calls his ideal the great-souled man, or the (properly) proud man.

This ideally proud man is a strong silent type who carries himself with great dignity and self-respect. He competently excels in every virtue and refuses to lower his standards even for life itself. He disdains things of little importance, saving his effort for things that matter. Good or bad fortune, power, wealth, petty dangers, the opinions of lesser men — none of these shake him to emotion, for he takes no trivial thing seriously.

He holds a high opinion of himself because he is truthful, assessing his own worth in an accurate way. (If he says anything false it is only "in irony to the vulgar.") He is appropriately gracious toward others, but he in no way depends on them except for friendship, which every good man will have. His truthfulness doesn't extend to blaming or speaking evil of others or even praising others, for all that sort of talk is trivial and idle.

He disdains the merely utilitarian and loves the fine and beautiful. But most of all he prizes his own worthiness to be honored by people wise enough to recognize true worth. He walks with dignity and speaks in a calm level way ("for the man who takes few things seriously is not likely to be hurried"). In short, he is a sort of ancient Greek Matt Dillon.

The Structure of Honor

Aristotle's ideally honorable man has competence, physical dignity, and strength and is in addition convinced of his own worth and deserts. In details of how he carries off these virtues, he differs from a modern counterpart, but the ideals have remained constant. For honor is the avoidance of shame, and shame arises over incompetence, ugliness, or weakness. Whenever anyone is trying to avoid displaying these defects, that person is using an honor norm to guide action. The corresponding virtues, then, lie at the heart of the structure of this limit norm. Different cultures and communities must constantly assess or reassess what things persons ought to be competent at doing and what grades of competence will be minimally acceptable. They must assess what ought to count as physical beauty or good physical presence. And they must assess what kinds of strength and competence are important and how they ought to be measured.

Consider, as an exercise, how much activity in American communities is devoted to these values and to debates over them. Even superficial reflection about this will easily show that honor (though we avoid the word itself) is a prevalent part of our normative thinking and concern.

Here are the main components in the structure of the honor norm. Individual codes of honor include these in various ways.

1. The ideals implicit in honor are competence, physical dignity, and strength.
2. A set of honor norms typically frames itself around ranking of people in some way.
3. Concern for honor reflects, in some degree, a concern for the opinion of others.
4. Honor norms have to do with self-regard or self-esteem, often related to the ranking.
5. Honor is the reciprocal of shame; that is, the loss of honor engenders shame, and so it has structural elements corresponding to the characteristics of shame.

Aristotle's ideas have thrown light on the first of these items, the ideals of honor. Each of the other four items needs separate discussion also.

Honor and Rank

Americans generally disapprove of social ranking. In a democracy all persons supposedly have equal opportunity to make a good life for themselves without worrying about what social class they are born into. It is a part of our code of decency to avoid making social distinctions.

In fact, however, there is plenty of social ranking in our country. *We rank people, professions, and people in the professions.* It is a volatile and complicated system, and we keep it largely covert, hidden even from our own view. But social classes there certainly are. Likewise, in smaller communities and groups like clubs and families, ranking of members typically develops. If a community is formed around a specific activity, like mountain climbing or waiting on tables or investing in stocks and bonds, that ranking falls smoothly into place on the basis of competence in the relevant activity. But even where no activity is specified and where values remain covert, a group will usually establish some kind of ranking. Even in a democracy, where no one uses the word "honor" without blushing, pecking orders are alive and well. Every preschooler already knows that.

Sociologists study how this pecking order, or idea of precedence, comes about. In ethics, or normative philosophy, we ask about the sorts of values that underlie that precedence. Are there standards telling when ranking is justified? Considering the structure of honor throws a partial light on the implications of ranking systems.

Certainly, up to thirty years ago, males outranked females in the United States: Sons outranked daughters, fathers outranked mothers. And there were badges of this rank. For instance, though it was all right for women to smoke cigarettes in those days, they must not smoke cigars — that was the prerogative of men. I once saw men in a restaurant, their faces transfigured with rage, as they stared at a foreign woman smoking a big, thick cigar.

Sometimes ranking occurs in a formal way, where its grounds are overt, clear, and well articulated. Branches of the military, for instance, carefully formalize their ranking system. Not coincidentally, military people are not as embarrassed about talking about honor as many other Americans are. The military follows fairly rigid rules about how one is to treat others in one's own rank and in different ranks.

The wife of a ranking officer will also follow a specific code about how to act around other wives. A story is told about a card game during which the colonel's wife said, "I believe I'm the ranking wife here." The nurse replied, "I believe I'm the only person here with any rank." Later the nurse was reassigned to some place in Alaska. She obviously didn't understand the actual pecking order.

The code these women were using is clearly not a moral one. Yet it is quite important as an action guide. Its grounds lie in the rationale for there being a military. Look at what the military community is supposed to be doing. What is its function, and how best can that function be carried out? The answer to that question will indicate how to evaluate the given code of honor and the ranking system implicit in it.

Again, in the academic world there is a formalized ranking. Grounds of ranking stem from the academic enterprise, and the code of honor provides that more honor be paid to full professors than to assistant professors. Many churches, too, have a definite formalized hierarchy (archbishops, bishops, rectors), as do governmental organizations, businesses, and some fraternities.

One point needs clarifying: The process of *achieving* a given rank is *not* action according to norms of honor. Rising in rank has rather to do with norms of glory or achievement. Those are another type of aesthetic, self-regarding norm. They are goal oriented. Norms of glory and of honor are closely connected, but they are not the same. Honor calls for limit norms. In later chapters we'll discuss goal norms of achievement and how promotion to a rank falls under them. For the present, take the pecking order or ranking as given or already established. In that context we can speak of honor separate from glory.

The rank a person holds determines how he or she ought to be treated by others. It also determines what level of performance others can expect of that person. Consider again Shakespeare's soldier Williams in *Henry V* (as discussed in Chapter 2). In his society's code, he is honor-bound to fight when challenged. Soldiers are supposed to do that. But he isn't supposed to fight the king, who far outranks him. As for the king's own part, he is expected to outperform a common soldier in the sense of commanding the army.

Since the king outranks Williams, he is bound by a higher standard of honor. But this doesn't mean that Williams is outside the code of honor; he is very much within and much concerned with it. His own rank figures as a part of his concern. It gives him a standing in the community that allows him either to act honorably or to disgrace himself. Remember that one of the marks of shame is fear of abandonment and alienation. As long as a person has some rank, that person is a part of the community.

Thus, no matter how low someone is ranked, the code of honor will still guide action, dictating limits to action. For instance, in some societies if an upper-level servant is asked to do the job of a lower-level servant, he must protest. There is severe ranking among servants. In the TV series "Upstairs, Downstairs" Ruby, the bottom maid, protested when she was trampled beyond customary limits. When she got the chance, honor required her to leave the relative comfort of her scullery job for the relative discomfort of war work. That preserved her self-respect.

Another example: In the musical play *The Student Prince* the enthusiastic prince tells his valet that they will be equals. "We shall *not!*" replies the valet. "If I am equal to you, then the third footman is equal to me. And the third footman is certainly *not* equal to me!"

Honor and the Eyes of Others

To speak of honor as giving strictly limit norms, we have taken personal rank as a given. In traditional class societies persons are born into a rank. In such communities and other organizations we have supposed an established ranking or pecking order. In any society children are raised to adults with a certain self-image of who they are and what sort of persons they are. They end up with various habits, competences, and weaknesses. Given these materials each of us develops a personal identity with which to face the world.

This personal identity, along with rank, is the make-up of a person's honor. Glory (including promotions) may be achieved. But honor is a given. Like innocence, it cannot be achieved or increased. It can only be lost. One sure way to lose it is by transgressing limits in the eyes of others (shame dwells in the eyes). Ranking sets limits and expectations, and so an honorable person must always appear to perform at the appropriate level. Society sets this level when it does the ranking, and the person consents to it by seeing herself as a full member of the community with a given rank. That is why honor is so closely associated with the idea of *reputation* or *name*.

Admittedly, reputation is just what other people think of you. In our individualistic culture there is a myth that merely what others think ought not to be a matter of importance. It's what you really are that counts, the myth goes. And there is a sort of wisdom in this. When someone pays too much attention to appearances and to the opinions of others, he risks losing his own ability to tell good from bad, right from wrong. That risk is especially high if the people judging are themselves poor judges of values.

On the other hand, the standing a person has in a community just *is* the rank other people see him or her as holding. Symbols of rank, like badges and hats and uniforms, are outward, visible means of indicating rank. They are only symbols, but they indicate what others can expect. They indicate a worth in the community. If a person relaxes too much about appearances, it is like walking out of the community. Then he may lose the opportunity to be active in meaningful and worthwhile ways. A Scotswoman in 1972 wrote to the newspaper: "University students used to seem worthy of respect. Now they dress like vagabonds!" She felt betrayed by these young people.

Consider these simple examples: If I am wearing a uniform that says I am a traffic director, then drivers will let me direct them. But if I wear blue jeans while directing traffic, drivers will most likely ignore me (they might even run me down). In order to direct traffic successfully, you have to convince people that you *are* a traffic director. Appearances serve as credentials, and without them it can be hard to find opportunity to develop one's self, or even to be one's self. Thus honor, the worldly worth of the self, is often equated with reputation.

This is also why insult is so painful and intolerable. In cultures where concern for honor (fear of shame) is open and unrepressed, people take great care not to insult each other accidentally. For public insult demands public revenge. Here is the logic behind that practice: An insult consists in making me look as if I don't belong in my rank. Because my personal worth is bound up with rank, the insult threatens the very core of my being. If I don't *do* something about it, then others will see me as lowered (because what others *see* are appearances). But, then, rank is in turn dependent on reputation, and reputation depends on appearances, so I just have to do something about appearances. Everyone expects me to do something. Therefore I (doubly) have to do something. In honor cultures, this is why people take care *not* to insult others, not to pick a quarrel with unknown consequences. In the roughest bars men are usually very courteous indeed.

Ruth Benedict relates an interesting encounter in Japan. An older American makes a slighting remark to a young Japanese. The young man replies that the American is "insincere" and leaves the American — whose criticism was quite sincere — puzzled. The youth meant that such slighting remarks made by a Japanese would deliberately risk a fight or a feud. The foreigner was insulting him frivolously, irresponsibly, unwilling to take up the quarrel that his remarks called for.

The American, of course, was raised in a culture that represses honor and fear of shame. Most Americans are taught to ignore the pain of being insulted: "Sticks and stones may hurt my bones, but names will never hurt me." After yelling "pig!" at sweaty, overworked, overweight policemen, upper-class hippies in the late 1960s were astonished that the policemen hit them with night sticks. These suburban youth had been taught that yelling names is free — but ethnic policemen may be quite sensitive to insult.

Moreover, Americans aren't by any means immune to the pain of insult. Imagine a man who lets a powerful person bully him, shrugging off the insult for the sake of promotion: This victim might then abuse his children. We often also hear of women who, battered by their husbands, beat their children in return. And consider, further, these questions:

• Why do Americans rant on more about the small chance of being mugged than about the much greater chance they take of being maimed in a car accident? Perhaps because there is no obvious insult in being hit by a car (though the driver may be careless or drunk), whereas the mere thought of the personal effrontery of the mugger provokes us to a primitive rage.

• Why do people assume it is worse to hurt someone than to refuse him help, even when the results are similar? Partly because we picture the help-refuser passing by uninsultingly and without malice, while we think of the hurter facing his victim, adding insult to injury.

• Why did our traditional reverence for youth turn sour for so many older Americans in the late 1960s? Young collegians showed contempt for their elders' achievements.

The distinction between insult and injury is closely related to the distinction between rage (or hate) and fear. Fear of injury is a sensible emotion if it does not turn into hate or rage. It is cautious, self-centered, interested in consequences, concerned with survival. But hatred is as unselfish as love — the ardent hater will willingly perish if his enemy goes down with him. Contrary to our myth, survival is not always the first human instinct. In our own culture there are many who prize automotive speed and convenience far more than survival. And there are many who love the sweet wine of revenge after an insult. So it's dangerous when people misdescribe their rage as fear: It is dangerous to underestimate the consequences of insulting others.

Honor and Self-esteem

In the structure of honor, reputation and self-esteem are two sides of a single coin. They depend on each other. Honor cultures have sometimes exaggerated this interdependence, saying that self-esteem just *is* protection of one's good name. Because honor can be lost but not won (achievement is a goal norm type whereas honor is a limit type), this exaggeration can go to bizarre extremes. In the works of Spanish playwright Pedro Calderón, the characters are so concerned with reputation that they seem to go around hoping for an affront — just so they can prove their honor. For them, having honor seems to depend on defending it frequently. One writer, commenting on Calderón, describes the old Spanish honor as

> the socially nurtured expression of self-esteem, which may be asserted only when challenged or assaulted. . . . It is the precarious just cause daily safeguarded in the cold war of social life, awaiting the trespass of a lurking enemy. . . . Having a sense of one's merit, or being virtuous, is not the same as being honorable; honor is achieved by successfully overcoming [a threat to honor].

But all this is a bit paranoid, and it has a wrong emphasis for honor generally. I include it because for many people the old Spanish code of honor has become a stereotype of honor norms. Calderón and other Spanish playwrights certainly used honor themes in fascinating ways, but the stereotype is too limited an idea of honor norms.

Aristotle spoke in a more moderate voice. He said that it is foolish to lay too much store on reputation because it makes you dependent on what others think. No self-respecting person is going to let his worth depend entirely on others. However — and this concession is crucial — to be thought well of by persons one respects is worth the effort. Why? Because being admired by worthy persons confirms one's worth.

A sort of mutual back-patting goes on here, but it isn't fraudulent or circular. Consider: Where can my sense of worth come from (aside from possible religious grounds) except what I think of myself and what others think of me? Now, if I pat your back *only* in order to get you to pat mine — and you *know* that — you will have good reason to disdain me. You certainly won't respect my back patting because it is insincere. It can do nothing to confirm your sense of worth. And you won't respect me either, because I am just a flatterer seeking after flattery. If you do pat my back then, it will be ironic, somewhat like Aristotle's proud man speaking in "irony to the vulgar." Therefore, if *I* have self-respect, I won't believe you any more than you believe me. So except when a fool lives in company with other fools, this situation gives people a dependable way to determine their own worth. I have an idea of my worth (my honor). If your idea of it varies much from mine, then one of us has got to be wrong. An important self-searching goes on as I try to decide who is wrong.

Further, if I respect your opinion, I will endeavor to be worthy of your high opinion. This is not just for the sake of getting your high opinion. It is mostly because I want to be actually worthy of it. Caring about competent critics could be seen as humility, while ignoring them could be seen as haughty pride. Especially young people *should* worry if observers see defects. Plato cited this point as one of the important contributions of love and friendship. The image of a lover's shaming eyes is so fearsome as almost to guarantee honorable behavior.

Consider now the idea of self-esteem separated from the opinion of others. That is literally the way an individual estimates his own value, his own self-worth. Just as people can be ashamed in private, they can also esteem themselves highly in private. Remember that in the experience of private shame, one perceives oneself *as if* through the eyes of another. High self-esteem works the same way. One pretends there is an audience, an imagined Someone looking on. In this case it is the self imagined *as another* looking on and judging highly. To have high self-esteem is to judge oneself as worthy of the good opinion of others. Furthermore, if those others want respect in turn, they had better be worthy of it. So justified self-esteem comes to this: I can esteem myself highly if I believe my rank is appropriate to my worth and if I stay within the limits the local code of honor assigns to that rank.

It is different with the ambitious person who wants to climb ranks and appear ever higher in her own eyes and in the eyes of others. Ambition commits one to goal norms of achievement more than the limit norms of honor. Not surprisingly, societies that repress honor tend to encourage the love of achievement. Honor provides us with a bond to community that no one can fully do without. Achievement can put us in competition with others in the community, and sometimes that isolates us.

Honor and the Avoidance of Shame

Shame and honor are reciprocals of each other. Honor is the avoidance of being shamed, and being shamed is the loss of honor. The structure of honor as analyzed above corresponds closely with characteristics of shame but does not cover all those characteristics. Here are some other properties of shame that further illuminate the structure of honor:

Shame wants to hide. When a person falls into a dishonorable situation he or she must do whatever possible to conceal that fact. It is shameless not to, for it means one doesn't care about reputation. This is somewhat paradoxical, as "having honorable intentions" usually means being honest and forthright. The dishonored, however, cannot afford honesty in respect of their shame. If dishonored, I can honor my neighbors only by keeping quiet about it. Honesty about it shows disrespect for others. If one is a coward in the face of dangers, one ought at least to keep quiet about it.

In Lope de Vega's play, *Justice Without Revenge*, a man finds that his wife has been unfaithful to him. According to the Spanish code of honor under which he lives, he must avenge the insult. So far, his disgrace is not public. No one knows about the adultery. Any act of revenge will make his dishonor public, so it seems he is dishonored no matter what he does. If he takes revenge, he publicizes the dishonor, which increases it. If he fails to move for revenge, he remains the victim of an affront to his honor, hence dishonored. The way this man actually manages his dilemma is by manipulating the "other man" into killing the wife. Then the *moral* code allows him to execute the offender — as a matter of "justice." This means he has his revenge but still has concealed the affront to himself.

Shame allows no excuses. The importance of reputation, mentioned above, partly covers this aspect of honor. A person who fears danger in a cowardly way probably can't prevent the fear, but the disapproval of that feeling is common among honor codes. One's reputation suffers.

Again, people cannot have complete control over their reputations, and yet reputation is nearly identical to honor. Much of the ferocity associated historically with "defenses of honor" comes from people's feeling helpless in the face of what others might think about them. Octavio Paz describes the Mexican male as living with "flayed skin," meaning that he is extremely touchy.

Consider the rape victim. In many famous honor codes she is so dishonored that, even if her brothers or father don't murder her, she has no hope of marrying or facing society again. Woman's honor in some of these codes amounts to little more than chastity. The refusal to excuse a rape victim still holds as an honor rule in some sections of our own culture, and groups of both men and women have been working to reform that part of our unwritten code.

Shame is closely associated with bodily affect. Surely no one should *blame* the rape victim, but there is no denying that the assault physically violates her in a deeply insulting way. In that sense she is in the same position as any other insulted person. It is, moreover, an insult difficult to redress.

Insult, the attack on honor, frequently shows up in bodily ways. A slap on the face, not particularly painful in itself, invites the victim to retaliate in furious rage. Again, when one person bows to another in traditional class societies, it is a bodily way of admitting that one's rank is lower. The bowed head recognizes the honor of the person addressed.

On a brighter side, people use physical symbols in order to announce rank to the public. Obtaining a higher rank is a matter of achievement, but announcing it has to do with honor. Thus a king dubs a man as knight by touching his head. In feudal societies, even condemned felons had special privileges of rank. Nobles got fancy executions whereas commoners might be garroted. In a folk song a woman laments for her felonious lover but is obviously quite proud of him:

Ah, my Geordie will be hanged in a golden chain,
'Tis not the chain of many;
Because he came of royal blood,
And courted a virtuous lady.

We still use physical signs for rank. A Bachelor of Arts wears a little hood, a Master of Arts a middle-sized hood, and a Doctor of Philosophy a great big hood. Campfire Girls get different colored beads to wear round their necks. Soldiers get badges (ripped off in case of court martial). In orchestras second violinists sit in a row behind first violinists. And someone puts a crown on Miss America's honorably beautiful head. This finishes my discussion of the structure of honor. Any examples from specific codes of honor were meant only as examples of that structure.

Honor and Chauvinism

I turn now to some common traits of specific codes. Chauvinism of various kinds is a dark side of many honor codes. If not in outright conflict with decency, it is often at least undesirable. It has given honor a bad reputation.

Bear in mind, however, that specific honor codes are not the same thing as an ideal, universal standard of honor. In speaking of structure, we've been speaking of the honor *standard*, the *type* of norm. Specific codes are particular applications of that standard or type. The distinction between norm type and code is similar to the one between theory and practice, where practice is a specific application of the theory. If I am right about the structure of honor, almost all specific codes will have that structure, but the way they apply that structure is quite individual. Honor codes are not necessarily chauvinistic unless somehow the structure dictates it.

Three common types of chauvinism found in specific codes are sexism, racism, and class or social snobbery. I will discuss each of these, asking whether the structure implies the chauvinism.

Honor Codes As Sexist.

"What a man's gotta do, a man's gotta do," goes the noblesse oblige honor rule for men. But women may vacillate, as they are supposed too weak to manage the honor demand for steadfastness: "It's a woman's privilege to change her mind." Honor sexism is rampant and far-flung.

Several aspects of the common structure can help explain this tendency. For instance, women typically could not defend themselves against bodily attack, and so defense measures fell to the men. As defenders of honor, the men naturally tended to become the holders of honor. Nor could women defend themselves against insults other than physical assaults. This meant that their own men, trusted to protect them from outside assault, could nonetheless insult them as they chose. If revenge against insults is necessary for maintaining one's social rank (given the structure of honor), then anyone incapable of revenge must lose hope of maintaining rank. Thus men would have all the higher ranks.

No community can tolerate this much inequality of men and women. To survive, men and women have to get along somehow, and even the most oppressively sexist cultures have figured out ways to manage this. Many writers have discussed this topic recently, so there is no need to say much here. But briefly, here are some ways that societies have softened the imbalance of male supremacy:

The community may develop stringent rules of etiquette and courtesy as a part of the honor code. Men are then required, as a point of honor, to treat women with special deference, and great is the disgrace of one who oversteps those limits. (Remember a parallel honor rule, "Don't be a bully," which serves to protect obviously weaker males.)

A woman can assume the man's rank as a part of the marriage contract, or she might hold a rank by virtue of her father. The wife or daughter of a prince is a princess. And in Germany the wife of Mr. Professor So-and-So is Mrs. Professor So-and-So. The husband or father still has freedom to abuse the woman, but excessive abuse would then reflect on his own worthiness. In systems like this it is evident why chastity became the female counterpart of honor. Where social rank comes from birth, men naturally must depend on their wives and daughters to guarantee the bloodline. In our own country many families are still horrified at the disgrace from an illegitimately pregnant daughter.

The women can resort to all kinds of power tricks of their own: conniving, having hysterics, being cute and sweet, being seductive, taking advantage of courtesy, and so on. An American woman, having married into lower nobility in a traditional society, found that the women manipulated men as pawns in their cruel power games. Such tricks are legion in sexist societies.

All these familiar methods are related to the physical differences between men and women. The structure of honor makes defense necessary and therefore implies important bodily symbolism. Defense often means fighting. As long as fighting depends on sheer bodily strength, then weaker-bodied persons will face oppression, even after the system tries to compensate. This is why it is important to remember the difference between the structure of honor, as a norm type, and specific honor codes. The gender chauvinism in many honor codes arises from the structure *plus* a specific incidental fact about women and men that can make an honor code flagrantly sexist. Julian Pitt-Rivers reports that the Andalusian honor code requires shy and timid behavior of a plebeian woman if she is to retain her femininity. Because honor and personal identity are closely linked, a plebeian woman in that society would be ousted for defending herself even if she had the ability. Even more extreme is the linking of honor strictly with having a male body. Such a code automatically excludes women from honor.

Gender, however, is not an essential part of the *structure* of honor. Where women are equipped and free to defend themselves against insult or aggression, or where (as with aristocratic women of Andalusia) a woman's honor is impregnable, the emphasis on honor as exclusively male could diminish.

Moreover, honor is not exclusively a male concern. Women suffer from affronts to their honor as intensely as men do. They are not necessarily concerned with chastity alone. Lily Bart, heroine of Edith Wharton's *The House of Mirth*, struggles to maintain her nonchastity honor — mostly nonmorally — and is in the end willing to die for it. Some years ago in Houston, the wealthy social matriarch Miss Ima Hogg used to walk regally onto the symphony stage after a concert and say to a hushed and awed audience what the near future of Houston's culture would be. She had all the feminine counterpart traits of Aristotle's ideally proud man.

Men have historically paid a high price for higher rank, binding themselves by sometimes absurd demands of honor. In American culture the stringent prohibition against males' weeping provides a poignant example. A few years ago a respectable candidate for the U.S.

presidency, Edmund Muskie, was eliminated overnight when he publicly shed tears of rage over an insult to his wife from an old man he could not strike.

"Male liberation" is the process of freeing men from such absurd demands, but it may imply giving up ancient claims to higher rank. Hence the backlash among some "hard-hat" males against male liberation prophets like Alan Alda.

Honor Codes As Racist

Chauvinism, in general, is excessive loyalty to one's own group. Racism is that particular type of chauvinism where the favored group is selected by bloodline. Racism is no more essential to honor than sexism is, but again the structure plus some factual premises produces a tendency to racial chauvinism.

The factual premise in this case is the specific method a community has developed for assigning rank. Where honorable rank depends on bloodline (often manifested by a person's physical characteristics), then we're likely to find a highly racist code of honor. If it depends on a particular talent or knack, then again racism will appear *if* the talent is seen as an inherited one. Sometimes these two factual issues combine to make race highly important in a specific honor code.

Consider how this lamentable tendency operates: Honor means both precedence (since it has to do with ranking) and virtue (since it has to do with worth). A person may maintain precedence by having power. The power can take a variety of forms, such as wealth, physical resources, personal connections. Any of those can be inherited, so it follows that precedence can be inherited. Maybe the heir in such a case is not worthy to be honored, but he has the power to enforce deference from others. Now add to this the biological fact that blood is also inherited. If people come to link bloodline (a biological fact) with power-enforced precedence (a historical happenstance), then they may well draw a racist conclusion. Their logic is obviously faulty, but people are not always logical. There are all too familiar examples of this illogical and disastrous racism.

Typically a racist community will also be sexist, putting a high premium on women's chastity. Anyone preoccupied with race will watch the bloodline scrupulously. Again, this tendency is incidental, not essential, to the structure of honor.

Honor codes and class snobbery

Because class distinctions presuppose honor, any honor code exist-
ing in a class society will encourage snobbery. Each class justifies its
status on the very grounds of being more "honorable," more "noble,"
than the classes beneath it. Class difference implies a difference in
honor standards. The term "noblesse oblige" stems from this idea. The
upper class is proud to be bound by stricter honor norms than the lower.

A vicious bit of upper-class Oxford doggerel sneered:

> The things a fella don't do,
> The things a fella don't do —
> These are not told to the scholarship boy;
> They are not revealed to the Jew!

The same sort of class snobbery (with a tinge of racism) is illustrated in
the movie *Chariots of Fire*. A rich Jewish athlete wants to hire a paid
coach so that he can achieve perfection in running. Two dons call him
in to warn him that this move is forbidden by unwritten "Oxbridge"
rules of honor. They tell him, "You're taking a plebeian attitude." The
athlete leaves, still determined to hire the coach; whereupon one don
sighs urbanely to the other: "Your semite, Hugh, worships on another
mountain." (They're both thrilled, though, when the runner's subsequent Olympic victory brings glory to the university.)

The structure of honor *does* imply distinctions of rank, and this
easily turns into class distinctions (often inherited by birth) because of
power struggles among subcommunities. The tendency is so rife that
societies that disapprove of class distinction (on decency grounds, say)
will likely disapprove of the honor norm itself. This has happened in
our democratic society, and so we don't like to talk about honor — or
shame or virtue. That is old-fashioned talk, for in our modern democracy, where everyone has equal opportunity, we don't like to dwell on
one person's being better than another. One American student, reading
a library copy of Aristotle's passage on the proud man, was evidently
offended by its antidemocratic tone. He wrote in the margin, "What an
asshole!" But however democratic, we still hate to be humiliated. We
care intensely about avoiding humiliation.

Self-regard and Self-interest

The typical modern American move for suppressing honor norms is to replace that concern with self-interest. "Look after Number One," goes the advice. Of course, it is all right to rank persons, as long as you follow two cherished rules (our code continues). First, you make sure everyone gets off to an equal start. Then you rank people on the basis of the merit shown by competition. After following these rules, society then rewards the meritorious persons (that is, the winners) by giving them money. After a while, having money is not just a reward of merit; it becomes a sign of merit. Looking after Number One means competing and trying to get money. Consider such sayings as "Money is the scorecard of life," and "Life is a game — the one who dies with more money is the winner." All rational persons look after Number One. So all rational persons compete for merit, which makes them deserve the money they are rationally trying to get.

The first violinists in the orchestra seem irrational because they haven't looked after Number One very well. They may sit honorably in front of the second violinists, but they don't get paid much more. Musicians almost never get paid much. In Wolfe's *The Right Stuff*, as noted earlier, the test-pilot heroes were irrational also, according to this code. Caring so much about the skill of flying and the right stuff, they committed themselves to the wrong competition and risked their own lives for low pay.

Fortunately, this is a parody. Our culture doesn't accept this "money-first" story wholeheartedly. People still volunteer to play the violin, to test airplanes, to teach, to study biology, even though these careers don't promise much pay. And we don't dismiss these people as irrational. At least, not all the time.

Self-interest is not the same as self-regard. Both are rational, but they are distinct concerns. One is the desire for long life, comfort, and wealth; the other is desire for personal merit or worth. Sometimes these coincide, but by no means always. Our dogma, parodied above, consists in claiming that they always coincide.

Honor and achievement are both self-regarding norm types, both concerned with desire for personal merit. In our country we certainly recognize and encourage norms of achievement, but we repress honor norms. Admittedly, honor does have dangerous tendencies, as discussed above. On the other hand, nobody can be achieving all the time, and almost nobody wants to. So we need to open discussion about that self-regarding, aesthetic type of norm that assigns merit by setting limits. It has the structure of honor, which people are embarrassed to talk about. But we need to debate about those limits. For one thing, people quarrel and even murder over issues of honor; these norms need to be clearly understood. Besides, there are probably some definite honor rules more sensible than getting even and not liking the color pink. For instance, one of these might be "Don't laugh too hard at the boss's jokes."

One further word about self-interest. In itself it is a perfectly innocent and rational guide to action. But what does it come to just in itself — without the addition of norm types like honor, decency, achievement, and beneficence? A beneficent person who has self-regard turns out to be interested in doing good things for others. A self-regarding decent person wants to hold to the rules of decency. A person emphasizing honor or achievement will promote his or her self-regard along those normative lines. So what is self-interest just in itself, without those forms of self-regard? What can it mean to look after Number One if one has no commitment to the value types of beneficence, glory, decency, or honor?

Well, after you take the four of those away, there is surprisingly little left. Humans, like other gregarious mammals, have certain basic needs. We need enough food and shelter to sustain ourselves. We need enough freedom to move around for exercise, enough security from danger to relax from fear and anxiety at least sometimes. We want and need at least some comfort, sex, and fun. These are the bare elements of self-interest. They are minimal indeed. Complicated human needs come about when we add peculiarly human norms and ideals to the standards of our conduct. Our concern goes far beyond money, which is only *one* indicator of human worth.

Chapter 7

Self-image and the Community

Shakespeare's King Lear had grown very old. He wanted to retire and enjoy his last years while his three daughters did all the work of ruling the kingdom. Somewhat dotteringly, he decided to make a show before the court of his daughters' affection for him. The two elder ones, out of malicious greed, flattered him with flowery speech about how much they loved him. Their hypocrisy disgusted Cordelia, his youngest and favorite daughter, so when her turn came to speak she simply said that she loved him. Cordelia's straightforward declaration enraged the old king. He was hoping to hear another flowery speech. He was so disappointed in Cordelia that he banished her and left the kingdom only to the two eldest daughters.

These two greedy women treated Lear badly once they started ruling. They deprived him of personal quarters, took his retainers, and found many other ways to humiliate him. Unable to bear more humiliation, he went out bareheaded into a raging storm and roamed in it, accompanied only by his fool, the jester who used to entertain him.

All of the kingdom had become as chaotic as the storm that Lear wandered in, everyone was as alone and unprotected as old Lear himself. Once the king had decided to stop acting like a king, his subjects got out of kilter, too. Fathers and children stopped being fatherly and filial, and masters and servants confused their roles. The faithless were treated well and the faithful badly. A raging social chaos swept the entire community.

Is Anyone an Island?

Community

I use the word "community" here in a broad sense, to mean any group of people with a more-or-less stable and agreed-upon set of ideals. To schematize what I mean, a group of people form a community if

1. they fill in the structures of honor and decency in roughly the same way;
2. they are aware that they do this;
3. they expect of each other that each is doing this;
4. they care about what the others think of them, feeling shame at being scorned;
5. they expect the emotional response, shame or guilt, from one among them who violates the ideals.

Keep in mind, however, that the ideals are only *roughly* stable and agreed upon. Some parts of a community's code might be more stable, commanding wide agreement, whereas others may temporarily "float," still open to debate. No sane person in the United States thinks it permissible for drivers to hit pedestrians, but there is much disagreement regarding sexual freedom, suicide, and killing animals for their meat.

Under my definition, a community may be quite small or quite large. In a sense our whole society is a community. We have laws about violence, property, marriage, and voting rights. We have rules of the road. But subcommunities among us sometimes differ in detail of customs and ideals. The Mormons, for instance, wanted to differ regarding their marriage customs, though they ended up complying with society at large to avoid being cast out of the mainstream. Some religious subcommunities in this country prefer not to send their children to school. They differ from what the society as a whole thinks proper.

Besides religious communities, we also speak of business communities, of intellectual communities, of towns and neighborhoods. Organizations like the Kiwanis Club are communities in the sense I've defined, as are street gangs, literary societies, corporations, some families and households, and even circles of friends. Often such smaller communities interlock, and most everyone belongs to more than one at a time.

Honor in Small Communities

In small communities honor, under whatever name, takes on particularly great importance. This is because its sanction — humiliation or shame — is such a personal thing. It dwells in the eyes and so takes on much force in communities small enough for people to meet face to face and know one another.

If I am visiting a city far away from home where I never expect to return, it will bother me somewhat if my clothes happen to come unfastened in public, damaging my sense of dignity. But I'll not fret about it afterwards. Those strangers will never see me again. My anonymity hides me. Suppose, however, that something embarrassing happens to me on the street where I walk to work every day. Then memory of that embarrassment may cut my spirit for some time. Those onlooking eyes that will see again threaten most. Some persons who are particularly fearful of shame prefer to avoid small, close communities, feeling safer alone or circling anonymously in a crowd.

Thus, we can expect to find concern with honor especially in small communities like the immediate family, circles of friends, long-term co-workers, and small social groups. This produces a paradox: Family members and close friends sometimes become quite careless in front of each other. A mother chides her son with, "That slouchy shirt is all right here at home, but you don't want to go out in *public* looking like that!" And a little three-year-old, having experimented with putting Vaseline all through her hair, was comfortable sharing the disaster with Mother but refused to go downstairs where Daddy would see her. He might laugh. If honor is most important within our closest groupings, how is it we can expose our loss of it in front of those who love us most?

Answer to this paradox lies in the positive aspect of shame that I mentioned in Chapter 3. Shame is fear of abandonment. As such it also bonds us together when we recognize in each other that fear. That brings about a tender acceptance and reassurance, and the people giving these become the ones we trust. An "approachable" parent or teacher or employer is a person of whom one can say, "It's all right to tell him. He will not laugh at me. He will not glare silently or call me a jerk."

Still, this acceptance has its limits. For example, in *Rebel Without a Cause* the teenager resents seeing his father wrapped in a frilly apron. It showed disrespect for the son's need to look up to his father. Confused and rattled, the boy can't articulate his resentment. Or a well meaning

89

stepfather tries to correct his new daughter's sloppy table manners. "You wouldn't want to eat like that even while alone," he ventures. It irks him the way her shameless manners take him for granted. She is taking advantage of his need to win her trust.

Trusting close friends and family does not mean that we forget about honor norms when in their company. Rather, we consign our honor to them, trusting them not to abuse our exposure. A breach of this trust spells personal disaster. Close friendships breaking, sibling rivalries, rivalries between parent and child, between husband and wife — these can be the sharpest and fiercest and most scarring encounters of all. They are hard indeed to speak of. Even Shakespeare, that supreme master of English expression, avoided speaking of them. He had his Julius Caesar grieve in Latin, not English, over sudden betrayal by his trusted friend Brutus.

Assault on Self-image

Remember again that shame dwells in the eyes. A person feeling shame is aware of an Other looking on, laughing or rejecting. Even if no one is there to look, emotion internally divides a person as he projects a part of himself outward, to become his own outside observer. As observer he is audience. What does he observe? He observes his actual conduct, judging how far it matches his (durable) self-image. If his self-image is quite low, there is little need to fear shame. A high self-image makes him vulnerable, easily insulted.

Of course, we do not go around observing ourselves all the time. Usually we are inside ourselves looking out at other things, not outside ourselves looking in. We go about our affairs without thinking of our self-image. We are then literally unself-conscious.

But suppose something suddenly happens that exposes the self. Then shame assails a person — perhaps not because of any particular blunder and not because of any particular weakness or deformity. It is rather because of a sudden isolation the person feels from disappointed expectations. The world fails to square with what he had prepared himself to be facing. Here are some examples:

Sam has just bought a handsome and expensive ski sweater after living many months without anything new. He proudly shows it to his wife and she is especially pleased. She is proud of him and proud for him. Continuing their prosperous mood, they go out to a nice restaurant for dinner that evening and Sam wears his fine new sweater. The maître d' at the restaurant says with hypocritical politeness, "This is very embarrassing. I will have to seat you in the anteroom as the gentleman is not wearing a coat and tie."

Lucy's daughter Jane has just married and enthusiastically begun her first adventures at managing a home for herself and her husband. Lucy and Jane enjoy talking and laughing about it. Lucy, wanting to participate and share, offers Jane a baking dish that has been one of her favorites for thirty years. "I don't want it, Mom," says Jane, "it doesn't have a lid."

These are fairly trivial incidents, but the feeling of shame provoked can be acutely painful because it comes on so suddenly. Sometimes the very triviality of the incident intensifies the pain because one is doubly ashamed to have been shamed by a small thing. It feels like a weakness. The meaning of such incidents can go far beyond their size because they bring into sharp focus how much the sense of self depends on community. We prepare ourselves to meet a world of some specific kind. The world turns out not to be quite the kind we had prepared for, and the effect is to isolate the self, putting it temporarily out of the safety of communication.

When the world goes awry like that, one thing a person can do is to declare the world wrong. Sam can get angry at the maître d' and say to himself that the rule about coats and ties is outrageous. Lucy can remind herself that Jane is struggling for independence in her new life and, consumed with her own needs, lacks tact and gratitude.

In other words, in both of these cases one can say that a feeling of shame was unwarranted. The world was wrong or awry, not the person pained by it. But shame allows no excuses. Honor norms are an essential part of the bond of persons in community. Whether Sam thinks himself foolish or the rule outrageous makes little difference in the isolation he feels. He is isolated either way. The restaurant owner may change his rules in the future — the code of honor constantly changes in light of the experiences and ideas that people have — but that doesn't help Sam at the time of his pain.

Here are two more examples. They are drastic instead of trivial, but the structure is the same as what we've been examining in that the world fails to square with what a person expects.

In the nineteenth century the Russian author Fyodor Dostoyevsky was arrested with a number of other men. After some months in prison, they were brought to a perfunctory public trial, ordered to strip and dress in eccentric, inadequate shirts in the freezing temperatures, and then told they would be executed. As they awaited the execution, a messenger rode up and announced that the czar in a "display of mercy" had spared their lives. One of them men, Grigoryev, lost his mind in reaction to the shock.

Nine-year-old Gretchen, who was half Jewish, attended primary school in Nazi Germany, where Jews were being systematically ousted from society. Though Gretchen was doing fine with her schoolwork, her teacher ordered her to sit at the back of the room and thereafter gave her bad grades. Gretchen handled this isolation by adjusting her self-image. She decided she was dumb, and that it is proper and fitting for a dumb person to sit at the back of the room. By adjusting her image downward she was able to see the world as having some order. Rather than isolating her from the community, her back seat gave her a proper place in it. It was many years before Gretchen found out she wasn't dumb after all.

Warrant

The four examples above give us pictures of *unwarranted* shame. The victims must make temporary adjustment in order to retrieve a place for themselves in the community, and sometimes these adjustments are painful and lastingly harmful. The world is *unfair* in these cases.

Notice that the words "unwarranted" and "unfair" are normative words. We are saying that the codes of honor and decency operative in czarist Russia and in the Nazi school were *wrong*. Now this presents a problem. On the one hand we all live in one or more communities. That commits us to certain specific codes of morality and honor. We can use their authority to judge right and wrong, fine and base. It is then a simple matter for us to say of some *other* code that it is wrong, if we find strong disagreement between it and our own.

On the other hand, remember we are judging by means of our own specific code. From the czar's point of view and from the Nazi teacher's point of view there presumably was no wrong. Likewise, I seem to be in no position to say that my own code is wrong. To do so I would have to speak from the point of view of some code besides my own. If I did that, then the code I am criticizing wouldn't be my code anymore. So it appears to be impossible to criticize one's own code.

Fortunately this just isn't so. Of course I can criticize my own code. People do that all the time. We all have normative insights that reach beyond our specific codes. Without them we could not manage all the new situations that constantly spring up. Our parents and teachers supply us with norms whose guidance works for a wide range of experiences. But life often takes us beyond that range. How do we then know what to do?

To answer this, imagine a simple conflict. Suppose someone has just called you a sissy, and the insult rankles you. Your honor code directs you to assail the offender. But you have promised a friend not to do any violence. You have given your "word of honor." You must now choose between two clear honor norms. The natural question to ask — and to ask quickly — is "What is *really* the better thing to do here? What is the more honorable thing to do?" The specific code you have won't tell you, it just presents you with the conflict. You must therefore go beyond that code. But how? By having insight into what your specific code aims at. You have a *concept* of honor that is a different thing from your specific *code* of honor. You've developed it over the years by thinking about your community's honor norms. With friends and family you've had conversations about what sort of conduct people should be proud of and what sort they should avoid. Often these conversations touch on mutual acquaintances, comparing and ranking them. Once you have the concept, you can make decisions that go beyond the code. That's why looking at the *structure* of honor is helpful. It helps one understand what the concept is about.

The same is true of the code of decency. When new situations arise, or when decency norms conflict with each other, we can make decisions (for better or worse) about what to do because we have a concept of decency distinct from the moral code we have grown up with. "That just isn't *right*," you might say of a situation that people have tolerated for years.

As long as we continue to grow and develop, our concepts of honor and decency also continue to change. They are never final. Only a deluded and arrogant person would claim to know with final authority what honor or decency really is. Most thinking people are fully aware that their insights will deepen and mature as life moves on. One may grow wiser just as long as one grows older.

To summarize; we use three distinguishable tools when making a judgment such as "The world is unfair in these cases":

1. A specific honor (or decency) code that guides action in simple, unproblematic cases
2. A concept of honor (or decency) that we get from thinking about the code after new experiences or conversations with others
3. Our knowledge that that concept is never complete

With these I can now explain what it means to speak of shame (or guilt) as warranted:

A specific (1) code of honor teaches me a distinct (2) concept of honor. With that concept I can recognize foreign codes as codes of honor even though they differ from mine. I can venture judgments about them. Likewise, I can criticize my own code, noting perhaps where certain reforms are needed. Suppose, after much public debate, the code does reform. Then we have a slightly different code, reformed in light of insights and public debate. Still, there is a concept of honor distinct from this new code. And so (3) we know better than to say that this new code is absolutely right in some final way. Warranted, yes: We've done all we could to make right-minded judgments. But finally finished and right, no: There is still a concept of honor, distinct from the code, hovering in our minds, guiding action and judgment and always changing.

The achievement of Martin Luther King, Jr., is a good example here. He sought to reform the decency code. For years (1) black people had sat at the back of buses. If there were no seats left there, these people stood. One day a Mrs. Parks, tired from a day's work on her feet, took a seat toward the front because none were left in back. That shocked people. It was against the accepted code. (2) One can imagine Mrs. Parks thinking, "It just isn't *right* that I should stand when there is an empty seat up here in front."

King had the same insight. It just isn't right that people should be denigrated, given lower rank, because of their race. Under his leadership reform took hold. Others saw the wisdom of that insight. There was protest, civil disobedience, violence, debate, legislation — reform is not a simple thing. The code has since then deeply changed, but (3) not enough. There is always a gap between the code and one's concept of decency. But we clearly are warranted in saying the insight was a good one. There is nothing mysterious in that.

Thus do codes change. That couldn't happen unless we distinguished between warranted and unwarranted judgments. Honor and decency as norm types, as ideals into which we have insights, differ from specific codes of honor and decency. We may not agree with the *values*, the specific tenets, of the Spanish or American West or Nazi code of honor. We may even want to say they are dishonorable. But we can still recognize that they purport to be codes of honor. That's because we have a concept that reaches beyond our code.

Audience

The audience of individuals and their actions consists of all the onlookers who judge according to the community's values. This can be anyone in the community, anyone whose opinion matters to the individual, including himself. All norm types are related to an audience. They are social. Even Robinson Crusoe, that famous individualistic achiever, judged himself. He was his own audience. Honor norms, however, present a special case, because there the presence of an onlooker or audience is especially important. In fact, it is built into the very definition of its sanction, humiliation. As we saw in Chapter 3, a person feeling shame divides himself in two: He is an Other, an onlooker, and he is also an object seen as ridiculous, pitiful, or disgusting. He is both the audience watching and the actor seen.

Thus we can expect of people who are concerned about honor that they will care a good deal about what other people think of them, for they identify with their audience. They care so much that often we find authors saying that honor and reputation are simply the same thing. When someone says, "My honor is at stake," it sounds as if he were talking about reputation.

On the other hand, surely it's possible for someone to have a bad reputation and yet be honorable. Likewise, one can have a superior reputation and be in fact a scoundrel or a slob. That is, the audience can be wrong about someone. So honor has to mean something besides reputation. It is not simply what people believe about one; it must also have something to do with the basis for those beliefs. What warrants the belief that a person is honorable? That would be the aesthetic virtues, the strengths that the person has. About these, whether my own or another's, I can be mistaken. The reality, so to speak, might differ from appearances.

In other words, sometimes a discrepancy occurs between self-image and reputation, and that isolates a person from the community. That is what happened to King Lear. He saw himself as independent of the kingdom, as ruling it from above. He thought of himself as an island, whose identity in no way depended on what others thought or did. But no one is an island. A sense of honor, which all but the shameless wish to have, depends not only on self-image but also on what fellow members see and judge. When these differ, one becomes isolated and lonely.

Discrepant Self-image

Reputation and self-image are two important sides of honor. (Notice they are not important for decency.) These can be discrepant from each other. But either or both of these can also be mistaken. To explain that we need to consider a third side of honor. I will call it "reality." By the "reality" of a person's honor, I just mean what strengths and virtues the person actually has. Here are some examples of discrepancies among all three sides of honor.

"Reality" and Sincere Self-image

Image can be better or worse than "reality." In *Henry V* the bawdy character Pistol seems deceived about his own valor. As he is cudgelled and humiliated by the officer Fluellen, he extravagantly vows revenge. But after Fluellen leaves, Pistol rationalizes, still seeming to believe in his own past worth: "Old do I wax, and from my weary limbs honor is cudgelled." Pistol thereby vows to turn cutpurse and beggar, renouncing his pretended gentle rank and its accompanying demands of honor altogether. With such rationalization Pistol can continue to deceive himself about his one-time honor, but he has never deceived others.

The Wizard of Oz provides several examples of characters whose images fall well below what they really are. Cowardly Lion, ashamed of his cowardice, consistently shows his courage. Tin Woodman, seeing himself as having no heart, is as kind as any person can be. Scarecrow, sad because he has no brain, does most of the thinking for the little company.

"Reality" and Pretended Self-image

The Wizard of Oz himself, however, shows a second kind of relation: One may pretend (that is, try to appear) to be better or worse than one's image. The Wizard sets up all sorts of appearances to impress people with his great power. He frightens the whole company with his tricks. But when they finally see him, they find an insignificant little fellow who mournfully admits his show of power has just been humbug.

And in one comic strip, Andy Capp is musing that he'll have to drop his new girlfriend: "She makes me so ashamed." Then he comments to the audience, "That's the feeling you get when you let yourself believe you're the man she thinks you are."

In *All's Well That Ends Well* the evil character Parolles wants to avoid a perilous mission he's been sent on, so he intricately plans to appear wounded in the line of duty. Unlike Pistol, he doesn't deceive himself. He knows from the start that he is a coward pretending to be a hero: "I must give myself some hurts, and say I got them in exploit: yet slight ones will not carry it; they will say, 'Came you off with so little?' and great ones I dare not give." Such cool plotting of a masquerade shocks the two lords who happen to be eavesdropping. One of them whispers to the other, "Is it possible that he should know what he is and yet be that he is?" Later, when Parolles is finally exposed, he shows little shame. He merely shrugs, "Who cannot be crushed with a plot?" Because he had a low self-image to begin with, he is almost invulnerable to shame.

In contrast there is Prince Hal, in *Henry IV, Part 1*, who establishes a reputation for being a profligate and ne'er-do-well by keeping lewd company, engaging in frivolous stunts and drinking bouts, and poking fun at his own royal rank. Hal wants to appear worse than he really is. His pretense is designed to make himself appear all the more glorious once events should call him to serious action.

Finally, a classic children's story, "The Emperor's New Clothes," provides a complex example where all the people in the community pretend to be better than they see themselves to be. The emperor loved beautiful, extravagant clothes. Two swindlers visited one day:

They told everybody that they were weavers and that they could weave the most marvelous cloth. Not only were the colors and the patterns of their material extraordinarily beautiful, but the cloth had the strange quality of being invisible to anyone who was unfit for his office or unforgivably stupid.

When the (nonexistent) "clothes" were finished, the swindlers went through the motions of dressing the emperor in them so that he could parade down the street showing them off. Of course, nobody could see the clothes, but all pretended they could. After all, it's bad enough to be unfit for one's office or unforgivably stupid. It's far worse if others find out about it!

A little child finally let the truth out that the emperor was parading with no clothes on. It was a truth everybody believed but couldn't admit. The emperor thought, "I must bear it until the procession is over." And he walked even more proudly, and the two gentlemen of the imperial bedchamber went on carrying the train that wasn't there.

Reputation and Self-image

Reputation can be better or worse than image. Think now about this story in another light. Suppose there were no storyteller who lets us listeners in on the joke. And suppose there were no child too innocent to know how much was at stake for the community. With those suppositions, "reality" drops out of the picture. What we have left is each person with a low self-image (unfit and stupid) and with *good evidence* that all the other people are both worthy and intelligent. In that case, reputation and self-image are systematically discrepant. This situation reveals something about storytellers and innocent onlookers, both of them viewers from the outside. Without that outside and distant view no one can judge with final authority what "reality" really is.

Therefore, this third relation carries special interest. It doesn't refer to "reality." It just refers to what people *believe* reality to be, and those beliefs are what we must live with. They are the basis of our decisions about how to act and what to value and approve of and seek. Maybe there is someone who is expert about what reality really is. But, even if so, it doesn't change matters for us normal humans. All we have to go on is what we believe. The expert cannot help us because we must ask, "Is this person *really* an expert?" An answer to that question just sticks us with our beliefs again. There is a parallel between this point and the process of warranting discussed above. No final expert can tell us about reality just as none can tell us finally about what is right. We can only fall back on our well-considered beliefs about what is true and right.

To make this clearer, let us use the story again with our two suppositions. Imagine that we are members of that community, so we are both pretending to see the emperor dressed in fine new clothes. Now suppose I whisper to you, "You know, I hate to admit it, but *I* don't see any clothes on the emperor. He looks naked to me." My confession will likely pull your thoughts in two different directions. On the one hand, you are relieved to hear someone else admit that she has the same perceptions as you. That gives you some confidence. On the other hand, maybe I am just shameless and brazen, willing to expose myself as stupid and unfit for my job. The first thought makes you friendly to me; the second makes you want to avoid me. You *hope* that what I say is true, but do you dare admit *believing* it is? Admitting that would risk your reputation as worthy and intelligent.

These matters of belief, truth, and reality are a difficult topic, but fortunately this third relation — that between reputation and self-image — lets us avoid it. When thinking about that relation, we need to deal only with what a person believes about herself and what others believe about her. That is the situation normal humans most often live with in "real" life. Perhaps for that very reason storytellers just love to deal with the relation between reputation and self-image. With it they can better address the normal human situation, in which we humans are trying, with doubt and uncertainty, to decide what to believe, what to do, and how to live our lives.

So in what follows I'm going to talk about two stories in which a gap occurs between image and reputation, between how one assesses oneself and how one appears to the community audience. The first is from the movie *Amadeus*, about the musician Antonio Salieri, whose image is lower than his reputation. The second, from Jane Austen's *Pride and Prejudice*, is about the character Mr. Darcy, whose image is higher than his reputation.

Salieri grows up desiring above all else to be a great composer. So high is his ideal that he wants to sing the glory of God, to express his religious devotion with sublimely beautiful music of his own making. He offers all his energies and self-discipline to that project. Such austere efforts get him the position of court composer in the court of Emperor

Joseph. There he is well respected. The emperor loves his compositions, his music is often played, and audiences respond with loud applause.

Unfortunately for Salieri, another composer arrives — a silly little twerp named Mozart. Salieri loves and reveres Mozart's music. It is truly, for him, the voice of God. He worships it, yet hates it — because *he* wants to be the voice of God. He has dedicated his life to being that voice, has made great sacrifices for it. But God, as Salieri sees things, is only laughing at him. There is that flippant, obscene little Mozart, writing heavenly music with such ease, as if he were taking dictation. And then there is poor, foolish Salieri, working long and hard hours, giving up the common pleasures of life to produce clumsy, ugly music, much applauded though inferior, destined to be forgotten altogether in a few years.

Now, the emperor *likes* Salieri's music, gives him good money and prestige for it. According to Salieri, though, the emperor "has no ear at all," does not understand music. The emperor might applaud, in other words, but does not have good judgment. God, the all-knowing judge, is laughing at Salieri — meaning that Salieri views himself as ridiculous, God's puny toy. "Why did God give me the desire to praise him with music," Salieri moans, "and then make me mute?"

Having God mock you is surely the ultimate height of feeling insult. Where the Other that a person experiencing shame imagines ridiculing and pitying him is one's mother, or a love, or a jeering crowd — that is most painful. But if one imagines the Other as God, surely that is unbearable. What is Salieri to do?

According to Schaffer's story (not meant to be historical fact), Salieri yearns for revenge against God. He takes steps to kill Mozart. More significantly, he maneuvers to keep the audience believing Mozart's music is inferior to his own. All the time he is convinced that Mozart's music is divinely inspired, far superior to his own. But he will have no part in sharing that insight with the community. He does not try to correct the gap between his self-image and his reputation. After all, he enjoys the audience's applause. It is a sort of compensation for his (self-image of) mediocrity.

In *Pride and Prejudice*, Mr. Darcy proposes marriage to a woman somewhat below him in social class. He thinks he is making a sacrifice and most generous gesture by doing that, but his main motive is not generosity. Rather, he is in love with her and therefore willing to forgo class restrictions. Elizabeth Bennet, however, rejects him, not so much because of his proud and condescending attitude but because she has got the impression from elsewhere that he has acted badly. She thinks he has deprived a Mr. Wickham of a deserved income, and that he has deliberately blockaded the marriage of her sister to a friend of his. She explains these as her reasons for rejecting Darcy. He departs, agitated and in a huffy frustration. Unable to face Elizabeth with a defense of himself against her accusations, he writes a letter and gives it to her, simply saying, "Please, read this." After reading it, Elizabeth admits to herself that *if* the defense is true, her prejudice against him is surely unjustified. The remainder of the story's events convince Elizabeth that the defense is true. With regard to the facts of the case, there is in the end no problem. They both agree that he is innocent of the accusations.

However, Darcy is not satisfied with just getting the facts straight. Elizabeth's rejection has changed his self-image regardless of the facts. We can imagine him thinking something like this: "If a person is able to think I have done such base things, then there must be something about me that allows that impression to take hold. I must not be as fine a man as I have been believing I was." Accordingly, Darcy's subsequent behavior is not merely to remain innocent of the charges. He goes beyond that by humiliating himself before Wickham (for the sake of Elizabeth's family) and opening the way for Elizabeth's sister's marriage that has been hindered before. After all has turned out happily, we find Darcy saying this to Elizabeth:

> I have been a selfish being all my life, in practice, though not in principle. As a child I was taught what was *right*, but I was not taught to correct my temper. I was given good principles, but left to follow them in pride and conceit. Unfortunately an only son (for many years an only *child*) I was spoilt by my parents, who . . . allowed, encouraged, almost taught me to be overbearing, to care for none beyond my own family circle, to think meanly of all the rest of the world, to *wish* at least to think meanly of their sense and worth compared with my own. Such was I, from eight to eight and twenty; and such I might still have been but for you, dearest, loveliest Elizabeth! What do I not owe you! You taught me a lesson, hard indeed at first, but most advantageous. By you, I was properly humbled. . . . You shewed me how insufficient were all my pretensions to please a woman worthy of being pleased.

Here we have a good example of how much self-image and reputation can modify each other. Darcy must first avoid the shame of having people think of him what Elizabeth reports in the beginning. But he must also face the personal question, "What am I really? Do I deserve the reputation that I have always thought myself worthy of?" And on having to answer himself, "No, not really," he goes about making a personal change in himself.

Notice that all we can talk about here is reputation and image. We have no access to a "real worth" in addition to these. But by the interrelations between the two we come (with Elizabeth) to see Darcy as a most honorable and admirable fellow in every sense. Both self-image and reputation have influenced him. The two together have created his growth into a finer man, one in whom the original pride is now well justified.

Adjusting the Image

Discrepant self-image isolates one from others. To get back into fellowship one must adjust one's image up or down. Above I told the story of little Jewish Gretchen in Nazi Germany. She adjusted her image downward, deciding she was dumb, in order the see the world as rational. Later she found herself needing to correct that. She had to adjust upward, and that was no easy struggle. Honors in college, her ability to speak three languages fluently and read several others, the respect and intellectual homage given her by teachers and fellow students — these were surely a help. But the assurances had to keep coming because her readjustment remained a little fragile. She can joke about it now with close friends. Sometimes, she admits, she falls back and still feels lonely.

Perhaps adjusting downward comes more easily even if it's more painful. It typically means giving up responsibility rather than taking on more. When the ancient Athenians were persuading the Melians to accept enslavement bloodlessly, they reminded them: "The contest [is not] an equal one, with honor as the prize and shame as the penalty, but a question . . . of not resisting those who are far stronger than you are."

The claim is that once the Melians correct their image downward, they will find no shame in defeat and enslavement.

The Greeks had a special word for bloated self-image: hubris. That meant a kind of blasphemy because one who had it was attempting to go beyond human limits. They saw a close connection between hubris and downfall. Their slogan "know thyself" reminded heroes not to mistake themselves for gods. Humans who forget human limits are apt to be painfully reminded of them.

Sophocles's play *Oedipus the King* celebrates this lesson. Oedipus is an arrogant tyrant, impatient and pushy with his subjects. He has in his youth killed a stranger at a crossroads. Later he marries a woman named Jocasta, who bears him several children. Events gradually reveal that the stranger he killed was his father and that Jocasta is his own mother. Oedipus continues his bullying ways, refusing to accept the revelations. The mistakes he made leading to such horrible crimes were only human ones, but he believes he is superhuman. Finally the revelations stack up so that not even his hubris can resist. Then he plunges into a deep shame as suddenly as the self-knowledge has hit him. He blinds himself so that he will see no one looking at him. He cries, "I beg of you in God's name hide me somewhere outside your country, yes, or kill me, or throw me into the sea to be forever out of your sight." He mourns over his two tiny girls, knowing now they are his little sisters as well as daughters. Conceived in incest, they have only misery ahead of them. Oedipus must leave the land but hates to leave the girls. The new king, Creon, says to him, "Do not seek to be master in everything, for the things you mastered did not follow you throughout your life."

Oedipus has by now turned into a lowly beggar. Once his self-image changes, with it change his standards of what conduct is shaming to him.

Rejoining the Community

The Thebans couldn't admit Oedipus back into their country because his crimes had dirtied it. There would be no rest or well-being for them until he had gone away as a beggar, abandoned by them. With no hope of redemption, Oedipus was a sort of sacrifice made for the health of the city. The gods were perhaps unfair about this, but — well, that's the way it must be.

Tony Morrison's prize-winning novel, *Beloved,* strikes the same hopeless note. Sethe, Beloved's mother, sees herself as dirtied by the whites who had made her a slave. Beloved would have to be a slave and would then be dirtied, too. It wasn't fair. The world was savagely unjust dirtying people who didn't warrant it. But that is the stringent point about how a community can determine honor. Sethe couldn't stand the pollution for herself or her daughters. She preferred to kill them rather than let them be stained. In a most stirring way Morrison's book faces head-on the dismal fact that shame allows no excuses — not even unwarranted shame, which this certainly was. It differs much from guilt in that respect.

Are there no ways out of such hopeless, dismal, disorderly predicaments? Thousands of books have been written about this question, and thousands of stories told. Our subject cannot extend to all those. But the question calls for some answer, even though I can give only the barest sketch. I will leave it to the reader to extend the sketch further.

Hopeful Versus Despairing Worldviews

Religions often address themselves to the question of how to discharge shame and restore honor. This is a sort of contradiction in terms, of course, because honor cannot be gained, it can only be lost. At least, that is the this-worldly truth. No wonder religions address the question: They can turn to other-worldly things.

Christianity offers its believers a special story about redemption. Jesus is given to the world as a sacrifice through which individuals are rejoined to community. The good news that Christians speak of is that anyone who sincerely asks to come into the Kingdom of God will be granted entry. Ultimately, no one need be lonely, isolated, or out of communication.

It is a symptom of our society's inability to think about and talk about shame and honor that even Christians often forget the social significance of Jesus' death. Straightforwardly, crucifixion was a punishment reserved for the most shamed elements of society, for slaves and criminals. It was a dishonoring, disgraceful way to die. Forgetting that — imagining that there was some kind of glory in being bodily exposed up on a cross — takes away much of the redeeming power of the Christian story. The idea that anyone can be saved from abandonment because of the suffering of one man, albeit a divine one, presents an optimistic worldview indeed.

Not all religions are optimistic about this. In one of the ancient Nordic myths the story goes that the best anyone can hope for in life is to be killed on the battlefield as a warrior. Women, children, and old men were out of luck. Their ultimate destiny was to end up in a dark, foggy, cold nether region. As for the killed warriors, they could expect that some day eons hence they would all be gathered together into a large army to battle with the giants. Furthermore, the giants would win! A most gloomy view of life.

From a secular approach, the Greek philosophers Plato and Aristotle took an optimistic view of life. They knew that human beings get themselves into binds as Oedipus did. They admitted that some people fall victims to outrageous misfortune like Morrison's Sethe and her daughters. But they didn't think all that *had* to happen. It was at least possible for persons to live their lives without inevitable conflict and isolation from the universe. Of course, given that there are so many conflicting norms, a fully good life was hardly easy. People feared missing the mark. Aristotle was deeply aware of that fear. He claimed that an important purpose of tragic plays, like Sophocles's *Oedipus*, was to give vent to that fear and relieve it for a while.

However, Sophocles himself rejected optimism. He thought conflict was inevitable in trying to respect all of at least four different types of norms: If someone were trying to avoid guilt, events could lead him into dishonor. If he sought both glory and innocence, eventually another ideal would crush him. A person with great political power had the means to be beneficent but was unlikely to improve the lot of others consistently and still maintain his power. And someone trying to uphold family honor might run into conflict with what is good for society at large. In other words, for Sophocles the universe was basically tragic. There was no way out for human beings. The disorder lay deep in their very existence. Nothing could save the individual from finally being cast out of communication into eternal loneliness.

Handling Guilt: Keeping Communication Going

If one could successfully transform shame into guilt, that would bring relief from it. I have mentioned earlier that people often try to do this. They want to talk about how guilty they are because that feels more dignified and less painful. That's because shame feels as if abandonment by others is warranted. "They ought to reject me, laugh, or turn away" is a thought one wants quickly to suppress. Remember Oedipus, who wanted to be hidden from view or thrown into the sea. He thought he ought to be out of communication.

Guilt need not bring on this loneliness. There are ways of handling it that keep communication going. Apology may serve for mild cases of guilt as long as one does not overuse it or become flippant. Certainly it is a form of communicating, often a kind that the wronged party will welcome graciously. Confession offers a strong form of communication. The guilty person can articulate what he or she did, bringing things out in the open. Even if a victim remains angry, at least a give-and-take still goes on.

If confession or apology don't go far enough, the wrongdoer can do penance or make amends. "I will make it up to you" comes as a promise both to the guilty and to the wronged. It keeps the former in company with others and gives the latter hope for compensation. Serious cases end up in court with perhaps millions of dollars at stake. Money cannot pay for loss of an eye or a leg or the life of a loved one, but if it's the best one can do, then society approves the measure and generally forgives.

When a judge sentences a convicted criminal to years in prison, the criminal then pays a debt to society. Many communities have used corporal punishment to expunge guilt from a wrongdoer. Though these processes are bleak, people do communicate by such means.

With shame the communication stops. Isolation and abandonment step in. One form of punishment is just that abandonment. The pain it brings may absolve the wrongdoer of guilt, but it leaves him to deal with loss of honor from which escape is harder.

Handling Humiliation: Help from Others

If shame has no excuses, leaving one abandoned, how can one escape it and start communicating again? Revenge offers one traditional way out. That is why revenge takes on such importance in honor cultures. Members of those cultures don't fear talking about shame; correspondingly, they accept revenge as a normal part of social life. Our society officially disapproves of revenge, and our repression of it often creates unpleasant bitterness.

But aren't there some peaceful alternatives to revenge? To answer this, remember the structure of honor: It sets up deep dependence between individual and community. Both warranted and unwarranted shame are painful because they come about by social rejection (or fear of it). Shame cannot occur without a community to threaten rejection since the feeling depends on community. A humiliated person must therefore look to his fellows to restore communication.

This point brings us back to the good-news aspect of shame. It is a highly social emotion, requiring the help of others if one is to escape it. Reassuring acceptance from another undercuts one's feeling of rejection. Hence benevolent, sensitive people can readmit the humiliated person. That is especially appropriate for unwarranted shame or for warranted shame that has gone on too long. But notice this requires the help of another. The victim of shame cannot reassure and accept himself.

Another form of social dependence occurs when shame arises from insult. If the offender apologizes for the insult, he disperses the shame. People in honor cultures observe this courtesy carefully. They otherwise leave themselves open to revenge. An apology sometimes works doubly well for avoiding a fight and relieving social tensions.

Handling Humiliation: Humor

In lighter vein, a good sense of humor serves to ease humiliation. It covers a wide variety of cases:

A man came as a dinner guest for his first time to the house of a woman whom he admired. The table cloth caught in his belt buckle so that when he got up glasses and plates of food tumbled noisily into a fine mess on the table and floor. He stood up and took a deep bow, saying, "And for my next act. . . !" They all laughed, making things OK.

Admirers of the psychiatrist Milton Erikson tell this story about him: A young girl was riding in a convertible, talking and laughing with her friends. Suddenly she got a blop of bird droppings in her open mouth from a bird flying overhead. Her friends saw it as funny, but she didn't. The more others laughed, the worse it became for her. Erikson, who didn't even know the girl, heard about how socially paralyzed she became after the incident. He sent her an anonymous postcard that said, "Beware of birds flying over open convertibles." After that she was fine. She had gone from feeling laughed at to laughing with. Somehow Erikson knew just how to make that change.

Classic slapstick artists serve society by offering themselves up to be laughed at, thus easing our fear of ridicule and humiliation. They play the part of the rejected, the incompetent, the foolish. Usually they exaggerate these weaknesses so that the audience can feel safely distant from them. These artists make a profoundly benevolent self-sacrifice.

They differ somewhat from comedians, who crack jokes and laugh with the audience. Groucho Marx was mostly a fine comedian who got people to laugh with him. He held slapstick to a minimum. But his brother Harpo was a clown, one to laugh at and deride. Try watching an old Marx Brothers movie. Harpo scampers around with his silly curly hair and idiotic smile. Truly ridiculous, he chases women whom he can't possibly catch. The audience can laugh and laugh at this ridiculous figure. At least once in each movie he finds a harp. Once he begins to play, his whole aspect transfigures. The pale curly hair becomes that of a saint. The silly grin changes to a profound look of selfless devotion. His beautiful harp-playing converts the once-laughing audience to religious seriousness. When he's through, the foolish grin comes right back. The audience starts giggling again, but now they do it with deeper understanding: Silliness is a human thing even when exaggerated. Anyone can blunder. Anyone can step into a wastebasket at precisely the wrong time.

King Lear's jester is likewise the redeeming clown. While making his master laugh at him he conveys wisdom about old Lear's foolishness. Clowns bridge a gap between the community and the outcast. A professional clown in my community put a bumper sticker on her car with this simple message of redemption:

CLOWNS ARE PEOPLE TOO

The bridge they build keeps shame from being hopeless. Shame allows no excuses, but we are only human.

Handling Humiliation: Ignoring It

In the movie *Nine to Five*, some women are trying to blackmail a man. One suggests, "We could photograph him in a whorehouse, and send him a print." The other woman says, "No, the jerk would print the photo on his Christmas cards!" This man is shameless.

One is not liable to shame unless one espouses community values. So one can avoid shame by just not caring — by being *shameless*. Notice the difference between calling someone shameful and calling him shameless. The reproach in the very word "shameless" suggests that liability to shame serves a helpful purpose. It sustains both love and self-respect. We saw how Parolles in *All's Well That Ends Well* hardly suffered when people saw through his masquerade. He was isolated, an outcast. But he didn't much care. Such a person does not hold values, does not mind being outside and alone. He has no respect for other people and none for himself either. It is as if someone were painting a picture without caring how it will look.

Too much shaming can drive a person to shamelessness, for one must find relief somewhere. Therefore, we must look attentively to how we reject or laugh at others. The community just loses a person who becomes shameless. The loss of a human being is always tragic. A more satisfactory way to avoid shame is this: Instead of shamelessly dropping all values, ignore only the limit norms. Take up a strong achievement norm to replace them. Get enough glory so that people forget about any warranted shame that lingers. After all, shame is a community affair. If the community forgets about it, then it's gone.

I will take up this subject in Chapters 8 and 9. But first, here are three case studies about honor in which self-image and the community lace into each other. They will give a chance to apply the ideas covered so far.

Personal Codes

Honor norms function for people in different ways. Some persons are more easily embarrassed than others. Some blush or fret faster. People disagree about what the code says and about how strictly to draw limits. Such variation allows the code to evolve.

Often individuals draw limits for themselves alone that demand more than the specific code. They hold high ideals. These may have their origin in the honor code; it is not as if individuals just create them on their own. But we often hear of someone, "He has high ideals and will not let himself fall below them." What people mean by this is that the person's limits, composing his personal code, are more stringent than what the community generally requires.

Holding Higher Ideals

Let us look again at Darcy as an example. Elizabeth accuses him of falling below the decency code by failing to give a man what was his due and by interfering in a courtship. With his letters to Elizabeth, Darcy is quick to defend himself, saying that in fact he has not passed these limits. Mere innocence, however, does not satisfy him personally. He demands more of himself, thanking Elizabeth for showing him "how insufficient were all [his] pretensions."

Right action ought to emanate from right character. Otherwise it is simply the following of rules — in our terms, just staying within the limits of the code. Darcy requires something of himself beyond those limits. Notice that no one else could have asked that of him, at least not directly. Members of a community can require directly only that each avoid violating limits. But the agent can, because of those limits, demand more of himself.

A personal code has much to do with self-image. Darcy sees himself as guilty of transgressing limits because in his own eyes his behavior, though right, does not rise out of a genuine character. Darcy gives us a clear example of someone who strives to uphold the community standards by making himself match the intention of the standards. His ideals correspond with standards of his community. As long as he acts in accordance with them he not only maintains the limit code in the sense of reputation but also lives up to those standards in the sense of real worth.

If a person's code disagrees so much with the specific code that he is likely to violate the specific code, then the person sets himself over against the community in some way. Either he is shameless in one respect or another, or he finds a way to get acceptance of his nonconformity. Short of these extremes, one has enormous freedom in what he may choose as ideals.

For other examples, consider ideals of health and cleanliness. These vary widely both in how high people set them and how they conceive them. One person may think avoiding sickness is quite sufficient. Another may be disappointed with himself unless he is able to jog forty miles a week. Someone may deem it foolish to spend time sweeping out a garage more than once a year, whereas another is upset when a drop of oil stains the floor. He gets some detergent and immediately scrubs it off. These personal differences shape a large part of our social interchange. Our choice and development of ideals influence how we live.

Inhabiting Two Communities

Now let us examine a case rather more complicated because it involves two communities. In Jack London's *The Sea Wolf*, a man named Hump, who is from a polite society, finds himself by misadventure on board a sealing ship where he must enter the society of rugged sailors. As a gentleman, unused to the ways of this new community and not at all prepared in the skills needed, he is of course low man in the pecking order. This delights the sleazy cook, who was previously low man. The cook pommels him unmercifully, happy having someone to pick on. This rattles Hump's pride, and Hump retaliates by taking up the rough ways of this ship community. He reverses the pecking order by outwitting the cook. The irony for Hump is that in order to bring about this reversal he must do things undreamed of in his genteel society. According to that society, Hump acts in a base way; according to the ship society, he scores some good points.

We can expect in this situation that Hump will have a confused self-image. For his own part, he seems to prefer the ways of his former community, but there is no possibility of getting along with and competing with the rough sailors by his previous, genteel rules. To survive, Hump must embrace some new rules even though he is ashamed to do that. Although the feeling of shame is peculiarly personal, peculiarly isolating, it always depends for its sting on some kind of community, on the eyes and ears of others. Hump doesn't forget his other values; they form part of him. But the genteel eyes and ears are far removed from the sealing ship, where he must deal with the eyes and ears of rugged seamen. They do not willfully force new and strange values on him. Rather, he must accept them as his present community, and that requires him to adopt some new values: "When in Rome do as the Romans do." (Here the reader may want to review the section on "Honor and the Eyes of Others" in Chapter 6.)

Suppose Hump preferred to maintain his gentlemanly ways, rejecting the ship community. How might his situation have differed? By asking this we can see again how much self-image and reputation connect. The newcomer who rejects a community trusts his self-image to values learned elsewhere. He tries to keep self-image independent of the eyes of the new community. If Hump had chosen that, the sailors would have killed him and thrown him overboard. As readers of London's story we can puzzle about whether Hump was "really" honorable. But Hump didn't have that luxury. He had to fall in line.

Rejecting the New Community

Nikolai Hel, the hero in Trevanian's novel *Shibumi*, provides a picture of someone who self-consciously decides to live according to a personal code. He holds his present community in contempt. The word *shibumi* means something like "having restrained, understated beauty and grace." In his youth Hel adopts that ideal from his Japanese teachers who train him in martial arts. He then generalizes it to cover all aspects of his life, from his manner of eating and dress, to making love, to creating a garden. It even determines how he assassinates political activists, which happens to be how he makes his living.

The novel gives a rather detailed description of Hel's training, circumstances, and trials under which he develops this ideal. The main action then takes place after he has retired from his vocation as assassin. He lives in the Basque country in his castle designed according to *shibumi*. Events pull him out of retirement and back into action. We see him fighting his enemies, dealing with his accomplices, managing adventures and difficult situations all for the sake of and in accordance with his ideals. Though he comes close to defeat, nothing makes him drop his adopted standard. His life is a work of art, created with *shibumi* as the guiding light. He avenges insults to himself and those under his protection. But he does this in no great hurry — one must carry out revenge with appropriate grace and restraint.

We certainly want to call this a personal code and a personal ideal. Hel sets limits upon himself that he would be ashamed to transgress. They are definitely honor norms because he cares about decency only for aesthetic reasons. Revenge, for a severe humiliation in his youth, is a lifetime duty he carries out methodically, with restrained grace. It matters little to Hel that *shibumi* sets him above other men. They just don't happen to follow the ideal and therefore fall below him. He considers only two other characters worthy of judging him because they can understand his superiority to themselves. Except for those two, he worries none about reputation. Yet this exaggerated hero lives by honor norms. Can honor break away so far from reputation?

No, it cannot. Hel and his two friends follow honor norms. They are aristocrats. The society around them, according to the storyteller, is not good enough for honor. They give him high reputation: a formidable enemy, a trustworthy friend. All respect him, though they don't understand his limit norms. They admire his achievements; they think he lives according to goal norms. So at this point the other two norm types come into view. In contrast to limit norms, we move now to goal norms.

Chapter 8

Beneficence and Achievement: Goal Norms

Everyone lives under a mixture of the four norm types, but individuals emphasize these norm types differently. Even a single individual is likely to change emphasis in different stages of life. The same thing goes for cultures, societies, and communities of whatever size. Our country has traditionally emphasized norms of the goal type. We care about results: "Just get the job done! Get the problem solved."

Remember, there are two types of goal norms — achievement and beneficence. Each of the two has a corresponding limit — honor and decency. Notice that if you typically emphasize results rather than restraints, you might be tempted to say that the restraints deserve attention only because they help get results. For instance, an honest merchandiser (we may suppose) is likely to get more business than a dishonest one. So honesty pays off. Yet I have assumed all along that the limit norms of honor and decency are distinct from their corresponding goal norms of achievement and beneficence.

In this chapter I want to talk about what goal norms are and to examine the question whether there are, after all, any limit norms distinct from these goals. I'll begin by reviewing the four norm types and some fairly obvious comparisons among them. For reference, here is a short version of the chart that you saw first in Chapter 4.

	MORAL NORMS	AESTHETIC NORMS
LIMIT NORMS	Decency	Honor
GOAL NORMS	Beneficence	Achievement

Under the goal norms of *beneficence* one aims to bring about happiness and well-being of other people as much as one can. Beneficence is different from decency in that no definite means of doing this are specified by a beneficence norm. Under the goal norms of *achievement* one tries to shine out among one's fellows by some accomplishment or excellence, or one esteems another for doing so. It is different from honor in that no specific constraints are laid down about how to manage a given achievement. The achiever finds his own way.

Beneficence and glory differ in that the former is the opposite of guilty behavior whereas the latter is the opposite of shaming behavior. One standard justifies moral self-respect; the other self-esteem. They also differ in the way we measure success in reaching the goals. We judge success in beneficence by looking to how much good a person produces with what means he happens to have. Thus the widow's offering of two mites that Jesus tells of in the Gospels shows as much or more beneficence than thousands of dollars given by a millionaire philanthropist. The widow gave everything she could, though it wasn't much.

Achievement works the opposite way. We judge an achievement by how much power some great deed displays. Oddly enough, the deed is likely to display more power if it suggests unused power behind what has been used. Voice teachers tell their students to sing below their limits of volume and range in order to give the finest performance. The pole vaulter who looks as if he could have vaulted another three feet is more glorious than one who succeeds with a look of strain. The bride's father who throws a lavish wedding party must act as if the expense were nothing to him if he wishes his generous wealth to shine.

But the two types of goal norms are also similar in several ways. For one thing, they bring up similar questions. Of both we need to ask what is timeless, "naturally" true about success under each norm. What features of beneficent or splendid success are common to all cultures? What aspects of each norm type are, instead, relative to culture — relative to place and time in history — left open for different cultures to decide on differently?

Of those aspects relative to culture, there is also a question about the quality of results sought in each case. A person trying to help people needs to ask what will count as happiness or well-being of those whom he seeks to benefit. Someone acting toward achievement must ask what sort of feat will count as true achievement. In other words, both types of goal norm raise normative questions about what the goal *should* be.

In addition, there are similar relations between the goal norms and their corresponding limit norms. Beneficence and glory emphasize results; limit norms of decency and honor put restraints on conduct or set definite duties. Limit norms say "Do this," whereas goal norms say "Get this done somehow."

These relations can be complex. I will examine beneficence first because just as people have talked more about decency than about honor, so they have talked more about beneficence than about glory.

Beneficence

Timeless and Relative Beneficence Norms

Beneficence demands that the individual work to improve the situation of everyone, thus avoiding guilt and deserving happiness. It orients itself to goals, of course, because it demands that we produce certain results. It is stated positively, whereas the decency norms are usually stated negatively. But clearly the results aimed at closely link with the ideals of decency, by which one is supposed to avoid harming others.

Consider once again the Golden Rule. Chapter 5 includes a list showing some of the negative versions of the rule that various great cultures have accepted. It is a timeless, nonrelative aspect of the decency norm type. There are also pervasive positive statements of the Golden Rule, which provide the timeless, nonrelative aspect of beneficence. Here are some of them:

All things whatsoever ye would that men should do to you, do ye even so unto them: for this is the law and the prophets. (Christianity)

No one of you is a believer until he desires for his brother that which he desires for himself. (Islam)

This is the sum of all true righteousness: Deal with others as you yourself would be dealt by. (Brahminism)

The true rule is to do by others as you do by your own. (Hinduism)

A man should go through life treating all creatures as he himself would be treated. (Jainism)

One should seek for others the happiness one desires for oneself. (Buddhism)

Regard your neighbor's gain as your own gain, and your neighbor's loss as your own loss. (Taoism)

Do to others as you wish them to do to you. (Shintoism)

Do as you would be done by. (Zoroastrianism)

Cultures that stress negative versions of the Golden Rule are probably more concerned with decency. Those that stress positive versions will be more concerned with beneficence. Noticeably, we can find both strains in every great tradition. Thus the promoting of good for others seems to be the timeless aspect of beneficence.

Assessing the Value of Beneficence Goals

Codes of beneficence, however, do not usually provide definite *rules* on how to achieve a beneficent result. That is one main feature distinguishing beneficence from decency. But a particular code of beneficence, which is the conventional or culture-relative aspect, does provide a fairly definite idea of what constitutes human happiness and well-being. Local ideas of happiness are not completely definite, just as decency rules are not completely definite. But in each culture there is some idea, some vision of what really benefits a person — as we can see by contrasting different traditions.

Here is an example: In a French film of Kazanzakis's *He Who Must Die*, one scene shows an elderly Greek patriarch dying in the company of his good friend, a Turkish patriarch. (The two different cultures are traditional enemies, but both stress honor. It isn't surprising that the old Greek feels at ease confiding in another man of his own rank.) The two men fell to comparing the two pictures of life after death presented by their separate cultures. The Christian Greek says he will be going to a place of sunlight in God's presence, to glory and choirs of singing angels. The Islamic Turk's picture of paradise also includes God and God's glory. But instead of choirs of singing angels, there are beautiful, celestial young women themselves made blissful by waiting on the deceased, and all the host are comfortable inside an airy room.

Both men display a touching wisdom about these mere cultural differences. Death being near, they are both more interested in the timeless aspect of human good than in whether their particular pictures are "true." As the old Greek spends his last breath, his Turkish friend says to him tenderly, "*Bon voyage*, my poor Patriarchias."

This little scene tells how much contrast can exist among different conventions about the details of human happiness. It also shows that the concept or ideal of happiness is importantly open-ended. A benevolent person must consider carefully just what sort of situation will count as good for another. This is not as easy as knowing what counts as harm. The positive golden rule provides a guideline but cannot settle finally what truly benefits another.

Yet anyone acting under beneficence must make some judgment about what counts as success in helping others. In order to act at all, one must answer that question. How to answer it is a matter continually open to creative revision and insight. I may seek for my daughter the finest education available and provide opportunity for her to meet many famous and stimulating people so that she will become renowned in an exciting career. But suppose she ends up saying, "Mama, I don't like being away at college. I want to come home and marry Glenn because I'm really in love with him and miss him too much." Then chances are I have failed to benefit her. No doubt my intentions were good and right. But for mere good *intentions,* others should say that I am a decent and moral parent, not that I've been really helpful to my daughter. At beneficence I have failed. And if my bungling attempts to help have actually harmed another, an observer might say sarcastically, "She *means* well. . . ."

Decency Reduced to Beneficence?

This point — the open-endedness of human benefit, the constant lack of finality about it — is clear enough. At the same time, there is something straightforwardly right and moral about trying to do good. On the surface, forgetting the deeper question about what truly is human good, it seems obvious that trying to achieve benefit, both for myself and others, is what morality is all about. "After all," we might reflect, "harm is just the opposite of good. If my moral obligation is to do good for others, then surely that *includes* not doing them harm. And so," we go on, "beneficence includes decency. There are not two separate norm types but only one. There is no limit norm type, only a goal that explains and justifies certain restraints. We can *reduce* decency to beneficence and simplify normative thinking enormously."

This sounds like a pretty good argument, doesn't it? Certain philosophers, called utilitarians, have indeed found it attractive. They claim we can reduce decency to beneficence. (Philosophers have neglected the honor/glory relation, but they have written thousands of pages on the decency/beneficence relation.) These utilitarians say that our moral lives can be reduced to a single overriding principle that explains *all* moral norms: Act so as to produce the greatest amount of happiness possible for the greatest number of persons possible.

The utilitarians claim that decency rules are justified by this single principle. For example, the rules against lying, stealing, and assaulting are good rules to have because people are better off in societies that have those rules. There would be much less happiness (or much more unhappiness) without them.

They point out that sometimes a person might need to lie in order to prevent a great deal of suffering. Certainly this is true. Sometimes, for instance, a doctor may consider it more kind to lie to a patient than to burden him or her with the knowledge of imminent death. Cases could come up where only a lie can save a life. Suppose an insane woman stomps into my house with a gun and demands to know where my friend is, who is hiding from her in my back room. Surely I ought to violate the decency rule against lying to save my friend.

Considering cases with this structure (and they do occur), utilitarians think it possible to summarize our moral beliefs in a simple way. They say that an act or decision is moral if it does more good than harm. So, for example, they would say that the decency duty of honesty is important only because, on the whole, society runs more smoothly and happily if its members are usually honest. They'd say dishonesty is wrong-as-harmful, not that it is just plain wrong.

Anti-utilitarians argue against this by saying that sometimes decency rules don't in fact produce the most possible happiness. Sometimes, for instance, violating a person's rights would make everyone happier except that one person. Suppose a whole town is paralyzed by fear and panic over a recent murder, and the sheriff can quiet those fears by jailing a person whom he knows to be innocent. It would still be wrong to jail the innocent even if it helped a great many people.

Or suppose there is some strangely bumbling rogue in the community who wishes that everyone were as unhappy as he is. Suppose this rogue is so inept that every time he tries to harm others he ends up doing nice things for them instead. Many people benefit from his presence in the community, only the rogue turns out unhappy. So utilitarians would have to say he is a good person to have around. His *intentions* may be bad, but intentions don't count ultimately in beneficence. (It's results that count. Just get the job done!) To most people this utilitarian view runs violently counter to their moral feelings and intuitions. It is *indecent, immoral,* to have such bad intentions. Most people wouldn't want the rogue around, regardless of the good fortune he brings.

Of course, we may retort that the situation I've drawn is so bizarre that it would never really happen. In fact, utilitarians have countered in precisely that way. They have argued that, as a matter of fact, people with bad intentions tend to do harm and those with good intentions tend to give benefit. That, they claim, completely explains the normal, decent person's revulsion from the rogue in the story.

On the other hand, the rogue story, though exaggerated, isn't entirely bizarre. Remember the story about Br'er Rabbit? That clever fellow pleads with Br'er Fox not to throw him into the briar patch. Br'er Fox, eager to be as devilish as possible, throws Br'er Rabbit into the briar patch — much to Br'er Rabbit's glee, as that is his home.

Getting away from fantasy, the recent Iran-Contra affair involved a bungling Colonel Oliver North trying to "encourage moderates" to undermine the Iranian regime. He ended up helping Ayatollah Khomeini's extremist regime while trying to harm it. With enemies like Colonel North, Khomeini needed no friends.

It isn't clear, then, that decency rules all fall under the utilitarian's principle of beneficence. Some deeply seated moral intuitions run the other way. I won't try to settle here the debate between utilitarians and their opponents. I'm more concerned with a practical, applied point that the examples above illustrate. It is just too hard to think through all the probable results of each act I am about to perform. When the insane woman threatens, I may see immediately the need to break a decency rule against lying. But I must struggle hard against my intuitions in order to believe that someone like Br'er Fox would be a welcome next door neighbor, even though he does good while trying to do harm. After such an intellectual struggle through much subtle logic, my normal feelings about morality have become pretty far removed. People must use careful reflection in order to act with integrity. But they also need right feelings to point the way in critical ventures that sometimes call for quick decisions.

So even if decency does reduce to beneficence in some subtle, long-run way, there is still good reason to think about them as two separate norm types. Decency rules give society a sort of minimum standard so that persons can get along. Beneficence is not quite so necessary. In fact, one of the greatest utilitarians, John Stuart Mill, quite agreed with this practical point and wrote eloquently about it. He believed that there are utilitarian reasons to consider decency rules separately, concentrating on their simple rightness. Thinking only about results can become so complicated that in ordinary life we might sometimes miss the point.

Achievement

That is all I will say about beneficence for now. As I mentioned, philosophers have written much about the relations between beneficence and decency, but they have neglected aesthetic, nonmoral types of norms. I want to turn now to achievement because it is a type of norm that dazzles Americans, even though, given our democratic values, we hesitate to talk about it thoughtfully.

If someone said, "I couldn't help failing because of external bad luck, even though I had the talent," that excuse might lessen the shame of failure. But slogans like the following condition us not to resort easily to such excuses:

- Winners are people who make their own luck.
- It's not the size of the boy in the fight, it's the size of the fight in the boy.
- It's a poor workman who blames his tools.
- It's not the aptitude, but the attitude, that determines the altitude.

These sayings express concern for achievement norms. In that type of norm, luck, not just good intentions or hard work, can be a legitimate route to success. A splendid actress gets no moral credit for her talent, but the nonmoral esteem that others accord her can be pretty personal. A young woman plain in looks might do as well as she can with what she has, but she won't win a beauty contest just for trying hard. An "A" for effort isn't ordinarily granted under the achievement norms (though sometimes it is granted under other norm types).

The reward of achieving is glory, esteem, and prestige. These rewards are logically scarce. That is, not everyone can get first prize. In this respect achievement differs from beneficence, whose reward is moral self-respect. (In an ideal world, everyone could be beneficent.)

There are many different ways to achieve, and contexts for achievement vary widely. Here are some examples to consider:

• Sometimes "what she did with what she had" counts for achievement, not the absolute degree of success. Adults applaud the baby's first steps, whereas they expect the three-year-old to walk. In boxing there is a separate championship for each weight class. And tournaments are designed to match winners against winners.

• The heavyweight boxing champion, however, has more prestige than the lightweight champion; the losing finalists in a tournament get more prestige than a winner at an earlier stage who had to drop out; and an assistant professor at Stanford has more prestige than a full professor at a state teacher's college.

• Our society pays lip-service to the slogan "Whatever you do, do well," but there is actually a fairly stable ranking of occupations. Young people trying to decide on a career are especially aware of this. A person far down on a higher ladder easily outranks, in prestige, a person high up on a lower scale. For example, a mediocre senator outranks a top janitor. So even if one cannot help it that one's talents happen to be in a less prestigious line, this doesn't really help in terms of prestige. (I'm from a small town. My big-city in-laws snickered horribly when a youth from my town won the national contest for grocery-bagging.)

• We'd probably scorn a person who sacrificed his or her family to some intrinsically worthwhile endeavor, say painting or poetry, if the results were paltry and inadequate. But if this person produced a masterpiece, most people would not think him a lesser artist for his immorality. They might call him a great artist but a bad man.

These are just a few examples of how varied and complex the achievement norm type can be. You have surely noticed that it hardly seems democratic! Actually, it is no more democratic than honor is.

But it figures heavily in our culture. Americans put great stress on getting the job done, so this type of goal norm deserves our serious attention.

In the following pages I'll ask the same questions about achievement that earlier in this chapter I've asked about beneficence. First, what are its timeless, natural aspects as opposed to those values supplied by community convention; and what happens when we are trying to decide whether something done counts as true achievement? And then, can we reduce honor to achievement as utilitarians suggest reducing decency to beneficence?

Timeless and Relative Achievement Norms

As with beneficence, the structure of achievement lies in the timeless or natural aspects of what makes some result count as an achievement. Again as with beneficence, little in the way of rules is available. Where rules dominate, we have instead the limit norm of honor. Achievement demands that an individual accomplish shining deeds, thus earning glory and avoiding shame of failure. Like beneficence, it is stated positively, whereas honor norms are usually stated negatively. A person genuinely concerned with beneficence is *benevolent;* a person concerned with achievement is *ambitious.* Both are goal-oriented. Both demand that we care about results.

To get at the timeless aspects of what an achievement truly is, I turn again to Aristotle's proud man for help. Review the section in Chapter 6 about the structure of honor. What I separated out there as the structure of honor had to do with the great-souled man's physical bearing: his dignity, competence, habits of walking and talking. These constraints make him noble, an image joyous to behold. But this proud man also attends to results: He stands ready to do truly worthwhile things remarkably well. (Big-souled as he is, he has contempt for trivial accomplishments.) Now if this man never *did* anything, others might still admire his dignity, but they could not appropriately give him glory. An ambitious person seeks glory for splendid deeds *done,* not just admiration for a great *potential.* From this we find the enduring central ideas of true achievement: Not only must the result be splendid, but also the act itself must be extraordinary in its beautiful execution. There is a competitive aspect of achievement — and an aesthetic one: People love to behold splendor.

The question immediately arises, "How do I tell whether a deed is splendid?" (It is very like the question we asked with beneficence: "How do I know what truly benefits another?") Not surprisingly, the achievement question is just as difficult to answer because defining achievement is open-ended, always inviting revision, never final. But again, cultural and community conventions give some guidelines for filling in detail. Aristotle's proud man knew, from his culture, what he was supposed to do. For instance, he should be splendidly formidable in battle. He could train for this by winning at athletic and war games.

In modern America, also, there are certain conventions about what counts as achievement. We, too, admire the athlete who wins swiftly, with agility. Our culture also puts great stress on earning and investing money. A successful businessman is one who executes good business decisions and manages money well, thus acquiring solid assets. In contrast, the splendid businessman makes millions by ingenious, uncommon insights leading him to remarkably clever decisions. A host of other people then copy him, but it is too late for them. They might make money, but the innovator gets the glory because his deed was uncommon, the creative exception.

On the conventional level, the culture-relative level of achievement, one must always be asking what a true achievement might be. What activities are worth excelling at? What is worth working hard to excel at? Are all achievements and excellencies appropriate for all people, or should people instead have only certain achievements available to them? (For instance, is it appropriate for women to excel at athletics; is it proper for an intellectual to be a skilled mechanic?)

Different societies disagree in answering these questions, and of course different individuals within societies also disagree, though not quite so deeply. Many men see achievement in limited projects where they can tell definitely if they've succeeded (while women may seek success in fostering relationships). In the movie *Parenthood,* a grandfather complains that fathering is never done: You never cross the finish line or score the goal. And in another movie, *A Touch of Class,* a middle-aged couple finally achieves sexual union. The next morning, the American man raves about how wonderful the experience was, inquiring dutifully, "How was it for you?" The crisp British woman says, "Quite good, and it will get better as we learn more about each other." Hours later she asks why he is sunk in depression. "Well," he sulks, "it's no fun to hear I struck out in the sack!" She's exasperated. At least he could see sex as a team effort, where *they* succeed or fail. Disagreements arise because the questions are open-ended. The achiever must innovate something in order to shine as extraordinary, splendid, and deserving praise. Such an innovation, by its very nature, creates new values, and then all the questions arise again. Answers to these new questions create revised conventions. In this way the code of achievement evolves.

The creation of new values — that others then follow — is a bold achievement indeed. But typically certain conventions are on hand purporting to guide even inventive achievements. If you want to find out what these conventions are in a society, look for those areas there where competition runs especially high, attracting a good deal of attention. Consider our relative rankings for soccer, baseball, and football. Unlike Europeans, Americans downrank soccer, and we've moved in the last fifty years from worshiping baseball to worshiping football. We can learn much about a society's values by asking about such rankings. In each society competitive intensity marks that society's version of high achievement. Once again, enduring aspects of achievement underlie local variations. Values differ from one community to another, and communities can be wrong about their values. (Americans are just wrong about soccer.)

Assessing the Value of Achievement Goals

Winning competition does not alone guarantee true achievement because a society might well become interested in valueless competitions. A friend of mine found herself among comrades who were competing tensely over who would get to have as houseguest an unexpected visitor. My friend left the gathering as soon as she gracefully could. She wanted to withdraw from the unworthy game. And the global community seems recently to have had second thoughts about the space race. For some ten years the United States and the Soviet Union poured millions of dollars into their respective space projects, each trying to achieve something more spectacular than the other. Then in the quieter 1970s Americans and Soviets sat back and wondered about the value of their countries' efforts. (Some critic of the space race has said, "Sending men to the moon is like farting 'Annie-

Laurie' through a key hole — the only possible reason to do it is to show it can be done.")

As a nation, we put great stress on goals and results, on getting the job done, and that indicates that we are very concerned about achievement norms. But this kind of norm isn't so simple as it may at first appear. It isn't just its difficulty that makes an action count as achievement (it is hard to wash a sidewalk clean with a toothbrush). And it isn't just how spectacular a thing is that counts. Political assassins get results and widespread attention, but they don't count as achievers.

Furthermore, following the achievement norm type doesn't mean just putting one's sights on a goal and then heading for it. One must also consider just what the goal *should* be. Mere success at reaching a goal, just getting a result, will not count as achievement unless the goal itself is somehow seen as worthwhile and praiseworthy. For instance, in a comic strip, Cudlow's owner comments to a friend, "He's not very talented." A wounded Cudlow thinks to himself, "You call stacking ninety-four beer cans NO TALENT?!" It certainly is a rare feat for a dog to stack ninety-four beer cans. And some "dogs" might even compete at it. But who wants a stack of ninety-four beer cans?

Another example: At a barbecue party with lively conversation the hostess began talking about how difficult — nearly impossible — it is to break a raw egg by squeezing it in your fist. "An egg cracks so easily against a surface," she said with coy dignity, "but it's just amazing how if you put pressure on the egg all at once in your hand, the round shape of the egg keeps it from breaking. You'd have to have a very strong fist to break it." One of the guests couldn't resist that challenge. He strutted over to the hostess. "I'll bet I can break a raw egg with my fist," he boasted. "I'll bet you *can't*," the hostess answered earnestly. "Well, get me one and I'll show you." The hostess fetched a raw egg for him. He squeezed it, and of course the egg cracked immediately so that its slimy insides oozed through his fingers and dripped messily to the ground. Everyone laughed, and the egg-breaker had to laugh, too, in order to cover his painful humiliation. He had tried to "achieve" a silly thing only because it seemed difficult.

So it isn't *just* getting the job done that counts as achievement. We also have to take account of what results we are going after. What job ought to be done? How can one decide what ought to be achieved? Even if it *were* hard to break an egg with your fist, who in his right mind would want a raw egg sliming between his fingers? It could never count as much of an achievement. In fact, doing trivial things obscenely well is more shaming than splendid.

This same point is made well in an important book, *Effective Versus Efficient Computing.* In this book mere technicians who "do the thing right" are contrasted with wise policy-makers who make sure they're doing the right thing.

It is one thing to say we need to be thoughtful about what goals we choose. It is quite another trying to figure out which goals are worthwhile. The normative codes of society provide a starting place. Those codes can be wrong, but they at least get a dialogue under way. Thoughtful, reflective, calm, and open discussion is then the way to go about assessing goals. Open discussion gives people a way to be cautious, to think before leaping into something that might have silly or tragic consequences. Because of the open-endedness of true achievement and splendor, it is not at all easy to decide what goals to seek. One can never be certain.

Many people, bristling with impatience, find it difficult to discuss openly and democratically something that has no final, pat answer. "Too muddled, too inefficient, too complex," they say, "and no answer promised in the end." But we can't ignore this most critical of concerns. What should we choose as goals? (The strange bafflement about this question marks it as properly philosophical. Philosophy deals with those questions that can't be answered patly and can't be ignored.) Although no answer is final or pat, some answers are far better than others. That was true in Aristotle's day, but it is especially true now. In these days we have super nuclear power and incredibly capable computers. Even if we avoid disaster, we must also worry about a life spent doing trivial things obscenely well. With our technology it is often so easy to "get the job done." If we don't discuss carefully and openly what job *ought* to be done, we could all too easily have a raw egg sliming through our fingers.

Reduction of Honor to Achievement

Above I mentioned that a way to find out a given society's code of achievement is by looking at its main areas of competition. Another guide is to examine the omissions or failures that most humiliate ambitious people in that society. People can even find out much about their own values by reflecting on which unfinished projects they most want to hide. Individuals will vary, but as always we take much from our local society's general code. Codes of achievement will then vary among different societies according to the way each society ranks activities and their results.

In our society a businessman is not ashamed to let his athletic abilities wither from lack of time to exercise. In fact, the saying goes, "If your golf game is too good, you've been neglecting your business." But in Homer's *Odyssey*, a Greek story written centuries before Plato and Aristotle, the character Odysseus is mortally insulted when a young stranger suggests that he has neglected his athletic training because he is a trader too busy making money. The stranger tells him roughly, "I suppose you are one of those grasping traders . . . who think of nothing but of their outward freights and homeward cargoes. There does not seem to be much of the athlete about you."

Though exhausted, Odysseus then decides to join in the games because the stranger's taunts have stung him to the quick. He would not be ashamed to admit that his running skills had deteriorated from lack of practice on shipboard during his heroic military adventures, but to lack athletic training because of greed for money would be, in that society, shameful indeed.

In the *Republic*, Plato brings a similar charge against merchants. They are poor at sports, he says, because they neglect training to concentrate on business. Also, they repress the splendid emotions necessary for athletic victory, for fear these might prove expensive. Traditional Greek culture clearly valued military ("heroic") activities highest, then athletic activities, and moneymaking lowest. From this kind of ranking of achievements a society derives a scale of dishonors, of things to be ashamed about.

The movie *The Americanization of Emily* suggests that today we should greatly downrank military achievement, and as we reassess it, we should rethink what shame physical cowardice deserves. In our age perhaps we should admire physical cowardice as leading away from worship of war. The suggestion here is that beneficial goals like peace should determine the demands of honor. This would be a revolutionary change: Traditionally, people have seen courage as essential to honor.

All these examples seem to indicate that honor, the avoidance of shame by respecting constraints, is a means to accomplishing results.

At the very least, honor closely links with achievement through the dreaded threat of shame. Failure to achieve provokes shame in ambitious persons. Lack of power — some kind of weakness or deformity — causes failure, and shame arises from weakness. Could it be that honor is really just a utilitarian part of achievement, that the former is subordinate to and derived from the latter? In Chapter 3 we saw that honor, though suppressed and often passed over, still figures in people's reflections about what they ought to do or be. But perhaps the limits and ideals imposed by honor are ultimately justified by the help they provide people in seeking their goals.

Are decency and beneficence really separate norms, or does the decency norm reduce to beneficence when you seriously think about it? We saw earlier that utilitarians agreed with this reduction. To get insight into the relation between honor and achievement, I want to examine these parallel questions: Are the two aesthetic norms, honor and achievement, really separate norms? Or does honor reduce to achievement when you seriously think about it?

The examples above suggest that we answer "yes." In addition, even Aristotle doesn't specifically distinguish the two norm types when describing his proud man. Not only is the proud man honorable in the highest degree; he also stands ready to do glorious deeds. The competence, self-regard, strength, and physical carriage that make up his honor also show his potential for splendid achievement when the occasion arises.

It might appear, then, that honor is valued only for the sake of results, only as a means for getting the job done. The Arabian racehorse, nervous and tempestuous even as it stands in its stall, is excitingly beautiful because every muscle quiver signals its readiness to win at the race. The power to do something great explains its beauty. Analogously, the weakness displayed in dishonor explains its ugliness. So dishonor might seem a mirror image of achievement, despicable merely as undermining achievement.

Few writers have examined this attempt to subordinate honor to glory, but Plato's *Gorgias* records that the philosopher Socrates did attempt that move. Socrates reflected deeply about values and norms. The greatest human achievement, he decided, is to live an authentic life in quest of truth and goodness.

In *Gorgias*, we find Socrates suggesting that there is no such thing as power in general — only individual powers. He saw a power as meaning "able to do so-and-so." The power to feed chickens means being able to feed chickens and means nothing more. The power to drive sixty miles an hour means being able to go that fast. Power over another person means being able to control that person's behavior. Socrates then concluded that the value of a power comes from the value of the thing done. The value of the end determines the value of the means.

Later in that same dialogue Callicles tried to shame Socrates for being unable to defend himself rhetorically against rascally accusers in the law courts. That is, Socrates didn't know how to use fancy emotional speeches to persuade a crowd of judges (there would be 500 of them in an Athenian trial) to acquit him. If Socrates were ever accused of bad citizenship, Callicles said, he would need eloquence to save his own life.

Socrates answered in this way: I agree that being unable to ward off important evils from yourself and your friends is truly shaming, but the discussion should get more specific. There are many kinds of evils we need to ward off, he said; real shame is warranted only for the inability to ward off the *worst* kinds of evils. So before we can decide whether I ought to be ashamed of my particular disabilities, we must first settle which evils (to be warded off) are in fact the worst.

Socrates had already shown in the dialogue (at least to his own satisfaction) that doing wrong is a worse evil than being wronged. A person is worse off, claimed Socrates, if he does wrong than if someone wrongs him. At this point he showed that to be a rhetorical success in corrupt Athens, you had to be as immoral and tyrannical as the riffraff that rules the city, for the riffraff heed only slobs like themselves. So anyone able rhetorically to ward off the lesser evil of being wrongly convicted will, unhappily, have to be immoral. In other words, you have to do wrong, and that's a greater evil than being wronged. It leaves you worse off.

What's worse, having rhetorical power means that you can do wrong with impunity because you can get people to approve of whatever you do. Socrates would wish that fate only on his worst enemy. Being disposed to do wrong and not being stopped, the successful orator will end up actually doing wrong, powerless to ward off this monstrous ill.

Paradoxically, rhetorical powers give a speaker a trivial power linked to an important weakness. Such success is reason for humiliation, and lack of rhetorical ability is reason for pride.

This argument is fairly complex. Here is a summary of the steps in it:

1. Doing wrong is a worse evil than suffering wrong.
2. Therefore doing wrong leaves one worse off than being unjustly convicted.
3. The worse an evil is, the more shaming it is to lack power to ward it off.
4. To persuade the mob in Athens to acquit one, one must be a good rhetorician.
5. The Athenian mob rulers are immoral; they behave ruthlessly.
6. "Good" rhetoricians have to be like those whom they persuade. The crowd will heed only a speaker with "the common touch."
7. Therefore Athenian rhetoricians have to behave ruthlessly.
8. Therefore being able to ward off unjust conviction is more shaming (a worse evil) than being unjustly convicted. The relatively trivial power to get acquitted is linked to a vital weakness: the inability to ward off wrong doing.
9. Therefore one should be humiliated to be known as a splendid rhetorician.

The weak stage of this ingenious proof is step 1, which many philosophers dispute. But Socrates's idea is sound that we must rank powers and weaknesses, the shame and glory they warrant, according to the worth of their corresponding activities and goals. Then we can decide, by reference to that ranking, if either shame or glory is warranted. Being able to do trivial things well warrants no glory, and lacking such ability warrants no shame.

Notice that the whole analysis depends on Socrates's idea of what a true achievement is. Then step 9 explicitly says that the honor demand (don't be a good rhetorician) depends on the achievement norm (ward off the worst evils). If *every* demand of honor depends on a goal, then honor is indeed reducible to achievement. Of course, the particular honor duty that Socrates arrived at might seem a little eccentric to some people. So to test further the idea that rules of honor come from the achievement norm type, let's take another case. Courage is a good example, because it belongs to most codes of honor. Imagine this dialogue:

Al: Why should anybody be brave?

Bert: Because anyone who isn't brave disgraces himself. People will laugh at him and avoid him.

Al: But why should they ridicule him? What good is bravery? (What goal does it help to accomplish?)

Bert: It helps win battles. If soldiers weren't brave they wouldn't fight. They would lose the battles. If union leaders hadn't been brave in facing managers, workers would still be living on poverty wages and working in horrible conditions. A coward can't defend his wife against a tavern bully. If a quarterback is afraid of being tackled, he will never succeed in throwing the ball accurately. Teams that take on challenges can't afford to carry the weight of cowards with them. They'd never get anything done.

Al: But now what you're saying is that people ought to be brave in order to achieve some goal. I'd agree to that. I certainly wouldn't want to be fighting in a platoon and have the guy next to me hightail it, leaving me to fight alone. So I'd sure say the fellows with me ought to be brave and I ought to be brave. So what you mean is that people ought to be brave in order to get some job done: to win a war, to make a touchdown, to get a raise in pay.

Bert: Of course. Cowards can't get important things done . . .

Al: Now it sounds as if cowardice would be OK except when people have some goal in mind. In other words, cowardice isn't ugly in itself. It's bad because it can make you fail when you've got a job to do. If you haven't got a job to do, courage and cowardice make no difference.

Bert: Oh, I suppose so, if you want to nit-pick. But you're not being very realistic. In real life . . . well, first of all, there nearly always is some job to be done. But second, you can't just turn courage on when you need it and off when you don't. Courage gets built into a person's character. It's got to be a habit. You can't rely on a man to be brave when you need him, unless you're sure he's got courage built right into his habits, ready to go into action when the situation calls for it.

What goes on in this conversation is that Al sees the honor norm as merely a means of following the achievement norm, because (according to Al) honor makes sense only when it aids achievement. Do you think Bert, in his last point, has begun to agree with that? If you want to find out, here is a good example to use to test Bert.

In Shakespeare's *Henry VI, Part 1*, King Henry rewards the noble Lord Talbot for brave and faithful services by making him earl of Shrewsbury. Near the end of the play Talbot is surrounded on a battle-field. His son John is with him, sharing in the doom. There is a chance for one of them to escape. Each of them tries to get the other to do so. Neither will do it because they both have too strong a sense of honor. Much will be lost if they both die: the chance to found a great new family, the chance to avenge old Talbot's death. But both Talbots find unthinkable any violation of honor for mere results.

Al and Bert continue their conversation, now using the Talbots as an example:

> *Al:* The Talbots couldn't possibly win and they knew it. So wasn't it pretty dumb of them to brave it out in that situation? At least one of them should have run, to save the family line.
>
> *Bert:* If one of them had run I wouldn't call him a coward, not when they knew the situation was hopeless. But I certainly don't think they were dumb to stand tight. Their courage was splen-did. Why do you say it was dumb?
>
> *Al:* Because it defeated their purpose! Look: The old man Talbot can boast of a real achievement — he has established his family name as an earl. Now all that gets lost if his son John dies, because there won't be anyone left to maintain his achieve-ment. Besides, they can't win the battle anyway. Their courage doesn't do them any good at all. It's just a loss all the way around. They should remember, "He who fights and runs away lives to fight another day."
>
> *Bert:* That slogan is too easy. Old Talbot didn't achieve his earldom just by winning battles. He was honored because the king knew his *courage* was reliable. If Talbot ran from this particular battle, he'd show himself to be unreliable. He wouldn't deserve the earldom. And if young Talbot runs, he wouldn't deserve to inherit the earldom. Flight by either would show he wasn't reliable.
>
> *Al:* Neither deserves the earldom now anyway. Just by their reck-lessness they've already undone the achievement.

Notice that both Al and Bert believe that courage is good because it is necessary for winning battles. That is like saying results (in achievement) make honor important. But Bert thinks cowardice is wrong even when some particular result doesn't require courage. Al thinks that unless a particular situation calls for courage, a person might just as well forget it — only results count.

Bert's point about habit and character is an important one. He seems to say that cowardice, whether resulting in harm or not, is just plain ignoble, just as dishonesty is just plain wrong. When we are judging people according to norms, it makes a difference what kind of character they have, what their intentions are, what we can guess about their motives and predict about their future conduct. In a practical sense it matters whether people are reliable or not. This practical point may be closely related to our concern about results. But it is not the same thing. Old Talbot and his son both die displaying courage. They lose much by it and achieve nothing, but their nobility of character still shines as something good in itself.

In fact, it is no clearer that honor reduces to achievement than it is that decency reduces to beneficence. I will say more about the complex relations between honor and achievement in the next chapter, but here is a simple example for the present: A talented sculptor must find some way to obtain the expensive marble he needs. Suppose he has a chance to get this marble by flattering a contemptible millionaire basely. We would hesitate to "absolve" him of the charge of baseness even if this shabby behavior were necessary for his art.

Ends Versus Means

Do saintly goals justify wrong means? Do splendid goals beautify base means? The question whether limits reduce to goals, in the case of both moral and aesthetic norms, is the familiar one of whether the end justifies the means. If honor reduces to achievement, or decency to beneficence, then desired results — and only those results — explain and justify the constraining rules of honor and decency, the limits on behavior.

Think back to situations where you have heard people pose this question of means and end, and notice that custom dictates we should answer saying, "No, of course the end doesn't justify the means." Quite recently, in the Iran-Contra hearings, one congressman reproved a bureaucrat, almost scolding him, with precisely those words. The bureaucrat didn't dare to disagree. It seems crass and insensitive, as well as immoral, to dispute the adage.

But what is a means anyway? It is a tool used or deed done in order to achieve some desired result. If a means were not a means *to* something, then it wouldn't be a means. So of course the end justifies the means. What else *could*? And given that it does, then why do people talk as if that were obviously untrue?

The answer to that should be apparent now. On a practical level — the one where we decide, act, and live out our lives — there are limit norms as well as goal norms. The former does not in practice reduce to the latter. Typically when a speaker says "the end doesn't justify the means" and expects everyone (even the feisty bureaucrat) to agree, this speaker is citing a *complex* of limit rules. Undoubtedly what the congressman meant is that we ought not to violate a limit rule (in this case, that public servants ought to obey the law) even if the end result is desirable. To be law-abiding stands out as a priority for public servants. Socrates wouldn't stoop to flattering a mob of thoughtless judges in order to save his own life because being honorable was more important than survival. John Talbot wouldn't desert his father in a losing battle because being noble was more precious than life or family name.

"The end doesn't justify the means" expresses a touchstone of limit norms. But from the viewpoint of a goal enthusiast it is obviously false. Living on a practical level, we must live with this paradox. Ends do justify means, but — there being many ends — often the price of the means is too high. Also, much uncertainty fills our practical affairs, calling for caution.

Sometimes, in emergencies, we must do wrong in order to avoid a worse wrong, but it still feels wrong. The end can justify the means even though it doesn't make the means feel right. Thinkers like Bert are quick to point out, however, that this slogan dangerously lends itself to easy abuse. Stalin supposedly justified his slaughters by saying coolly, "You can't make an omelet without breaking a few eggs." And in terms of honor, the slogan, "The man who fights and runs away lives to fight another day" gives a convenient rationalization for the coward who plans to run away on *all* days. Falstaff, for instance, justified his own blatant cowardice by piously announcing, "The better part of valor is discretion."

If I *know* that the end is worthwhile and if I *know* that my wrong means will achieve it and if I *know* that the end is worth the price of the means, then I am sure that the means is justified. But mere humans rarely have so much knowledge. Before killing millions of humans with modern weapons, modern governments have sometimes just aggressively announced that the slaughter is necessary. They don't discuss the vexed question openly and democratically. That is much too careless.

Chapter 9

Tensions Among Aesthetic Norms

In practice, as I noted earlier, the demands of honor cannot be reduced to mere corollaries of achievement. A noble goal doesn't always beautify base or ugly means. So when honorable, ambitious people must stoop if they hope to conquer, poignant clashes are common between the two types of norm.

Cyrano de Bergerac wrote great plays, but he could get them performed only by seeking the favor of ruthless potentates whom he despised. Shakespeare's Coriolanus gets the noble office of consul only by basely "showing his wounds" and begging for the votes of those greedy cowards, the commoners of Rome. Brutus could gloriously topple the tyrant Caesar only by basely kneeling before him as his friend and setting him up for the assassins' knives. Many young employees have managed to get promoted, so that achievement would become possible for them, by laughing too hard at the boss's jokes and letting the boss win at golf. As someone noted, "Ambitious climbing is often just diagonal crawling."

Reprinted by permission of NEA, Inc.

The Risks of Achievement

Failure and Defeat Versus Mere Nonachievement

If a person sees failure to achieve as merely losing glory, then it's not hard for him to resist temptations to ugly, base conduct. An honorable man or woman would easily prefer the mere loss of glory to the positive humiliation from loss of integrity. Cyrano scorned success as a playwright that would befoul the white plume of his honor. And Coriolanus at first would gladly forgo the chance to achieve as a consul if he could thereby avoid flattering the contemptible commoners. He said he would rather be ruled by them in *his* way than to rule *them* in *their* way.

There seem to be three choices open to an ambitious person: glory, shame, and — in between — the zero state of forgoing glory while avoiding dishonor. But often an ambitious person doesn't see the three choices as open to him. For one reason or another, he commits himself to some great project. Once that happens, he faces either the glory of success or the shame of failure.

The witches tempt Macbeth simply by predicting plausibly that he will be king. At once his sights are raised, his heart is committed to attaining the crown. From then on, not getting the crown will count not just as lacking glory but as humiliating failure. Similarly, Richard III deliberately goads himself to action by deciding to view not getting the crown as a failure: "Counting myself but bad till I be best."

Honor Versus Achievement

Hector, in Homer's *Iliad*, faces a terrible conflict between honor and achievement. He is called to the achievement of leading the Trojan people in defending their city against the Greeks. Of course, this achievement will be made impossible if he perishes in single combat against superhuman Achilles. But if he flees that awesome foe's challenge, he will be humiliated. His father reinforces the call of achievement. He should save himself in order to save the city: "Come, then, my son, within the city, to be guardian of Trojan men and Trojan women."

Hector's dilemma is complex. He can't run into the city because he fears the women's scorn over his previous tactical folly and their added scorn if he should back down from this duel. Nor can he try talking reasonably with maddened Achilles, for fear of being killed "naked, like a woman." He fantasizes that he might manage to kill Achilles, or at least be killed by him gloriously with an audience looking on at his valor. But his mother reminds him of the likely outcome: She predicts he will be killed in enemy territory, far from the Trojans' admiring eyes, and that dogs will eat his corpse.

In the event, Hector adds two elements of humiliation to his fate. First, in a panic, he runs from Achilles, circling the city three times. Besides this shaming flight, Hector begs his enemy not to desecrate his body. This begging is quite base, since earlier Hector has shown every intention to desecrate his victim Patroclus's corpse. Besides, the plea is useless, only adding to Achilles's vindictive triumph.

Later, on the other hand, when Hector realizes he is alone and doomed, he turns to an achievement norm again and determines to attack even if it means perishing: "My doom has come upon me; let me not then die ingloriously and without a struggle, but let me first do some great thing that shall be told among men hereafter."

Hector's call to achieve by saving Troy clashes tragically with the demand of his honor not to shirk the hopeless duel. Even so, the conflict might have been mitigated by Hector's foresight that Troy was doomed anyway, by the enmity of the gods. Ultimately, his main mission must meet with failure anyway.

In Shakespeare's story of this war, *Troilus and Cressida,* Priam's family is debating whether to end the bloody, pointless war. Why not just give Helen back to the Greeks? Helen's abductor, Paris, blocks this peace move by reminding them of the humiliation they will all face if they back down ignominiously from the glorious theft of Helen. On the Greek side (in Homer's version), Odysseus uses a similar war rhetoric of failure shame: It's shameful to set out on a project — recovering Helen — and then to withdraw without success.

We may smile at primitive man's vulnerability to such crude rhetoric. But there are a number of recent examples of the same sort of pressure. During the Vietnam War, peace moves were blocked by similar rhetoric: "Maybe we shouldn't have gotten into the war; but once in, we can't back out now!" Eventually, we had to resort to a humiliating retreat.

The Soviets, amazingly, learned nothing from our grim experience. Marching into Afghanistan, they were stalled there for years, afraid to back out and face humiliation. Finally they, too, failed anyway. And British boys have been dying in Ireland for 700 years. Most British now see that Ulster is a dead loss. Still, even British professors will tell you, "We can't just bug out; we've made a commitment." It's amazing how little change in the human ego is visible after 3,000 years! (Or is it just the male ego?)

Self-image and Achievement

We've seen that it's dangerous to commit oneself to projects one cannot complete. After commitment, nonachievement counts as humiliating failure. In *The Magic Flute*, Papageno has a realistic self-image as a nonhero; when he flunks the test for noble glory, he just shrugs and says he can live easily with comfort and family love, without glory — as most people do.

We saw how the witches tempt Macbeth by raising his self-image to royal levels. Similarly, in *Julius Caesar*, Brutus goads himself into action by recalling how his ancestors drove away the tyrant Tarquin. Brutus has no chance of defeating Caesar in open battle, as his ancestors did the old tyrants. Brutus has thus saddled himself with a fatally unrealistic self-image. A counselor warns Oedipus not to push the investigation about his background, but Oedipus has a superhuman self-image as problem-solver; he must push on in the inquiry until it destroys him.

A satirical book, *The Peter Principle*, suggests that in big organizations, everyone tends to get promoted to one level above his actual competence. This model presupposes that each worker *wants* promotion beyond his real competence. It's interesting to ask why so few American males — even the apparently successful ones — seem contented with their actual level of achievement. It's as if our society has decided that all active youths should be *trained* to aim unrealistically high. After all, it's literally true that you never know what you can do until you try. Maybe the sum of actual achievement in society is increased if everyone aims a little higher than he realistically should. If each youth constantly remembers the plucky ant who toppled the rubber tree plant, he'll live in high hopes. However, the price finally paid for these ambitious dreams is widespread humiliation. The full professor at a state university sees himself as a failed candidate for a post at Harvard.

One view of the "male menopause" phenomenon is this: In his forties, many a man is surprised at how disappointed he is in his level of accomplishment. He thought he had set his self-image down to a realistic level. At forty he is shocked to realize that he has been cultivating half-conscious, inflated dreams that have made his non-achievements look like humiliating failures. If inflated dreams are the price of high achievement for the society as a whole, the inevitable result is wholesale humiliation. Dreams are fine, but inflated dreams are costly. One can ask if the demoralization from such inflated dreams is not too high a price for increased achievement.

Shame as a Goad to Achievement

We've noted how a high self-image can motivate a person to try for high achievement. Paradoxically, a low self-image can have the same effect. A person who is humiliated in childhood might strive mightily for a success so glamorous that observers will forget his ignominious past. People with drive are often people who are driven. Everyone wonders if Napoleon wasn't overcompensating for his short stature in his attempt to rule Europe.

Two problems can arise here. The anxious achiever might fail, compounding previous humiliation. Perhaps his neurotic need for compensatory vindication has led him to commit himself to unrealistic projects, making fresh humiliation inevitable. Or the audience to his childish humiliation might be no longer available to revise their view of him and applaud. An ambitious man once admitted, "I'm the fifth of nine children; my mother often called me Freckles, which was the name of the dog. I seem doomed to spend my whole life trying to get my mother to notice me." And the aged composer Igor Stravinsky once told an interviewer, "Everyone I wanted to impress is dead."

Cutting the Knot: Accepting Dishonor

Once nonsuccess is seen as failure, then the agent will be sorely tempted indeed to use base means to succeed. After all, he'll be humiliated in any case: either by failure or by his ignoble acts. Aufidius, after being thrashed repeatedly by Coriolanus, turns ugly:

> Mine emulation
> Hath not that honour in't it had; for where
> I thought to crush him in an equal force,
> True sword to sword, I'll potch at him some way,

An important point comes up here about the psychology of temptation. A naturally optimistic agent will be more strongly tempted to go for the base means, hoping that ultimate success will be so splendid as to blot out the ugliness of his earlier behavior. Shakespeare's optimistic Henry IV sees blustery weather on the day of battle as an ill omen for his opponents, not for his own side. He says of the bad weather, "Then with the losers let it sympathize,/ For nothing can seem foul for those that win." But if an agent is pessimistic, he'll look ahead to the likely double humiliation of acting basely and then failing anyway; this bleak foresight will lessen his temptation. The odd prediction here is that ambitious optimists are more likely to act basely or ruthlessly than are ambitious pessimists.

Consider the person who has already behaved basely or ruthlessly in pursuit of a goal. Having already lost innocence and integrity, he may feel that he has nothing to lose (in terms of feeling guilty or humiliated) from more bad conduct. Indeed, if the person has already adjusted his self-image downward, he will hold himself to a lower standard of honor, will be less open to shame feelings as a deterrent from shabby conduct. For instance, in Graham Greene's novel *The Power and the Glory*, a peasant betrays a priest for profit. Later he is not even embarrassed to demand that the priest help guarantee that he won't be cheated of his reward. Such shameless persons are especially to be feared and avoided. Having nothing to lose in terms of dishonor, they have no honor limits to restrain them.

Cutting the Knot: Giving Up Achievement

Honorable youths who foresee vividly the pressure that ambition will put on their integrity might decide to drop out altogether from the life of attempted achievement. Why not maintain honor and, like Voltaire's disenchanted Candide, spend their lives cultivating their own garden? In the late 1960s, hundreds of elite American youths dropped out of the middle-class career world with just that intention. Concern for their integrity was often reinforced by their suspicion that success — say, in advertising agencies — would actually count as doing trivial or harmful things obscenely well. One lad said he'd prefer unemployment to malemployment.

Such a decision has some noble precedents. Cyrano "dropped out" of the playwright's profession, abhorring the courting of loathsome potentates involved in that profession. The dialogue *Gorgias* could be read as Plato's defense of Socrates's decision to drop out of the public political "game," which most Athenians saw as appropriate for any talented citizen. Socrates considered political success in Athens as shaming, not glorious; he bragged that he didn't even know how to call the vote.

The dropouts of the late 1960s, though, on reaching their thirties, discovered that this option was emotionally more costly than it had looked. Living on food stamps or from vegetables discarded by supermarkets quickly became unbearable for most of them. Bosses may treat janitors and carpenters with contempt because it is so easy to replace them. These elite young people found they didn't enjoy being looked down upon. A middle-class upbringing had also planted in their souls the sting of greed, so they found their frugal lifestyles too grinding in the long run. Needing so many *other* luxuries, they could hardly afford the luxury of integrity. Besides, they suffered boredom from not using their minds in their dull, routine jobs.

Most of these young idealists went crawling back to the middle classes, ending up as stockbrokers and the like, and now recall the 1960s with nostalgia. Middle America has enjoyed snickering at these backsliders ever since, but this wave of backsliding has not logically discredited the decision to preserve integrity by dropping out from the career world. This option deserves realistic discussion, not propagandistic ridicule. We should strive mainly to reform the professions, so that worthy young men and women can aspire to success without fearing an inevitable loss of integrity.

Not all dropouts are worthy of respect. Youths who are simply too lazy to study find themselves later unqualified for middle-class careers. And then there are neurotically competitive people who somehow fear the shame of failure more than they aspire to the exhilaration of success. These people avoid ambition for less than splendid motives. They often pose as stalwarts of honor too pure for the rough-and-tumble world of careers.

Honest honor dropouts must face the prospect of being taken for one of these latter, pathetic types. Before taking the dropout option, they should ask themselves if their self-esteem is sturdy enough to survive the easy, snickering contempt that others will show them.

Aesthetic Norms and Women's Liberation

A special case of tension between honor and achievement arises in the modern feminist movement. As noted earlier, a person feels bound by stricter honor norms as he sees himself possessing a higher rank. Practically all the classical literature on honor simply assumes that honor is inappropriate for women, slaves, and perhaps merchants. Only upper-class men are worthy of undertaking to live by honor norms. Women, it was admitted, are capable of heroism when motivated by love, religion, or decency — but not by honor. Shakespeare's Helena blatantly rejects limit norms in favor of goals in her ambition to move into the noble classes: "All's well that ends well: still the fine's the crown;/ Whate'er the course, the end is the renown." This may feel strangely upsetting. In point of fact, lower-class men were impelled to the same choice of goals over limits if they wished to rise in society.

When Lady Macbeth tempts her husband to behave basely as well as wickedly, she scorns him as cowardly and unmanly for his hesitations. He snaps back, "I dare do all that may become a man;/ Who dares do more, is none." In the traditional view he might have said instead, "Who dares do more is woman."

The liberation movement has two concerns that exactly correspond to the two aesthetic norm types. With regard to honor, feminists are seeking an end to the continual barrage of insult inflicted on women as a matter of course, often by their closest loved ones. Subtle slights permeate our language, our lore, our customs. For instance, a wizard is just a male witch. But wizards are wonderful and splendid, whereas the stereotype of a witch is an ugly old woman on a broom with her nose touching her chin. The insult is not lost on a three-year-old listening to a fairy story. When she is thirty she finds it still rankles along with countless other insults. Or perhaps she has become insensitive.

With regard to achievement, modern women seek to shake off traditional fetters imposed by their male-dominated society. Women have always achieved, but traditional woman's work has in our history and culture been systematically belittled, judged as trivial. And the trivial achievement was supposed to be private — in the home. Many women now opt for public achievement of some kind. Will they redefine traditional codes of achievement? Or will they show themselves more coldly efficient in seizing power than men are, in the fashion of Margaret Thatcher? Or can we hope for some sane moderation?

Suppose liberated women buy into the code of achievement but reject the code of honor that has traditionally tried to limit the single-minded pursuit of success? Suppose they follow Vince Lombardi in deciding that winning is the *only* thing? A powerful new force would then be unleashed in the world, for good and for ill.

No one would want women to imitate, in the current male honor code, those flagrantly stupid norms: never weeping, never asking for directions, never backing off from even a pointless fight. But if women achievers are not ashamed to get ahead by flattering the powerful, then honorable competitors (both male and female) will be left in the dust. Our changing society must give careful thought to this question: How might we modify present codes of honor to fit women's situations, without abandoning those codes?

The Dangerous Demands of Revenge

The cases of tension between honor and achievement we've examined above are relatively optional. In these cases people can choose not to face the stark alternatives of winning glory or facing shame. With the demand for revenge, however, the agent *must* face those alternatives. For revenge is by definition an honor norm: One seeks it in response to insult, a blow to self-esteem or to the community from which one takes a sense of identity. Yet once one accepts revenge as a project, it also becomes a matter of achievement: One must somehow accomplish the punishment of the person or group who did the harm. Failure at revenge warrants shame, not just loss of glory. And brave, clever success at revenge warrants glory, not just escape from shame.

Henry James's novel *The American* sketches a poignant tangle of norms. A tough U.S. businessman clashes with some cold and ruthless French aristocrats who have blocked his marriage to the woman he loves. The businessman obtains a paper showing that the haughty matriarch murdered her husband. He might seem to have a duty in decency to expose this crime; instead, he tries to pressure the aristocrats to get his beloved restored to him. When they won't yield, he then wants to use the paper to destroy them, for revenge. But he can't bring himself to perform an act that resembles blackmail, violating his naive code of honor. In the novel's first edition, James suggests that this failure to revenge himself might count as weak queasiness.

In our society there is general disapproval of the revenge norm, but everybody knows the feeling of wanting it. On the legal level, we pay too little attention to that common feeling. Our society represses honor and therefore belittles the harm of insult. If we are injured in body or property we can bring suit against our offender, but our courts provide no realistic way of redressing an insult. (A nine-year-old was recently charged with aggravated assault for punching a boy who tormented him about being fat.) It's often too humiliating to sue for defamation. But since an act of revenge violates decency, conscientious people victimized by insult must repress their warranted rage and let it smolder. This is not a healthy situation. It causes much suffering.

Codes of honor and codes of achievement both urge revenge, each with its special stringency. In societies where this norm is influential, a person who has been insulted or wronged cannot just choose to lose the glory of successful revenge. Nor can he choose to let the insult drop unattended. Thus, if he tries for revenge and *fails,* he is mortally humiliated under the achievement code; if he fails to *try* for revenge, others will hold him in complete contempt.

Sad experience over millennia has taught us, though, that private revenge is in the net socially harmful, especially to families caught up in escalating revenge spirals. The vengeful terms of the Versailles Treaty after World War I did not benefit France in the long run. And self-appointed law-and-order groups, like vigilantes and the Ku Klux Klan, have in the end done much more harm than good. To keep things under control we need the due process and restraints of law, even though the law ought to be more enlightened about the seriousness of insult.

Revenge in Traditional Societies

Milovan Djilas's book about bloodthirsty feuds in Montenegro is aptly called *Land Without Justice.* Djilas says that in Montenegro around 1900 a family that wasn't formidable for revenge was a family "whose blood could be shed like water." One Montenegran youth in America said that his family must never return to their homeland. Decades ago his grandfather was drinking with an old friend. In a rage the friend called the grandfather an old woman, and was promptly shot dead. Sixty years later, if the killer's relatives were to show up in Montenegro, the victim's family would still feel obliged to kill them.

In Homer's *Odyssey*, young Telemachos is rousing himself to avenge the wrongs done to his family; he recalls Orestes, who killed those who killed his father: "The Achaeans applaud Orestes and his name will live through all time for he has avenged his father nobly. Would that heaven might grant me to do like vengeance on the insolence of the wicked suitors." This sounds as if he sees being wronged as a happy occasion for winning glory. But Hamlet feels the project of revenge is forced on him, and he resents the burden: "The time is out of joint. O cursed spite,/ That ever I was born to set it right!" And Calderón's heroes often howl with frustration at the "tyranny" of the code of honor laid on them, which mainly demands revenge. Calderón's Spain placed a heavy duty of revenge on upper-class families, though there was concern to keep this code from being interpreted in an excessively bloody way.

Shakespeare's characters sometimes talk as if the very norm of revenge is pathological. In *Troilus and Cressida*, Hector lumps revenge in with brutish passions during the war debate. Troilus, wanting revenge, responds by cleverly deemphasizing vengeance as the main reason to continue the war: "Were it not glory that we more affected than the performance of our heaving spleens, I would not with a drop of Troyan blood spend more in [Helen's] defense." But then he pretends to agree with Hector that revenge as such is a bestial motive.

Surprisingly, though, Hamlet in one mood thinks he's called to revenge by his *higher* nature, while his sluggish animality holds him back:

> How all occasions do inform against me
> And spur my dull revenge! What is a man,
> If his chief good and market of his time
> Be but to sleep and feed? A beast, no more,
> . . . I do not know
> Why yet I live to say, 'This thing's to do'
> Sith I have cause and will and strength and
>   means to do't.

The Rationale for Vengeance

Why has the revenge norm held so stringently in these traditional societies? As noted before, where the law can't be counted on to punish wrongs, a family would not be safe unless would-be transgressors were deterred by fear of revenging relatives.

After Hamlet murders Laertes's father, King Claudius asks Laertes, "What would you undertake/ to show yourself your father's son in deed/ more than in words?" Laertes volunteers, "to cut his throat in the church!" And earlier, Laertes fairly froths with murderous rage:

> To hell, allegiance! vows to the blackest devil!
> Conscience and grace, to the profoundest pit!
> I dare damnation: to this point I stand,
> That both the worlds I give to negligence.
> Let come what comes! Only I'll be revenged
> Most thoroughly for my father.

The revenge norm binds Laertes more stringently than moral or religious duties, more than any other kind of rival honor demand.

A puzzle here: What social purpose is served by conditioning youths to display such crazy rage when revenge is called for? There is a tendency among aggressive men to assume fallaciously that their foe is rational enough to yield to superior force. Let's consider the question from the perspective of game theory, where one's strategy includes manipulating the opponent's beliefs. In one moment of game-theory analysis, I as player (that is, a given family in a traditional honor culture) find that this countermove is indicated: It pays my group to convince would-be aggressors that our response to their aggression will be mad, crazy, unlimited. A family will be safer if others see its males as ferocious madmen who, once aroused, will strike back at any cost to themselves. And my family can assure this image of "mad when roused" only if our young men are in fact trained to *go* mad when roused.

A son has even stronger reason to display wild eagerness to revenge his father. Machiavelli cynically advised a murdering king not to confiscate a slain enemy's estate: The victim's son and heir, as the beneficiary of the killing, would tend to object to it only mildly, as he would like to get the inheritance. But he wouldn't want anyone to believe that. To block suspicion (even in his own mind) that his devotion to revenge might be adulterated by his prudent joy at inheriting, the son must whip himself up to a murderous frenzy.

Revenge in Modern Society

Do these strange social customs have any relevance for our advanced society? Most people think we have outgrown such primitive codes of revenge. But when people today feel that the law will not punish those who seem to have wronged them, the honor demand for revenge is still powerful and dangerous. Cool macho men in our popular action movies mutter, "Don't get mad; get even!"

In a supposedly idyllic American college town during one recent year, eleven people were killed by middle-class men seeking revenge against women who had left them. One wife left town after the split; her husband tracked her for three years. He murdered her, served a short time in prison, then married again. One has to warn one's daughters: "Most romances nowadays crash, sooner or later. The first thing to find out before getting close to a man is whether he will shoot you if you leave him."

Many wives feel wronged when their husbands leave them for younger women, and are legally obliged to pay little alimony or child-support. Such a woman might seek revenge by blocking the visits of her former husband (and also, sadly, visits from his parents). She is willing to harm her own children in order to strike back at the man. To justify her objections to his visits, she might even be tempted to accuse him falsely of earlier sexual abuse of the children.

A policeman near Denver was enraged by his wife's tough, female divorce lawyer and told several people he intended to "get" the lawyer. He shot her right in the courtroom with a bullet designed to cripple her permanently and was later convicted on a fairly light charge. His desk sergeant admitted that he had heard about the murderous plans but said he ignored the ranting because "my men often talk about shooting some woman if she gets in their face."

Recalling those Muslims who have taken U.S. hostages, many Americans would be delighted to hear that the United States had bombed *any* Muslim country. These Americans, blinded by thirst for revenge, forget decency: Millions of Muslims have *not* taken hostages.

Until the recent thaw, the whole system of Mutual Assured Destruction (MAD) assumed this: If the young officers in missile silos or in submarines hear that their own nation has *already* been destroyed, they will not hesitate to level the cities of the enemy (the old women and the children and the pets) in simple revenge. The actual revenge might seem pointless, but *readiness* to seek revenge has a clear point: Only such a "mad" readiness can actually deter the enemy from a first strike.

The United States has been in a position even more bizarre: The government professed willingness to launch a first nuclear strike against the Soviet Union, if it were to invade Europe. Washington said that in revenge for such an invasion of Europe, it would provoke a Soviet counterstrike that would wipe the United States off the map. For the Soviets to be deterred from invasion, as mentioned before, they must believe our young officers are really that crazy. For them really to believe this, we must train our officers to be just that crazy — but not crazy enough to "push the button" inappropriately. Officers successfully conditioned that way would make Shakespeare's Laertes seem like a cautious, middle-aged wimp!

Many people approved of MAD as a rational, though deplorable, system of deterrence. Yet these same people tend to think that the code of revenge is important only in studying sixteenth-century Spain. In fact we must undo the current repression of discussions about norms of honor and revenge; we must understand these strange standards for evaluating conduct, standards that impel modern people, just as they impelled the ancients, to behave in awful ways. People go to such lengths for revenge (as they always have) because they believe that if they can't wipe the smile off a smug enemy's face, they will count as pathetic and contemptible.

Chapter 10

Relations Between Aesthetic and Moral Norms

We have seen now that conflicts can arise between the norm types honor and achievement, and that the relations between these types can become extremely complex. I don't mean to imply by this that there are no conflicts within the codes that represent the types. In Chapters 5 and 6 we saw norms within the code of decency and within the code of honor sometimes conflicting.

Suppose I have promised to keep a secret, but I can do so only by telling a lie because in this case keeping silent would give away the secret. Then I face a conflict between two decency duties. "Don't break promises" and "Don't lie" conflict with each other here. I mentioned similar conflicts between honor duties.

There are also some lurking conflicts within codes that fall under the goal norm types. A beneficent person could well see the duty to remain in a political office because his projects benefit society and yet see also that his teenage children need guidance and care he has neglected.

Conflicts Within the Achievement Norm

Someone wanting to write a scientific treatise on soil microorganisms and also wanting to have the most immaculate garden in town clearly faces hard decisions about priorities. This would be an obvious conflict within the achievement type of norm.

Love of Noble Projects

Ivan Morris's book *The Nobility of Failure* studies a puzzling tradition in Japan, a history of Japanese heroes whose failure seems to increase their honor. At first the tradition appears to be concerned with the relation of achievement and honor. But on closer inspection most of the tragedies of these failed heroes arise because the heroes took on impossible projects.

These tragedies actually come from a conflict of two achievement norms: "Choose noble projects" and "Don't fail at your projects." Both of these lie in the timeless aspects of achievement. The *heroism* lies in this ironic point: If you work hard at a project, competently do all you can to accomplish it, and then fail, then the failure shows how noble your project was. To strive toward an ideal totally beyond even competent powers shows a reverence for ideals that transcend the human condition. The kamikaze campaigns of World War II are a recent example of this.

The story of Mishima, Japan's beloved postwar novelist, provides an even more recent example. Mishima tried, through an audacious civil act and the spectacle of hara-kiri, to turn his country back to the military samurai ideals of centuries past. For the consummation of his plans he dressed in the finest military attire he could get (especially designed for him in Paris) and girded himself with an authentic sixteenth-century samurai sword. He had no chance of succeeding, of course: His country didn't want to turn back. (A Japanese friend of mine reports that the people now feel uneasy about this modern hero. They are uncomfortable talking about such an eccentric.)

Such stories suggest that there is a strand in Japanese culture that weights "Choose noble (that is, impossible) projects" more heavily than "Don't fail." That strand contrasts with the celebrated fear of dishonor and failure shame that the Japanese are usually presumed to have.

Avoiding Failure

Some people would definitely reverse these priorities, insisting that it is foolish and wasteful to aim at an achievement beyond hope of success. Jesus warned his followers not to be like the man who started a great building and then became humiliated in failure when he ran short of materials.

In the *Iliad* Hector stands outside the walls of Troy and faces the murderous and angry Achilles. He could run inside the walls to temporary safety, but shame inhibits him. The shame involved arises from Hector's having taken on a project greater than he could handle. Hector's foolishness lies in his not sounding a retreat when Achilles comes forth again to fight. He manages badly the code of achievement.

Conflicts Between Aesthetic and Moral Norms

There are, then, conflicts within each type of code, and these can come from timeless aspects of the norm types as well as from conventional rules and ideas that make up any particular code. Likewise, there are conflicts among the nonmoral or aesthetic norms, and conflicts among the moral norms. I have given many examples of these. Now I want to talk about conflicts between the aesthetic and moral norm types. That kind of tension is especially important to consider, for these reasons that you know well by now:

1. Guilt is the enforcer of moral norms, both limit and goal. Shame is the enforcer of aesthetic norms, both limit and goal.
2. Guilt and shame are different and distinct emotions, though it is possible to feel them both at once for some act both shaming and wrong.
3. Guilt and shame overlap in many cases because norms under the different norm types overlap often.
4. People often forget to distinguish guilt and shame both because of the overlap, and because society often uses shame, the more powerful of the two emotions, as a way of punishing immorality.

That shame and guilt overlap in many cases makes it confusing to talk about the relation between aesthetic and moral norms. To keep things simple at first, I'll stick with cases where guilt and shame are clearly distinct.

Honor Versus Beneficence

If one loses honor for the sake of beneficence, will that expunge the dishonor? Imagine a competent, saintly person, one who loves and cares for his country. Suppose that the country now lives darkened under the tyranny of a cruel king and that our beneficent hero has a chance to stay at the court of this king and overthrow him. In order to overthrow him he must endure some horrible humiliations. He must flatter loathsome courtiers in order to get information he needs. He must prevail on his wife to dance sweetly with the king at a formal ball. He must pay homage to the king even in private, speaking to him in the most respectful tones. All this to overthrow the tyrant and free the country. Triumph at that would give him moral credit for beneficence. I should hope his honor would be vindicated by such credit, washed of the pain of all those humiliations, though that isn't guaranteed.

It would be easy to imagine a proud woman sacrificing her sexual honor to a seducing king in order to get him to change some harmful policies. In a society in which chastity-honor looms large, this would be a clear conflict between beneficence and honor.

In Shakespeare's *Julius Caesar*, Brutus thinks that Caesar, now ruling, is becoming an arrogant and tyrannical autocrat, violating the Roman tradition of shared power. So Brutus believes he has a beneficence duty to eliminate Caesar, and he plans to assassinate him. He pictures the killing as a beautiful sacrifice, the death of a splendid man for the sake of Rome. He claims to love Caesar more than anything except the welfare of the city.

In the *Iliad*, before his fight with Achilles, Hector speaks with his wife, Andromache. Clearly, he has a beneficence duty to protect his family. This requires surviving. Andromache, trying to stem his sense of honor in this case, reminds him that all her other relatives are dead, that he is now father and mother and brother and husband to her, inheriting all the duties these relatives would have to protect her.

His father, Priam, also pleads with him to come inside the gates, so that he will survive to lead the Trojans. A warrior, Priam says, could be honorable as he lay slain in battle, but an old man slain by conquerors would end up degradingly torn apart by his own dogs.

Against such appeals Hector chooses honor over beneficence in this situation. In fact, he knows that Troy is doomed anyway and that Andromache is destined to end up in slavery. Perhaps this knowledge weakens his sense of duty to save Troy: That beneficence goal calls less loudly in its hopelessness. Maybe his honor urges him to die in that vain battle with Achilles rather than live on in the hopeless task of war.

Otherwise, he risks living to hear, while lying half-dead in the field, Andromache's screams as the Greeks drag her away captive. This would be a strong motive to choose honor over beneficence duties.

Achilles has two reasons for contending against Hector. First, Hector is an enemy Trojan prince, mightiest of the Trojan warriors. Second, Achilles craves personal revenge, for Hector had killed Achilles' dearest friend. As you may have guessed, Achilles does kill Hector. But he doesn't stop there. He drags Hector's body round and round on the ground in order to mutilate and desecrate it.

This treatment of his son's body is devastating to King Priam. He hates Achilles more than any of the Greeks because he has lost so many sons to that super fierceness. Yet he has a beneficence duty to rescue Hector's body from that final shame Achilles doles out. Priam therefore kneels before Achilles and kisses his hands to beg for the return of Hector's body. Surely this is terrible humiliation for the sake of beneficence.

Tensions Between Achievement and Moral Norms

People have said much about ambition as a temptation to wickedness. One vain author described his priorities clearly:

And when I die,
Of me may it be said:
"His sins were scarlet,
But his books were read!"

Goethe's hero Faust feels pangs of remorse when he realizes that he has poisoned many people by giving them mercury as medicine. But Goethe doesn't picture Faust as merely a kind and wise old man. Rather, he is the very prototype of an achiever, "demanding from heaven the most beautiful stars." He even goes to the extreme of selling his soul to the devil in order to achieve. (The result he strives for is some moment free of boredom.)

Near the beginning of Goethe's epic play we find old Faust hard at work in his laboratory. He experiments, wonders, tinkers. Perhaps he distributes the poisonous medicine because he wants results from all that tinkering. Later he has the self-insight to know that the experiment was a deplorable failure of beneficence.

Likewise, an atomic scientist who was in on building the first

157

atomic bomb describes his decision to go ahead with this work: "That night I decided against the purity of my soul and in favor of a livable world." This formula sees the code of decency ("purity of soul") pitted against the demands of beneficence ("livable world"). But elsewhere in his article the man admits that there was little concern for conscience among the scientific workers and that one of their great concerns was the Faustian desire to find out if the thing would work.

When we ask if the end justifies the means, we are considering whether a beneficent end justifies a wrong means; we would never claim that the nonmoral pursuit of glory *morally* justified the use of wrong means. When Assistant Secretary Elliott Abrams finished his testimony to Congress at the Iran-Contra hearings, he asked permission to read a closing statement. It was an eloquent justification of his actions in the name of beneficence. Think how odd it would have sounded if he had spoken instead in terms of achievement.

In a pep talk to his officers before battle, Henry V speaks for the code of achievement, eloquently describing the logical scarcity of glory: "We few, we happy few." Victory brings more glory for each if fewer share in it. He predicts that the names of the victors in this coming battle will live forever in men's tongues:

> And gentlemen in England now a-bed
> Shall think themselves accurs'd they were not
>   here,
> And hold their manhoods cheap whiles any speaks
> That fought with us upon Saint Crispin's day.

But earlier the plain soldier Williams had noted two distinct types of conflict between the glory of war and decency norms. One is that the war itself is either just or not. If not, then the war violates the decency rule of justice. This, says Williams, the common soldier simply cannot know; it is for kings to judge. The soldier can only obey, and so any guilt of fighting in an unjust cause (Williams's friend adds) falls not on soldiers but on kings who start the wars. Henry's invasion of France probably was not just. And in our own century we seriously debate the truth of Williams's point. Many claim that obedience does not absolve the individual soldier from guilt in an unjust war.

But then Williams has a second point. In his code of decency a dying person must repent for all sins. What about all the petty, common sins that a rough soldier is likely to have on his conscience? "I am afeard," he says, "there are few die well that die in a battle; for how can they charitably dispose of anything when blood is their argument?" That is the residual problem for the soldier.

Now this second point gives rise to a special conflict for the king himself, for he orders these men into a situation where they might die without repenting. He is responsible for his men. King Henry, who is disguised as a plain soldier in this scene, replies, "There is no king, be his cause never so spotless, if it comes to the arbitrament of swords, can try it out with all unspotted soldiers." Soldiers in that place and time just didn't come unspotted. In Henry's army, soldiers were commonly inclined to murder, seduction of virgins, and pillage. It's interesting that, whereas the previous suggestion goes unchallenged (that the king must shoulder the whole guilt for killing done in an unjust war), Henry responds to the second suggestion with a nervous lengthy rejoinder. Perhaps the first problem can simply be dissolved by insisting that one's cause is just, but the second problem cannot be so easily evaded in a culture that prays every day for help "now and at the hour of our death," a culture in which final repentance is the main hope of ordinary sinners.

Moralizing Shame

Such tensions show the distinctness of moral and aesthetic or nonmoral norms. Happily, there is also some overlap between them. Many times it is an achievement to perform a beneficent act. Many times immoral acts stem from weakness, which violates honor. Still, honor and glory are distinct from morality. When overlap occurs, we simply act on more than one norm at once, and there is nothing inherently odd about that, when different norms happen to prescribe the same conduct.

But there is in our normative talk and thinking a prevailing tendency to overlap them *all* the time. I have often talked to people who look utterly puzzled when I point out a difference between guilt and shame. I believe they are thinking, "Oh, I know all about guilt and know what she is talking about. As for that word 'shame,' it's the same thing of course. I wish she wouldn't bring up the word, though. We don't need it when we have a good word like guilt instead, and anyway, it's so *embarrassing.*" In other conversations I hear these people say such things as "I feel guilty about not winning that race," or "I feel guilty when I wear a shower cap in the bathtub." Well, who cares? It is important to have a good self-image and think your appearance is acceptable. But how could such a concern as this possibly have anything to do with morality? Do the walls have eyes that the shower cap offends? No. What happens there is just a typical aspect of shame. A person feeling that painful emotion is broken and self-divided, looking upon herself as the imagined Other. But to describe herself as shamed is itself painful. It is much more comfortable to say "guilty," and in self-deception to believe it.

Now this prevalent confusion has me deeply concerned. For the confusion is not simply a matter of words. If it were, then the word "shame" wouldn't carry such a sting. Rather, a mechanism takes over that collapses some aesthetic norm into a moral one, where there is hope of relief and forgiveness. What worries me is that whenever that happens it *dilutes* the moral norms. The more a person piles aesthetic norms in with morality, the less chance morality has to get a hearing. So painful and punishing is that feeling of shame that it can overpower conscience if allowed too much space.

An older man told his former classmate that he was despised in eighth grade for wearing glasses. "I couldn't see," protested the former classmate. The first man responded, "What kind of excuse is that?" I can imagine the taunted classmate as years go on saying, "I feel guilty because I wear glasses." This "guilt" he thinks of as part of morality — then so much the less energy he has for authentically moral concerns.

From many corners in the United States today voices decry the slippage in our morality. On Wall Street, in government, in the media, the universities, and factories, achievers gasp in amazement when caught having violated some simple rule of morality. After all, they were doing what they were supposed to do, namely trying to achieve. How can people call them immoral? They do have a point. We have neglected to discuss and think about honor and achievement as normative. But they are normative. Moreover, their enforcer, shame, dominates and crowds out the delicate voice native to conscience.

I overstate all this to emphasize my point. If the picture were exactly as I have described, the United States could never have got under way and lasted for two centuries. Nor could our Western heritage have maintained itself for thirty centuries. Something, then, must inhibit, at least a little, the mechanism I describe. What could be powerful enough to keep shame, the enforcer of honor and achievement, from overpowering conscience? Only shame itself! Fight fire with fire.

Seeing the dangers of the process I've described, societies typically moralize shame. They harness its power to morality so that it assists conscience in enforcing decency duties. It is like fighting fire with fire. The parent, the teacher, the state threaten potential evildoers with shame. "Shame on you" will almost certainly teach four-year-old Sally not to lie. She is too young to understand conscience and honesty, but she knows about shame. She has felt it before many times and doesn't like it at all. If she comes to feel it whenever she lies, then she'll avoid lying. And a recently convicted sex offender was ordered by the judge to put a sign in his front yard that clearly told all passersby of his offense. I suppose that gives a double social benefit: It keeps him from repeating his offense, and it provides a good threat to others who might have indecent tendencies.

This process of teaching morality by means of shame is age-old. It provides another — and very strong — cause of the frequent confusion of guilt and shame, for the teaching associates them. But please remember they are not the same thing, not the same emotion. The one is fear of punishment; the other, fear of abandonment. The eyes of the Other, often the imagined Other, reject as they look on. Abandonment is punishing, so the threat of it may well keep people in line. But one can certainly have that fear without violating morality. Having a facial blemish, being a sucker, coming in last in a race can all bring on that fear, although maybe they ought not to bring it on. That is, maybe such shame is unwarranted. We can only decide by discussing it more openly.

We typically moralize shame by linguistic fiat, by choosing words that associate shame with immoral acts. By saying "Shame on you!" Sally's mother will probably stop her lying, her cruelty to the cat, her sassiness to her grandfather, and so on. Language provides an effective control because the word "shame" easily — but not always — calls up the punishing emotion. If not, then perhaps Sally's mother will resort to humiliating punishments aimed at tightening Sally's association of the word "shame" with the painful feeling she wants to avoid. Parents should use this powerful control cautiously. Too much shaming can produce a cowed and clumsy adult with stunted moral sensitivity.

Overuse of this power of speech also whittles away at its own effectiveness. The process of moralizing shame linguistically has gone so far in the United States that hardly anyone ever uses nonmoral words like "shaming" or "shame-making" at all: If an American had to take abuse from a tavern bully, he'd say that was "humiliating." And of course "shameful" to many people just means "very wrong."

In those rare cases where the word "shame" is used aesthetically, it still carries a good wallop. That is why people hesitate to use it and dislike hearing it. But we have so completely moralized some glory-shame words that their shame-glory meaning — and therefore the desired effect — has disappeared. In this regard I have already discussed the word "virtue" (Chapter 5). It used to mean manly excellence and fearful prowess in battle. Imagine the powerful effect this word must once have had when someone told a growing boy that he must strive for virtue. Then, over the centuries, this word became totally moralized. By the beginning of this century only sweet maidens had virtue, and people noted that only when the maidens lost it. In this century, with better contraceptives and Freudian psychology, even that last vestige disappeared. (Contemporary philosophers, though, have been exhuming the word.)

Similarly, we can assume that "fair" and "foul" were once primarily aesthetic words, describing nonmoral success and failure. Now they have become moralized except for the archaic usage in *My Fair Lady*, and our occasional reference to "foul smells." Today, when a child says indignantly "That's not fair!" he means only that it violates rules of justice. The desirability of playing fair is no longer reinforced by the idea that it is just ugly not to do so. And in the United States it is perfectly respectable for a basketball player to commit small fouls deliberately for some tactical advantage, cheerfully accepting the penalty. There is no resonance of disgust left in the word "foul." Except for smells, foul things are not ugly any more. "A foul ball" just tells us where the ball went. And when one hears the word "gentleness" today, no one thinks of "*strength* displayed in kindness," which is what it used to mean.

These attempts to moralize pride and shame linguistically date back at least to ancient Athens, when the phrase "good man" was apparently moralized. Socrates noted this oddity: In aesthetic uses of "good," as in "good dancer," the dancer who makes a wrong move deliberately is a better dancer than the one who makes a wrong move involuntarily. A good cook innovates by changing a recipe, doing it "wrong." The good

NANCY   **Jerry Scott**

Reprinted by permission of NEA, Inc.

dog trainer can get a dog to *not* do tricks. Steve Martin, in *The Jerk*, danced to rock music ever so slightly off rhythm, not an easy feat. It is like this for all the straightforward uses of "good" to describe expertise.

Socrates noted, however, that it is different when we call someone a good man. Here one who does wrong involuntarily is a better man than one who does wrong voluntarily. We know why this oddity is so: Someone is labeled "a good person" simply according to his moral good will, not because he's "good at" any activity that requires skill. If a person does wrong deliberately, that means he doesn't have that good will. So if a good person does wrong, it has to be involuntary, not deliberate.

We can refer nonmorally to a good artist or to a "fine specimen of a man" who seems to near physical perfection. Or we might speak of "a good man to have on your side in a fight." But in our society as well as in Plato's Athens, the sole criterion for judging someone a "good *person*" is his conscientious will to do rightly. We have no simple, classic way to praise the person who is physically and mentally splendid but wicked.

The paradoxical result is that "good person" and "goodhearted" may no longer *praise* effectively. They may even convey a faintly patronizing scorn. Try these examples. In an old movie, a woman tries wittily to tell off a man. He replies scornfully, "Look, dear, you be good; let those who will, be clever." Then there is the story of the little girl who stares admiringly at the gorgeous blonde wrapped in sables. "My," says the child, "I'll bet you had to be a very good girl to get that coat!" "Honey," replies the woman, "to get a coat like this, you gotta be *excellent!*" Here the aesthetic word "excellent" (proficient at some skill) has all the glamour. Finally, the efficient criminal in another movie comments dryly about the totally incompetent saint, "You have to admire him — even when you don't."

We seem to have an "official" linguistic line that moralizes shame-glory words completely. But satirical reminders of another, subversive, nonmoral value system undermine the moral praise. The moralizing linguistic tricks, then, don't work well to encourage morality in the long run. They weaken the language rather than strengthen moral habits. People care about being handsome and fine and competent, about achieving and about avoiding shame. So we just forget the original meanings of these now-moralized words. Our language changes, not our allegiance.

Later on I will use the phrase "splendid villain" to describe the sort of person willing to be guilty in order to be nonmorally excellent. This phrase carries no air of paradox in current language. For late medieval people, however, it would have meant something like "shining serf" — a true paradox. A villain used to be someone economically and legally bonded to a villa, an estate. The villains were low on the social scale, with no power or education. They depended for their survival on the lord of the estate in return for their hard work there. They were uncouth (that is, didn't know much), so if someone called you a villain, that was an insult. Eventually, the word became moralized.

Since moralizing shame just by use of words isn't effective in the long run, some people have tried more substantive ways to harness that powerful emotion to morality. For instance, we might announce that cruelty is *always* a sign of weakness or ugliness or incompetence. My brother, in grade school, had been told that bullies are always cowards. Seeing a fellow intimidating a smaller boy, he said, "Let's see you pick on someone your own size." "Fine," said the bully with relish, and proceeded to pound my brother.

Or else we may say that wickedly ambitious people are merely compensating for an inferiority complex. Unfortunately, this tactic could discredit *any* strenuous achievement, noble as well as wicked. Someone sneered about Bobby Kennedy, with his eleven children, "What's he trying to prove?" "I dunno," was the answer, "but he's sure proving it." And Shakespeare's Richard III, pitifully ugly with his deformed, hunched back, epitomizes the conscienceless achiever. Shakespeare may have had it in mind that someone with so much physical shame might go to extremes to overcome it.

In *The Art of Loving*, psychologist Eric Fromm takes the line that aggression is always a sign of insatiable hunger, which he says could be construed as a weakness. But this is arbitrary. Hunger doesn't always appear as weakness. That voracious look *adds to* the splendor of the prowling Siberian tiger. Glamour still attaches to mythical male satyrs, with their insatiable appetites for sex. The story of womanizer Don Juan still crops up in our movies and literature. Recall also the French story of a youth who confessed to sinful intercourse the night before. "How many times?" snapped the waspish priest. "Please, Father," demurred the youth, "I came here to *humble* myself!" Again, recall how unglamorous is the fading sex drive of a middle-aged male in tavern jokes, a figure of sport and sneering. (For instance, there was the man whom his wife saw packing. "Where are you going?" she asked. "To Germany," he replied. "I just read that single women there are desperate and will pay $30 for each servicing. But now what are *you* doing?" "I'm packing, too," she said. "I want to be there to see how you can live on $45 a week.")

Thus, although the moves to moralize shame can be powerful, people can slip out of them. They do that not only by going underground to jokes and satire but also forthrightly by sheer gall and rebellion. The moves are not logically tight. We can always claim that they are just linguistic tricks after all, just ways of redefining and redescribing what we don't have to accept if it is too inconvenient to be moral.

Plato gave us the first systematic attempt to moralize shame, trying to go beyond mere linguistic fiat. He wanted to subordinate honor norms to beneficence norms. "Only the useful is beautiful," he said in one place, "and only the harmful is ugly." In this remark he was obviously not reporting common usage of the words "beautiful" and "ugly" but proposing a reform of honor standards. His immediate concern was to defend the idea of old women-warriors exercising naked in public, useful to society though physically ugly. But clearly he hoped to apply his principle broadly to completely moralize honor for the purpose of social welfare. Any custom helpful to the state would thus no longer count as ugly and shaming, would no longer be barred by an (enlightened) code of honor.

When Socrates in prison awaits his execution, his old friend Crito tries to get him to escape. Socrates refuses. Crito reproaches him by using the code of honor. Socrates's refusal, argues Crito, will bring dishonor on his friends. People will say they were too timid or stingy to effect his escape. Crito also suggests that Socrates is dishonorable for letting down his sons, "taking the line of least resistance" and leaving them as unenviable orphans.

Socrates calmly reminds Crito that the only shame and glory that count are the evaluations by expert critics of conduct. What the mob might say does not count. It turns out that the standards of that expert critic, Socrates himself, bar the shaming of persons acting out of duty to the state. That means Socrates's refusal to escape cannot count as violating an enlightened code of honor, no matter how many enlightened honor norms Crito might bring up. All this, of course, reflects Plato's continuing attempt to distinguish warranted from unwarranted shame. In the moralized standards of shame and glory that Plato argued for, only immoral acts would count as dishonorable.

Plato's is a noble attempt at moralizing shame, one well worth thoughtful study. But remember, we are fighting fire with fire. If fear of shame can get people to act morally, but if "shameful" and "wrong" don't at a deep level *mean* the same thing, then fear of shame can just as easily get people to act *immorally*. It is a powerful tool of control. How could one shame a conscientious person into violating the code of decency? Taunt her with how queasy she is, weakly submitting to restraints fit only for cowards and slaves. Remember that Iago sneers at the honest servant who

Wears out his time, much like his master's ass,
For naught but provender, and when he's old,
        cashier'd;
Whip me such honest knaves.

And in our own day, a Tank McNamara cartoon shows a decent man expressing distaste for the brutality of boxing — whereupon a companion snickers to the group, "We've got the Bambi complex going here!"

Suppose you were out on the town partying with Friday-night friends. The group decides to make a little joke out of a tired-looking, middle-aged woman sitting alone at the bar. The plan is that every five minutes one of the group will go make conversation with her, tell her how beautiful she is, and then end the interview with some insulting disclaimer. Suppose you refuse to go along with the game. How would it feel if one of your comrades asked you, "Why are you such a wimp?"

Shame is a powerful tool of control. Ambitious hands can apply that tool toward wicked as well as toward beneficial ends. One celebrated pair of ambitious hands belonged to Shakespeare's Lady Macbeth.

The Story of Macbeth

A brave warrior of decent and well-meaning habit, Macbeth is returning from battle with his friend Banquo when they encounter three weird and surly witches. These strange witches prophesy that Macbeth will, among other things, someday be crowned king. Of Banquo they prophesy that his descendants will be kings.

Shortly afterwards a part of the prophesy comes true, quickening Macbeth's trust in what the witches have said. He likes the idea that he will become king and writes a letter about it to his wife, and she likes the idea, too. She reflects, after reading the letter, that they should help fate along with a bit of direct action. Knowing her husband well, though, she figures his decent and honorable ways will inhibit him. She knows how to handle his vacillation, though: Use shame as a tool against the restraints of honor and decency. In her reflections she says, as if to him,

            Hie thee hither,
    That I may pour my spirits in thine ear,

And chastise with the valour of my tongue
All that impedes thee from the golden round.

As it happens, the current king, Duncan, requests the Macbeths'
hospitality for an overnight stay. What a good opportunity to help fate
along, thinks Lady Macbeth. Just assassinate Duncan and his heirs while
they are staying here in our castle. She says to herself,

> Come, you spirits
> That tend on mortal thoughts, unsex me here,
> And fill me, from the crown to the toe, top-full
> Of direst cruelty! make thick my blood,
> Stop up the access and passage to remorse,
> That no compunctious visitings of nature
> Shake my fell purpose.

Sure enough, Macbeth falters in his plans. Duncan is such a kind
and good king, and he has been generous with his kinsman and subject
Macbeth. Here is what the valor of Lady Macbeth's tongue has in store
for her husband to take care of that queasiness:

> Art thou afeard
> To be the same in thine own act and valour
> As thou art in desire? Wouldst thou have that
> Which thou esteem'st the ornament of life,
> And live a coward in thine own esteem,
> Letting 'I dare not' wait upon 'I would' . . . ?

In other words, she calls him a wimp. Macbeth protests that he is not
a wimp: "Prithee, peace:/ I dare do all that may become a man;/ Who
dares do more is none." Lady Macbeth responds to this by asking why
he ever told her about the matter in the first place if he wasn't going to
go through with it anyway.

> What beast was't then
> That made you break this enterprise to me?
> When you durst do it, then you were a man;
> And, to be more than what you were, you would
> Be so much more the man. . . .
> . . . I have given suck, and know

How tender 'tis to love the babe that milks me:
I would, while it was smiling in my face,
Have pluck'd my nipple from his boneless gums,
And dash'd the brains out, had I so sworn as you
Have done to this.

With that she wins the debate. They plan to kill old King Duncan while he sleeps and make it look as if his guards committed the murder. Macbeth asks, but what if we fail? She answers, well then, we just fail. But, she tells him, "Screw your courage to the sticking place, and we'll not fail."

Macbeth has been shamed by his wife into breaking certain rules of decency, and certain rules of honor (notice the overlap, as shown in the table below).

Rules of Decency	Rules of Honor
Don't kill your king.	Obey and protect your leader.
Protect your houseguest.	Protect your houseguest.
Don't tell lies.	Don't use trickery and deceit to succeed at your projects.
Don't break promises.	Keep your word.
Don't kill anybody without good reason.	Don't kill a sleeping old man.
	Don't let others take blame for your deeds.

So it may not be such a good idea to rely overmuch on the force of shame to enforce morality. Fighting fire with fire can backfire.

Chapter 11

The Spectre of the Splendid Villain

"To be weak is miserable doing or suffering," says Milton's Satan at the beginning of *Paradise Lost*. Satan has, with certain other angel friends, revolted against God. He has been envious and humiliated at God's great glory. In response to the revolt God has cast the rebels out of heaven and thrown them into hell. Satan reflects on their future:

> To do aught good will never be our task,
> But ever to do ill our sole delight,
> As being contrary to his high will
> Whom we resist.

His aim is to frustrate any attempt of God to create something good:

> If then his providence
> Out of our evil seek to bring forth good,
> Our labor must be to pervert that end,
> And out of good still to find means of evil.

The Challenge of the Splendid Villain

The perennial presence of the devil in our heritage shows that we are aware, in our culture, that good doesn't *necessarily* triumph over evil. Most of us just hope it will. Jesus called the devil "the Prince of this world." And a doggerel verse tells our worry about the prospering of evil we see every day:

171

God made things fine, in beginning;
Adam ruined it, by sinning;
We hope that the story
Will end in God's Glory,
But so far, the other side's winning.

If good were sure to win all along, then hope would be trivial, and so would moral concern.

Although we admit this easily enough, it is more difficult to think about it in bald terms. In our habits of speech it sounds strange and paradoxical to say that something wrong ought to be done. Milton's Satan articulates his intentions straightforwardly, but, after all, he is the devil, the very lord of evil. "I am the spirit that negates," he says in Goethe's *Faust*. We might expect mere humans to have more trouble being so open about purely evil intentions. Even accomplished, sophisticated criminals typically have family or clan whom they are friendly with and at pains to protect, so they talk guardedly. It is rare to find a Richard III with his articulate, incisive self-knowledge.

The Start of a Splendid Villain

Imagine Shakespeare's Richard III as a boy. He has just played a cruel, clever, and successful prank on his brother, which ended with George half-drowned in a barrel of wine. The duchess, their mother, scolds Richard, "You ought to be ashamed of yourself!" Richard says nothing to her. Instead he delivers an aside to the audience he always recognizes and loves to share his thoughts with: "I ought to be *ashamed?* Well, perhaps yes, if 'ashamed' just means 'guilty.' But I don't really mind feeling guilty. Guilt is my destiny anyway." He goes on, "If shame means humiliation, however, then I fail to see why I should be ashamed. My conduct displayed no weakness or incompetence." The mother scolds on: "You can't be very proud of nearly drowning poor George!" Richard then muses, "Why not? I managed the affair beautifully. It required courage, daring persistence, and a good deal of intelligence. And the trick succeeded beautifully — George will never cross me again. I *am* proud of that."

The mother goes on railing at him, "Sometimes you behave like a proper villain, like a moral monster." Then Richard comments to himself and the audience, "Hardly! 'Villain' means slave or servant. That's why it's supposed to shame me. But it would be really slavelike to let George tease me the way he was trying to do. If I had let it go on, *then* I'd be a 'villain.' *Then* I'd be ashamed and humiliated. Instead I struck back so terribly that he'll never cross my will again. From now on I'll be George's master and he my villain, my slave. As for being a moral monster, I'm already a physical monster anyway, with my deformed torso. It's only fitting I should be a moral monster as well. Anyway, 'handsome is as handsome does.' This trick I pulled off displayed mental strength and agility. So it makes me handsome. I'm a veritable athlete of cunning!"

He reflects further, "Now, no one has to tell me that I ought to be ashamed of my deformed back. I'm automatically ashamed of that. And no one now needs to tell George he should be ashamed of his defeat by me. He's naturally ashamed of that. There is something fishy about being told that you 'ought to be ashamed' of this and that. Something arbitrary and conventional about it. Society uses it as a trick to hobble splendid minds and spirits like mine. Society takes powerful words like shame and pride and twists them from their natural uses. That is supposed to brainwash us into respecting the conventional norms of justice and decency."

Richard sees how completely our ordinary language has moralized shame-glory words. He will not be fooled by it for a moment. He and Satan are what I call splendid villains, persons who coolly do what they know is wrong, accepting great guilt but no shame. Such persons grant that their action is morally wrong. But is there any way to show that they are *irrational*, missing some significant point about life? Is it illogical to reject the idea that being guilty automatically makes one shameworthy?

Analysis of the Challenge

Let's look back once more at the four types of norm in chart form:

	MORAL NORMS	AESTHETIC NORMS
LIMIT NORMS	Decency	Honor
GOAL NORMS	Beneficence	Achievement

I have been arguing throughout that these norms are distinct. They can conflict, and they interrelate in intricate ways. In order to argue against the splendid villain we will have to argue that somehow, ultimately, honor and achievement are automatically connected with moral norms. We must show that Richard III, ultimately, deceives himself. We will have to show that the existence of a splendid devil is logically impossible, that he is like a round square: There just can't be one. The spectre of the splendid villain, we must argue, is only a spectre. If we understood it deeply enough, we would recognize that it is mythical, like flying horses and goats with men's torsos attached to their shoulders.

Can we meet that challenge? Can we show that no *real* splendid villain can exist? Linguistic fiat certainly doesn't work. It fails or back-fires. Human society has tried other ways to meet the challenge. It tries to catch and punish deceptive villains so that they won't seem so splendid, sitting in jail.

Actually, many theorists have said that the real function of legal punishment is not to deter would-be criminals but to reinforce respect-able people in their law-abiding habits. The idea is that punishing criminals assures the law-abiders that they are not bungling suckers for staying within the rules. The punishment ritual then eases a conflict that anyone might feel between decency and nonmoral honor, between guilt and humiliation.

But this legal method carries no guarantee. Billy the Kid, mythical outlaw of the Wild West, is a hero whom many have admired and found exciting. The movie *Bonnie and Clyde* celebrates as lovable heroes those two outlaws because of their indomitable spirit. Marlon Brando played his role of Mafia godfather as a strong, wise lawgiver and statesman.

The Criminal Who Doesn't Get Caught: The Secret Stigma

Here is a deeper analysis of what the law may be trying to do. Maybe it will work. We could try this move: Criminals who don't get caught carry around with them a secret. They deceive the force of law, hiding their villainy. Shame wants to hide. An honorable person has nothing to hide. Just as I can be ashamed of an ugly birthmark on my back that I always keep covered up — some deformity others never see — so also the deceptive villain must be ashamed of his secret villainy. Suppose he succeeds in passing himself off as a fine person, loved and admired by all, a pillar of society. Yet he knows that the loved and respected person is not the real him. If they knew him as he really is, they'd loathe him. In the play *The Foreigner*, a preacher, respected for his goodness and authority, turns out to be leader of a brutish chapter of Ku Klux Klansmen. His fiancee covers her face in horror and disgust when she sees him exposed.

But I can imagine this situation reversed, with a decent person keeping his decency secret from rascals in the society where he finds himself. Imagine that in Nazi Germany among the notables in the hierarchy there lives a high-minded young revolutionary. He goes disguised among his Nazi friends, aware that they would loathe him if they really knew him. This consideration would upset him if he wanted their friendship, but he'd console himself that their standards of "correct loathing" are completely wrong, that they *should* admire him for what he really is.

In the same way a secret villain could tell himself that he is splendid and praiseworthy by *true* standards of what is fine and splendid. If the people around him are so deceived by sissy conventional morality that they are conditioned to despise villains, then so much the worse for them. He'll prudently conceal his villainy and perhaps long for an intimate who would understand and admire him correctly, truly appreciate his splendor. Notice that he need not come to doubt the correctness, the true splendor, of his villainy.

In *The Sea Wolf*, Captain Larsen sets out to *train* young Hump to admire his villainous strength. Hump is the first associate Wolf Larsen has ever had who is worthy to be his audience, his admirer. Toward the end of the story a woman named Maud arrives. Hump's love for her saves him from the role Wolf Larsen planned for him. This loss of audience doesn't change Wolf's heart at all. He still dies unrepentant, convinced as ever of the truth of his antimoral philosophy. This "secret stigma" consideration, then, doesn't seem especially helpful in refuting the splendor of villains.

A Religious Answer

One can understand why society, in a world darkened by corruption and brute power, latched on to Christianity as a counter to the splendid villain. In the Christian view, that villain will burn forever for his crimes. Hence, he is a fool to do wrong, even if he gets away with it here on earth.

In fact, the Christian myth has even more power than my brief statement displays. After all, a person like Macbeth might be willing to "jump the life to come." He might even be willing to suffer forever for an immortal name in glory, as are Richard III and Milton's Satan. But consider the peculiar significance of the Last Judgment, the general judgment, in Christian teaching. Already at death God judges each person as innocent or guilty, saved or damned forever. Then why do Christians add on the idea of general judgment? What function is left for it? Well, on that great day, the deeds of each person will be manifest to all men and angels. More importantly, those deeds will be manifest under the divine perspective of what is truly beautiful and glorious, what is truly ugly and base. Then "splendid villainy" will appear frozen forever in its actual, leprous ugliness. *That* should deter the proud would-be villain.

But it doesn't. Judgment Day is a long way off. The Christian responds, "Ah, but even now the deceptive villain, who seems a saint to others, is seen accurately at every moment by the cold appraising eye of God. His glorious success is even now ugly to the top aesthetic expert on warranted glory and shame." A *full* believer, then, will not be strongly tempted to admire or envy the splendid villain.

The trouble is, few people have ever fully adopted this convenient myth as part of themselves. Even the Psalmist admits: "My foot almost slipped, so I should envy sinners." And almost nobody today fully internalizes this myth. Can philosophy do the social job that theology has failed at? Can we find arguments, not needing "God" premises, to show that wicked achievement is automatically inglorious? That is what we need to show. Here are several ways to say it:

- No wicked triumph can count as true achievement.
- Decency is a necessary precondition for true glory.
- Immoral means automatically spoil, deface, the end.

Now we could just assert dogmatically that a wicked triumph is not truly a triumph. But that move isn't very helpful. It won't make a dent in the minds of Satan or Richard III. We need to argue in *their* terms if we are going to convince *them,* just as Socrates argued against rhetoric in the rhetorician's terms.

The Glory Spoiled?

Try this possibility: Achievers (both noble and wicked) want to win. Satan wants to overthrow God. Richard wants the crown. Now, sometimes it happens that there is a difference between really winning and only apparently winning. A real competitor would be furious to realize that his opponent is just horsing around. He wants to match himself against opponents at their best.

Achievers like to win in fact, not just apparently. To see this clearly, think of the other types of norm. A person whose well-intentioned bungling has harmed people would deserve no moral credit for beneficence. (We saw Faust in that situation.) Again a decent person would feel guilty if he negligently let justice miscarry. Honor also must be genuine; merely apparent honor is a sham — indeed, maintaining such a sham itself breaks a timeless rule of honor. So it is with the competition of achievers. The fervent competitor, one who genuinely cares about the game as worthwhile, will not accept a sham victory. If the pseudo-winning means that glory isn't glory to him, then the glory is worthless. The fervent achiever, then, will not cheat to win in a way that taints the winning.

This isn't to say that luck can't be a part of winning. The boxer who got the lucky punch honestly won. The winner of a beauty contest is probably lucky to be endowed with at least something of natural good looks. But the boxer whose opponent is set up to receive the punch hasn't won. Snow White's wicked stepmother, even if she had succeeded in killing Snow White and getting the mirror to call her the fairest of all, would not by that have been beautiful. She would just have knocked her competition out of the game.

So the luck to be more talented doesn't stain winning, but cheating does. Cheating negates the game itself, makes its competitive aspect and the skill needed, pointless. Cheating at solitaire provides one of the clearest examples of this point. To cheat there is utterly silly: No one gets defeated, no one triumphs and shines to others, nothing is accomplished except piles of cards. The whole point of the game, if there ever was any, disappears.

Amelia, in *Vanity Fair*, wants nothing so much as to be loved by her handsome soldier husband, George. That's what succeeding means for her. So Captain Dobbin, loving her so and wanting her to have the feeling of triumph, buys her a piano and makes it look like a gift from George. This thrills her. But what if she had found out that her triumph was a sham? Think how quickly her triumph would have turned to ashes.

Let's apply this now to Richard and Satan, for I think this tack would work against them. Suppose they thought they had won in their endeavors. Richard is happy with his crown now that he has killed all those people to get it. Courtiers abound, people do obeisance, high-ranking ambassadors come from foreign countries to pay respect. Then Richard finds out that Lord Hastings had just pitied him because of his ugly hunchback. At great expense (I keep pretending), Lord Hastings had kindly set up an elaborate charade so that Richard would feel as if he were king. He would be devastated. I recoil from thinking about what he might do to Lord Hastings. If achievement by wicked means were automatically made into a sham like this, I've no doubt Richard would just as soon be a decent person.

We can imagine the same with Satan. If God were beneficent, even to Satan, to so great a degree that he let Satan believe himself to be king of the universe, and Satan in his apparent glory found out about that beneficence, it would be the most mortifying and enraging blow of all. And if Satan learned that such a sham was the only way even to *appear* as winning in his revolt, then I suspect even Satan would reform.

Shabby Means Leaving Glory Intact

I take it that the achiever cares about the goal itself and won't be satisfied with what merely looks like success, no matter how much glory people bestow. In both these previous cases the *means* to glory cancels out the glory. We saw in Chapters 9 and 10, however, that dishonorable or indecent means to glory do not *as such* taint or diminish the achievement. What about cases where such means are not closely tied in with the goal but merely happen to be a way of getting to it?

Consider somebody who wants a million dollars. There are a number of different ways he might succeed in getting it. He could be lucky at gambling or on the stock market. Or he could invest thoughtfully and wisely. Or he could win at the lottery. Or he could work hard in a well-planned business. Or inherit it. Or steal it or blackmail somebody without getting caught. Or pull some clever, shady deal. Success in any of these methods will let him count as a millionaire.

Regardless of how he got the money, he can spend it as he chooses. A million dollars stolen will buy just as many yachts as a million dollars honestly come by. Of course, if he set up a press and counterfeited the bills clumsily so that retailers recognized the counterfeit, then he would not count as having the money. *That* form of cheating would negate the goal, because it wouldn't produce spendable dollars, only pieces of paper.

This example exposes a trouble spot in our dealings with Richard and Satan. They are fervent competitors, pure in their dedication to winning. Like the wealth-seeker aiming at a definite and single goal, they have nothing in their value system to deter them from any means that helps achieve the goal. The only deterrent possible to these single-minded achievers is something that undermines the goal. Short of that no holds are barred. Cheating is allowed under the pure achievement norm type as long as the goal remains intact.

A temptation to cheat will press especially hard on the authentic, fervent competitor *if* the cheating in no way negates the winning itself. Suppose a competitive person faces a formidable and arbitrary obstacle that prevents him from getting into the big game at all, and suppose he can evade this obstacle by cheating. When a person feels sure he could perform well in a certain high role (if he could only *secure* that role) then he'll be tempted to cheat, slander rivals, or flatter superiors to *get* that role.

If the obstacle he faces seems closely related to the skills needed for the game itself, it would be self-defeating for him to evade the test. He might end up in a game he should have discovered he is not fit for. However, in a complex society like ours the screening criteria for a high role often seem arbitrary, unrelated to the role itself. It seems to the young person as if he were being asked to pass a singing test in order to qualify for a foot race. It is then that he will be tempted to cheat in the singing contest. Here is a story about that.

Seeking a Specific Goal

Thirty years ago I was in the Dominican Order as a novice-student. I left after two years and went out to teach in a college for steelworkers near Gary, Indiana. Meanwhile, I was still finishing a master's thesis for the Dominicans, as an external student.

The boys at this college just wanted to get out of the steel mill and into the steel company offices. Corporation leaders had decreed that a candidate have a bachelor's degree to get in the running for that more prestigious job. Yet the Irish, Italian, or Polish mothers of these boys would not hear of their going to a godless, secular university. So these boys had to go to a Catholic college.

At that time, Catholic colleges required every student, even business majors, to take hour after hour of Thomistic philosophy and theology. Put all these factors together now: The end is to get to work in the company offices. The *means* seem not related at all. The young men found that to get from the steel mill to the steel mill office, they had to pass tests on the Thomistic distinction between essence and existence. They were baffled and outraged. I met a former student several years after his graduation. After a few drinks, he said solemnly, "Professor, I want to confess that I once cheated to pass your metaphysics course. It has tormented me ever since. Never mind that this cheating got me my degree, and a fine job, where I'm very happy. What good is money and success [snicker] when I know I did wrong?" I was offended at the fellow's cheek, because I thought then that Thomistic metaphysics was a good thing for everyone to learn.

Now it happened at this same time that *I* needed to get an "A" for my M.A. work for the Dominicans in order to qualify for a fellowship to go on for a Ph.D., which I needed to get a university teaching post. The old priest who would judge my work was saintly and unworldly but rather vague mentally. He read my thesis, wrote me that it was superb and should be printed. When I went back to the House of Studies for my defense, however, I discovered that he had written merely a "B" on the thesis. Disaster!

Then came the temptation. I remembered some Machiavellian advice from an old business professor. He'd maintained that professors don't like best the student who always *agrees*. The student they love is the one who first disagrees and then lets himself be convinced. This sort of student shows himself as independent-minded but intelligent enough to appreciate the prof's brilliant refutation.

My eyes narrowed . . . I went up for my oral defense. The old priest looked bored and perfunctory, until I innocently advanced a plausible *mis*interpretation of Aristotle. He awoke from his boredom and set out with zest to demonstrate my error. I resisted vigorously; he drove me back, step by step. He refuted me, triumphantly! I went downstairs to await his verdict. Almost at once, word was sent that my examiner was so impressed by my oral defense that he would change my overall mark to an "A." So I got the fellowship. I got the degree. I got the academic post. All because I was willing to basely flatter an unworldly superior.

After that, I saw the undergraduate's point. It's maddening to be deprived, in what seems like an arbitrary way, of the chance to enter a race where you feel sure you'd do well. It's a powerful temptation to evade the obstacle, using any methods.

The moral here can be generalized. Universities that admit students who need the degree mainly to qualify for a middle-class career can expect that even "decent" students will cheat. In many American schools I've heard about, cheating has progressed beyond tragedy to farce. The point here is not that the student is morally excused for cheating in such a situation. That's not the issue. The point is that, feeling that this obstacle (the degree) is not intrinsically related to his real goal, the student won't feel it's silly for him to cheat in the way a solitaire player should feel that cheating would be silly. If the person cheats to get in a race and then legitimately *wins* the race, his victory is not really invalidated by his earlier cheating. So completely innocent conduct is not a necessary precondition for true achievement. Wrongdoing won't always bar true glory. Sometimes it can even help get the glory.

The Half-met Challenge

We have above two cases that are similar to the splendid-villain model in displaying willingness to transgress limit norms without scruple. The students violated decency; the professor violated honor. You may want to respond that these achievers are not exactly splendid. What is so great about working in a steel mill office? What is so great about being a professor? But I hope you will recognize both the students and the professor as would-be achievers. Both are motivated by that type of norm. What we have in these cases is the splendid villain in miniature, a willingness to bypass limit norms for the sake of a specific goal, without the feeling of shame. They show that the splendid villain is possible, that people can rationally perform immoral and ignoble deeds for the sake of a splendid goal. Shame need not deter us from ugly means and often enough does not. Although none of the people in this story makes a *career* out of being a splendid villain, as Satan and Richard do, the piling up of such little violations can erode a society's moral strength.

The splendid villain rarely appears in pure form, perhaps never except in myths and stories. But the spectre of such a person is not a fuzzy, impossible illusion. It is just an exaggerated picture of thousands of daily violations. I have offered three ways to blot out the spectre; each of them has a fatal weakness.

Solution for blotting out the spectre	Weakness of the solution
Undetected villains carry a secret stigma, which others would loathe if they found out about it.	But others could be wrong in their loathing. The secret stigma *could* be something fine instead of evil.
A true believer can find religious sanction against using immoral means to achievement.	But it's hard to believe, and there's no answer to the successful achiever who does not believe.
Certain means to glory ruin the glory, keep the achievement from counting as winning.	But shabby means *arbitrarily* related to the goal may not diminish the glory. (The achiever could even consider them de-uglified by his later success.)

So I have found no logically tight way to argue with an ardent achiever who single-mindedly sets his sights on a wicked goal. I have found no way to bolster conscience in face of a person who has decided not to worry about any norm except the achievement norm he has chosen.

Help from Multiple Norms in Discrediting the Splendid Villain

But there are *four* types of norm, and we live by juggling these around, grappling with the conflicts that we find within ourselves. In most cases the different types of norms provide some other motive as well as a "conscience" to support moral action. I'll review here how this occurs.

Some achievements are worthless and silly. Some "achievements" are silly in themselves. In certain "games" victory is inglorious and automatically shaming.

Thomas More describes somewhere a spirited contest among greasy clergymen to see who can flatter a rich cardinal most extravagantly. It would be cold praise indeed to say of a man, "He's no good at fighting but a veritable Hercules at fawning!"

In *A Man For All Seasons*, Rich has testified falsely against More to get a post in Wales. More says to Rich scornfully, "You should not sell your soul to gain the whole world. But Rich, for Wales . . . ?!"

Some achievements are dishonorable. Everyone agrees that shame and guilt — honor and decency — do in fact overlap considerably. So a sense of honor can bolster conscience in its battle against wicked achievements. If I attempt a wicked coup and then blunder and fail, my act counts as wicked and also as shaming because I both attempted to do wrong and mucked it up.

Coriolanus tries to flatter the base plebes, and fails totally. We surely think better of him for failing.

Socrates didn't want to save his own life by persuading the mob with effective rhetoric. He knew that the crowd wanted as rulers people like themselves, that the crowd was shrewd enough to see through any aristocrat pretending to be base and common. So the very success of a politician in Athens showed his deep baseness.

Many corporate bureaucracies offer degrading success, and so do schools that emphasize unmeasurable achievements like "good teaching." The alleged good teachers are often, in practice, the teachers favored by their superiors. Success is thus limited to what looks like success.

Good administrators are often equally difficult to pick out objectively, which means that the aspiring administrator must pick up skills of flattery. One professor at my university has rugged good looks. You'd expect him to be independent and brutally blunt. But this man hoped to be made a dean. I once heard him say to a powerful vice-president: "Good morning, Dr. Prentice." I can't convey the sweetness of this greeting, which had six notes in it, like the mating song of a lark.

Moral and dishonor shame often overlap. If we consider all cases of immorality instead of just spectacular ones, we will see that most of them come not from purposive action or evil intentions. Most come from weakness, laziness, not thinking quickly or carefully enough. With a slip of alertness I hurt a friend's feelings. I tell a lie for lack of courage or simply because it's easier. I break a promise because I forgot, or because I decide making the promised phone call is just too much trouble. Such weaknesses and deficiencies are genuinely shaming. If guilt doesn't deter me from these slips, shame is likely to because I fear and avoid it. Thomas More, in danger at court for his integrity, came home cheerful one day. When asked if the pressure was off, he said, on the contrary, that he was relieved because he had that day committed himself publicly to his principles: If moral principle now were too weak to hold him to the line, sheer shame at backing down would reinforce it.

The Motive of Conscience

With varying degrees of commitment, most people try to do right. People know what the word "wrong" means and know it is at least relevant in deciding what to do or not to do. Most wrongdoing comes from weakness, cowardice, clumsy bungling. People try to live morally, so for typical people their wrongdoing does count as a shaming failure at an attempted project, namely failure to do right.

The spectre of the splendid villain, however, means we cannot say that everyone tries to avoid what he accepts as "really wrong." We cannot say that actual wrongdoing counts as failure. But real psychopaths — people who accept no acts as really wrong — are rare. It is hard to imagine someone who sincerely accepts the idea that cheating or murder is wrong, and yet considers that judgment as giving no direct reason at all to avoid cheating and murder.

That is why, thinking about the quotation from Satan at the beginning of this chapter, I mentioned that there is something rather odd about it. What an odd thing, to set out deliberately and purposely to pervert good and do wrong. It is odd because deciding to *do* something seems to imply that you have judged normatively that the thing is good to do. Likewise, judging that an act is evil or wrong naturally gives at least some reason not to do it. Satan may not be a contradiction, but he is, as philosophers put it, logically odd. Consider a statement such as "You ought not to cheat, so go and cheat." This sounds odd by itself because we feel the need for a *reason* for doing what we ought not to do. Consider some possible reasons people could give: "Cheat, though you ought not to

   ... because you'll be a wimp if you don't;

   ... because your family depends on your passing this exam;

   ... because getting the job you want requires passing this exam;

   ... because you are a devil-worshiper and Satan wishes it;

   ... because you are dedicated to beating the system."

Each of these cites a normative concern in advising someone to break the decency code. Each of the concerns falls into the pattern of one of the norm types. The first is honor, the second beneficence, the third achievement. The fourth is a perverse notion of decency by which someone is supposed to be loyal in his commitment to a leader.

What then is the fifth? It interests me especially because it shows how important it is for us to discuss openly all of our norms. The fifth looks to me like an instance of the achievement type, with someone whose goal is to subvert the stabilizing rules of his community. But why would anyone want to do *that?*

Watered-down Decency

I suggest the reason lies in this: We talk about decency norms, at least giving lip service to them. But we don't talk and debate about our achievement norms, which often conflict with decency. That leaves the spirited achiever, the natural leader, alienated and without help in deciding what ends are worth achieving. He consciously sees decency as the sole type of norm because that gets talked about. But he *acts* on the unspoken norms of achievement. The decency code then loses its punch, appears sissified and effeminate, to be followed only by those too weak to rebel. "Conscience is but a word that cowards use," sneers Richard III, "to keep the strong in awe."

An example of a decency code enraging to natural leaders comes from a local child care center. Their newsletter quotes from Robert Fulghum's book in this way:

> Most of what I really need to know about how to live, and what to do, and how to be, I learned in kindergarten. . . . These are the things I learned: Share everything. Play fair. Don't hit people. Put things back where you found them. Say you're sorry when you hurt somebody. Wash your hands before you eat. Flush. Warm cookies and cold milk are good for you. Live a balanced life. Learn some and think

185

some and draw and paint and sing and dance and play and work every day some.

Take a nap every afternoon. When you go out into the world, watch for traffic, hold hands and stick together. . . . And then remember the book about Dick and Jane and the first word you learned, the biggest word of all: LOOK. Everything you need to know is in there somewhere. The Golden Rule and love and basic sanitation.

And so on. If *that* is all I thought decency could amount to, *I'd* rebel also. It's not that the norms mentioned are themselves bad. They have merit. The compassionate golden rule (not sanitation) stands at the very core of decency. But stated so simple-mindedly they just sound puny and cute, humiliating when put forth as a fulsome philosophy of life. They contain nothing of adventure, nothing of splendid action. They squelch and deny rather than inspire and encourage.

This collection of norms makes up the stereotypical decency code that Mama teaches. In order to grow up, everyone has to break away from identity with the mother. Psychologists tell us that this is not so difficult nor quite so important for little girls. For little boys it is not only difficult but absolutely crucial as they become men. Thus, if a child identifies the decency code with his mother, identifies it with female passivity, there'll be a temptation to reject that code — and also to show fear and resentment toward women.

Suppose I fail to distinguish between the *code* of decency, and the norm *type* of decency. Then when I reject the code I'll reject the norm type as well. People often take this step. I have read many editorials scoffing at moral concern. They say it is soft-headed and unrealistic, that to be realistic (that is, manly) you must suspend all that sweet morality when the going gets tough.

But morality doesn't have to be sweet, dainty, and passive. Decent men who must separate themselves from their mothers, and decent women to whom for centuries exciting public achievement has been denied, want and need headier stuff. They want to accomplish more than doing the laundry that Mr. Fulghum takes delight in. They need a code of decency strong enough to take achievement and honor into account. The four codes always conflict from time to time. But until they come out together in the open where we can discuss them all as legitimate norms, I fear the decency code will sometimes lodge at lip-service level, appearing pale and sallow.

The Lingering Challenge

Decency must compete not with achievement as such (for we don't want to lose that norm type) but with the spectre of the splendid villain, someone who can accept genuine, intense guilt without feeling *any* humiliation about some action. Plato made this spectre explicit to us in his *Republic*. He drew the picture vividly, creating an imagined character who had the special power necessary for not getting caught at his wrongdoing. Plato wanted to show that this person would be better off avoiding wrong, independently of the penalty for getting caught, because it is always shaming to do wrong.

But we can continue debating whether Plato succeeded in his project. Our pictures of Shakespeare's Richard and Milton's Satan show that wrongdoing does not always arise from personal weakness. Sometimes it arises from an energetic and spirited appetite for action. Such action can be splendid, the opposite of shaming. Splendor *can* be moral, but it is not automatically so. We cannot deglamorize naughty achievements simply by announcing that naughtiness automatically, *logically* undermines achievement.

Milton's Satan accepts tremendous guilt for his rebellion. He admits that God is completely in the right. But he feels no failure shame over starting the rebellion because he was *not* committed — all things considered — to the project of avoiding wrongdoing.

He might well admit that since rebelling against God is really wrong, there is that one forthright reason not to rebel. After all, decency is a type of norm. But norms of honor and glory, he thinks, give him far stronger reason to rebel. So he is not committed overall to avoiding this form of wrongdoing. It's not that he accepts no norms. When he first appears in Milton's epic, he refuses on principle to betray his troops and sign a separate peace with God. He would not even vacillate dishonorably by repenting at all. Weighting shame-glory norms far more heavily than moral norms, Satan is absolutely committed all along to doing wrong. He feels shame only at defeat. And he is not very shamed by that: He reminds his troops that it took an omnipotent enemy to beat them.

Chapter 12

Concluding Remarks

In this book we have been contending that there are two schemes of human reaction to others' behavior — an aesthetic one and a moral one. Both these schemes are normative: People approve or disapprove of what others are and do. In both of them the normative judgments may be either warranted or unwarranted. Normative judgment is not just a matter of feeling or opinion.

Summary of the Two Normative Schemes

The moral scheme is a world of punishment and reward. We consciously and deliberately offer benefit or harm to agents who have helped or hurt others. When doing this we often use the agent's intentions as a criterion for how much reward or punishment there should be. Did the agent display benevolence? Or did the agent display malevolence toward others? In a moral scheme we esteem benevolence highly, think ill of thoughtlessness and cruelty. Moral estimation of ourselves, when not biased, follows the same patterns. My attitude and actions toward others provokes in me feelings of innocence, of guilt, or of moral credit. If my estimation is rational and careful, following the process described in Chapter 7, then these feelings are warranted. If biased by favoritism or neurotic influences, they may not be warranted at all. There are objective standards for self-esteem.

In the world of aesthetic norms our reaction is either admiration or contempt. We spontaneously display admiration for and sometimes award prizes to those who truly achieve — those who do better things better. Society also encourages people who display the talents, training, and character traits indicating potential for doing better things better. Conversely, we show pity, amusement, or contempt for someone who violates honor limits or fails visibly at what he or she undertakes. Again, as we estimate ourselves, what we see as defect or success summons up feelings of humiliation or of triumph. These feelings, too, are either warranted or unwarranted. They, too, match or miss objective standards.

Guilt is the sanction proper to enforcing moral limits and goals; humiliation is the sanction proper to aesthetic limits and goals. Humiliation is, for most people, far more painful than guilt, far more to be feared. Because of that, the fear of humiliation is a more powerful motivator than fear of guilt. Sometimes we try to manipulate the offering of admiration or contempt deliberately, understanding how powerful it is as a sanction. When someone wrongs us cleverly, we hide our rage (which that person might enjoy) and say, "I'm sorry for you; you're really sick." This usually is a pathetic, flat lie if our admiration patterns otherwise show that we admire aesthetic proficiency. And we tell naughty children they "ought to be ashamed of themselves." Notice we never say this to children with birthmarks or other defects not of their own doing. Such defects are automatically humiliating, and we try to draw attention away from them.

Aesthetic norms, with their more stressful sanction, are likely to carry more personal urgency than moral norms. Morality can easily go by the board in such a competition. For the last two centuries philosophers debated through many volumes about morality, but recent philosophers writing in English have scarcely remarked about honor and glory. Outside the universities conversation about standards of conduct show the same lack. It feels so undemocratic to ask which achievements are better.

We are fairly comfortable talking about excellence at a given activity: "Peter is a good administrator, but Paul is a better one": "Joe is the best player on the team." Americans accept, even if sometimes a bit squeamishly, the importance of these evaluations, and the search for fair standards goes on. But we shy from openly asking what sort of activity is better to administer or which game is better to play. Everyone must answer such questions in order to decide how to live, but the answers come at a mostly uncritical, even nonverbal level. We don't openly search for fair standards regarding them. Social scientists discuss pride, triumph, humiliation, shame; but they avoid speaking of objective standards warranting such feelings.

Rationality of the Schemes

Every normal person desires to feel self-respect and to shine before others. These are perfectly rational desires. The meaning of life would be much impoverished if it weren't rational to seek to be the best people we can be. This matter is so personally important that even when openly recognized it can jeopardize morality. Its sanction, humiliation, is stronger than the moral sanction of guilt. But both aesthetic and moral concerns are rational. They both call out for a rational hearing.

Since each scheme has both a limit and a goal aspect, we find four general types of norms in all, each with a different structure. Frequently the norms of different types conflict with one another. Everyone's life is in some way affected by each of these types, but typically people will emphasize one or two of them more than the others. We have seen how achievement-lovers can be tempted to neglect decency and honor norms. Honor-lovers sometimes forgo glory and decency. People conscientious about morals sometimes forget that aesthetic norms legitimately guide action.

Someone who recognizes all four types of norm and cares about them all undertakes a high challenge indeed. Imagine a person who wants to be splendid at doing a fine thing, wants to be honorable, wants to be decent and beneficent. Such a person is quite vulnerable to conflict, and that sort of conflict lies at the heart of many tragedies.

We saw how Macbeth only reluctantly gives up honor and decency for the sake of achievement. Once committed, he loses the restraints that had kept him upright. He becomes single-minded about success. Later, foreseeing defeat (everything has gone wrong for him), he reflects that life has no meaning. Macbeth despairs at all that effort to live up to so many conflicting norms: It comes to nothing — we all die anyhow.

Such despair is understandable rationalizing in a man who has forsaken all values except one and then failed at that one. He has become shameless and friendless, acting brutally and desperately to survive against impossible odds. No wonder he saw no meaning in life anymore. Our ability to respond to aesthetic and moral sanctions is in large part what gives our lives meaning. When pride is warranted — when we have done something truly splendid — then certainly we ought to be proud.

People fear talking about shame because it is such a painful emotion, and many people are even ashamed to admit that they fear it. But a fear of warranted shame makes for a self-respecting person. That sanction, rationally regarded, steers us to right ways and conduct. For that reason we need to discuss it, asking which occasions warrant it and which do not. Let us fear shame — for we ought to do so; but let us not fear talking about standards that warrant it.

Remember again that shame, as feared and as universal among humans, provides several positive services in human affairs. Not only does it protect us from ugly conduct by sanctioning against it. It also creates bonds among people in a community, and it is a main component in the development of personal identity, of self-esteem.

Here is a final example of the beneficial aspects of shame. At the end of the *Iliad,* Achilles, acting fiercely on a revenge norm, kills Hector and then drags his corpse about on the ground to dishonor it. Under the stringent aesthetic norms of Homeric society, no fate could be worse. Even the gods are horrified by it. Hector's father, Priam, therefore humbles himself by going to Achilles, giving him ransom gifts, and begging to have Hector's body back for honorable burial. Achilles never sways from his fierce warrior role. But Priam's situation is one he can well understand, and it moves him to pity. He also admires Priam's courage in crossing enemy lines. He has Hector's body washed and wrapped in a clean shirt and lays it safely on Priam's wagon. He treats Priam graciously, as a guest. When Achilles asks Priam how long it will take to celebrate Hector's funeral properly, Priam tells him eleven days. So Achilles calls for an eleven-day truce. The two enemies have supper together that night and are friends. Tragic as this situation is, a bond of community develops even across the line of a harsh war.

What Remains To Do

Throughout this book I have used many examples from Homer and Shakespeare. These bards were particularly aware of the conflicts among the four types of norm — decency, beneficence, honor, and achievement. We should try to make these four codes consistent with each other. People shouldn't be faced so often with tragic conflicts where, whatever they do, they will violate some norm. The only way to improve our normative consistency is to talk about all four codes and aim for reflective agreement about them. That means including achievement and honor in the discussion along with the moral norms. Those aesthetic norms, so personally urgent, have lain underground far too long, exerting an unnoticed, powerful influence. How can we reach consensus on these topics when real discussion of them has been taboo? Here are some ways to make a beginning.

1. *Discuss what activities are better.* Although demands of honor don't reduce completely to the ideals of achievement, we still can't help noting that clear thought about pride and humiliation depends on clear thinking about true achievement. If you and I disagree on whether a certain inability really warrants humiliation, we probably disagree also on whether that is an *important* disability. It cannot be important to be able to do something unless that something is worth doing.

Mere proficiency at something may win applause, but it doesn't warrant applause. "Whatever you do, do well!" is an indulgent slogan that blocks any intelligent concern for doing the *right thing* vs. doing the *thing right*. We should replace it with the counterslogan "Whatever is worth doing is worth doing badly." For if something is worth excelling at, then it's worth an honest try. We might also add the slogan "Doing trivial things obscenely well is rat-race."

2. *Discuss when humiliation is warranted.* "Shame [is] that gift that hinders mortals, but helps them too," says the god Apollo in Homer's *Iliad.* Wrongheaded humiliation can wreck a person's life; the need for revenge can drive one to murder. Misdirected ambition can fuel war or predatory conduct in business. We need reflective standards that distinguish the healthy fear of warranted shame from the wrongheaded kind.

Truly shameless people, who simply don't care what others think, are dangerous. They won't hesitate to do revolting and wicked things. And we find a person pathetic, not tragic, who simply cannot assert his or her rights and insist on respect for his human dignity.

Certain lines of accomplishment are beneficial for mankind. It is sad when talented people drop out of achievement from laziness or neurotic fear of failure or ridicule. Some people misunderstand the honor norm that says "Don't be a sucker!" They seem to think that only a sucker would pursue a line of hard, steady work. Thus, they never feel the exhilaration of meeting a worthwhile challenge.

3. *Discourage socially harmful admiration.* We can't just dismiss social norms that allocate admiration and contempt in observers, provoking pride or shame in performers. Their power in determining conduct does not depend solely on our approval. We need to understand the complex logic of such unwritten standards. We need to discuss the present standards of our society, compare them with the standards of other societies, and try to improve them.

Philosophers from Plato through Adam Smith struggled with the problem of the splendid villain. This project still lies open. Many societies have been misled by their charismatic leaders. We must learn at the very least to recognize villainy when it occurs with dazzling splendor. Even better, it may yet be possible to show that the splendor is fake. Short of that, we can at least control splendid villains, once recognized, by effective legal punishment.

But villains are not the only threat to society. Well-meaning, sincere fools and fanatics can also be enormously destructive. So we must state the problem more generally: We tend to admire courage, self-control, and cleverness, even when these traits are harnessed to foolish or wicked goals. Such admiration is socially harmful. Admiration is not free. It has consequences. What is admired, said Plato, will be imitated.

A thoughtless eight-year-old can perhaps be trusted with a bicycle, but not with a car. Today we have unbelievable technical power to achieve spectacular results. Overnight, as it were, we've become able to use gunpowder, explosives, drugs, fertilizers, fossil fuels, rockets, robots, and nuclear energy. We're proud of our new powers; our nation would be ashamed to fall behind other nations in their development. These splendid assets can facilitate foolish as well as wise actions. They magnify harmful as well as beneficial actions. With little effort we can thoughtlessly destroy our atmosphere, our oceans, and our ground.

This proficiency makes it all the more urgent that we quit admiring power-as-such, and give our applause instead to wise application of power. Know-how is worthless without know-whether.

Notes

Page 9:   King Henry's practical joke
           William Shakespeare, *Henry V*, in *The Complete Works of William
           Shakespeare*, ed. William Aldis Wright (Garden City, NY: Doubleday,
           1936), act 4, sc. 1.
Page 10:   Williams's protest
           Ibid., sc. 8.
Page 11:   The murderers' "assignment"
           Shakespeare, *Richard III*, act 1, sc. 4.
Page 11:   Iago's scorn for conscientious servant
           Shakespeare, *Othello*, act 1, sc. 1.
Page 12:   Hamlet's call to revenge
           Shakespeare, *Hamlet*, act 2, sc. 2.
Page 13:   Hamlet's chance to kill Claudius at prayer
           Ibid., sc. 3.
Page 21:   Erikson on shame
           Erik Erikson, *Childhood and Society*, 2d ed. (New York: Norton, 1963),
           p. 252.
Page 22:   The right stuff
           Tom Wolfe, *The Right Stuff* (New York: Bantam Books, 1980).
Page 30:   Dick Gregory's story:
           Dick Gregory with Robert Lipsyte, *Nigger* (New York: Dutton, 1964),
           pp. 43–47.
Page 37:   Sartre on "The Stare"
           Jean-Paul Sartre, *Being and Nothingness*, tr. Hazel Barnes (New York:
           Philosophical Library, 1956), part 3, chap. 1.
Page 38:   Aristotle on shame
           Aristotle, *Rhetoric*, tr. W. Rhys Roberts, in *The Basic Works of Aristotle*,
           ed. Richard McKeon (New York: Random House, 1941), book 2,
           chap. 6.
Page 38:   Blinding the horses in Equus
           Peter Shaffer, *Equus* (New York: Avon Books, 1974)
Page 38:   Villain blinding the witness
           Shakespeare, *King Lear*, act 3, sc. 7.
Page 40:   Philip's clubfoot
           Somerset Maugham, *Of Human Bondage* (Garden City, NY: Doubleday,
           1936), chap. 11.

Page 40: Hump's shame
Jack London, *The Sea Wolf* (New York: Bantam Pathfinder edition, 1960), p. 32.

Page 41: Lynd on the positive aspect of shame
Helen Merrell Lynd, *Shame and the Search for Identity* (New York: Science Editions, 1966), p. 66.

Page 41: Shame understood by another
Somerset Maugham, *Of Human Bondage*, p. 117.

Page 42: Vlastos on human dignity
Gregory Vlastos, "On Justice and Equality," in A. I. Melden, *Human Rights* (Belmont, CA: Wadsworth, 1970), p. 56.

Page 42: Miller on human dignity
Arthur Miller, *Death of a Salesman* (New York: Viking, 1949), p. 56.

Page 43: Augustine stealing the pears
Augustine, *Confessions*, tr. Edward Bouverie Pusey (New York: Oxford University Press, 1982), p. 29.

Page 43: Child abuse repressed
Gershen Kaufman, *Shame: The Power of Caring* (Cambridge, MA: Shenkman, 1980), pp. 178–185.

Page 43: Not admitting shame
Helen Block Lewis, *Shame and Guilt in Neurosis* (New York: International Universities Press, 1971), chap. 9.

Page 46: Husband's refusal to ask directions
Judith Viorst, ". . . So My Husband and I Decided to Take a Car Trip Through New England," *New York Times*, February 15, 1989.

Page 47: Males and not naming puce
Joanne Greenberg, in her *Rites of Passage* (New York: Holt, Rinehart & Winston, 1972), pp. 8–9, tells of someone who "was despised not for ignorance but for the degrading things he knew."

Page 51: Jesus' curse
Matthew 25:41–45.

Page 52: Aesthetic norms
The term "aesthetic" in connection with human excellence is suggested by R. M. Hare in *Freedom and Reason* (Oxford: Clarendon Press, 1963), pp. 139–151.

Page 56: Negative Golden Rule
Holmes Rolston, "The Golden Rule from Different Traditions" (mimeograph, 1980).

Page 58: The cannibalism dilemma
Henry Carlisle, *The Jonah Man* (New York: Alfred A. Knopf, 1964).

Page 59: Pollard's responsibility
Notice that Pollard's position puts him under a goal obligation of beneficence as well as the limit obligation of decency required by a sense of justice in the way he carries out his beneficence duty.

Page 65:   Aristotle defines virtue
           Aristotle, *Nicomachean Ethics*, tr. W. D. Ross, book 2, chap. 6.
Page 69:   The big-souled man
           Ibid.
Page 75:   The Japanese/American misunderstanding
           Ruth Benedict, *Chrysanthemum and the Sword: Patterns of Japanese Culture* (Boston: Houghton, Mifflin, 1946), pp. 159–161.
Page 76:   Touchy Spanish honor
           Edwin Honig, *Calderón and the Seizures of Honor* (Cambridge, MA: Harvard University Press, 1972), p. 185.
Page 76:   Aristotle on moderate care for others' opinions
           Aristotle, *Nicomachean Ethics*, 1095b, 1125b, 1148a, 1159a.
Page 78:   The dilemma of Lope's cuckold
           Lope de Vega, *Justice Without Revenge* in *Five Plays*, tr. Jill Booty, ed. R.D.F. Pring-Mill (New York: Hill and Wang, 1961).
Page 79:   Touchy Mexican honor
           Octavio Paz, *Labyrinth of Solitude* (New York: Grove Press, 1985), p. 30.
Page 80:   Geordie's golden chain
           "Geordie," in *One Hundred English Folksongs*, ed. Cecil J. Sharp (New York: Dover, 1975), pp. 24–25.
Page 80:   Outward manifestations of rank
           Julian Pitt-Rivers, "Honour and Social Status," in *Honour and Shame: The Values of Mediterranean Society*, ed. J. G. Péristiany (London: Weidenfeld and Nicolson, 1965), p. 25.
Page 82:   Shyness in poor women
           Ibid., p. 42.
Page 82:   Automatic dishonor for females
           Labyrinth of Solitude (p. 33), Paz writes that in Mexico "the ideal of manliness is never to 'crack,' never to back down. Those who 'open themselves up' are cowards. . . . Women are inferior beings because, in submitting, they open themselves up. Their inferiority is constitutional."
Page 82:   Honor of Andalusian aristocratic women
           Pitt-Rivers, "Honour and Social Status," p. 71.
Page 82:   Lily Bart's honor
           Edith Wharton, *The House of Mirth* (New York: University Press, 1977). For commentary see Dan Lyons, "The High Honor of Big Lily Bart" (mimeograph, 1987).
Page 83:   Illogical racist honor
           For an example of the faulty logic carried to absurdity, see Julio Caro Baroja, "Honour and Shame: A Historical Account of Several Conflicts," in *Honour and Shame: The Values of Mediterranean Society*, ed. J. G. Péristiany (London: Weidenfeld and Nicolson, 1965), pp. 101–109.

Page 84: Oxford jingle
Jan Morris, ed., *The Oxford Book of Oxford* (New York: Oxford University Press, 1978), p. 317.

Page 85: Self-regard vs. self-interest
Jann Benson, "A Legacy of Ethical Atomism," *Canadian Journal of Philosophy* 13 (June 1983), p. 193.

Page 91: Dostoyevsky and comrades at the scaffold
Geir Kjetsaa, *Fyodor Dostoyevsky: A Writer's Life*, tr. Siri Hustvedt and David McDuff (New York: Viking, 1987), pp. 86–89.

Page 96: Pistol rationalizes
Shakespeare, *Henry V*, act 5, sc. 1.

Page 97: Shameless Parolles
Shakespeare, *All's Well That Ends Well*, act 4, sc. 1.

Page 97: Parolles shrugs
Ibid., sc. 3.

Page 97: Vain king swindled
Hans Christian Andersen, *The Complete Fairy Tales and Stories*, tr. Erik C. Haugaard (Garden City, NY: Anchor Press, 1974), p. 77.

Page 101: Darcy after reform
Jane Austen, *Pride and Prejudice* (New York: Dell, 1959), p. 365.

Page 102: Athenians and Melians
Thucydides, *The Peloponnesian War*, tr. John H. Finley (New York: Modern Library, 1951), book 5, p. 333.

Page 103: Oedipus agonizing
Sophocles, *Oedipus the King*, in *An Anthology of Greek Drama*, tr. and ed. C. A. Robinson, Jr. (New York: Rinehart, 1951), p. 96.

Page 103: Creon's response
Ibid., p. 100.

Page 103: The defiled slave-woman
Tony Morrison, *Beloved* (New York: New American Library, 1988).

Page 105: Pessimism of Sophocles
Alasdair MacIntyre, *After Virtue: A Study in Moral Theory* (Notre Dame, IN: University of Notre Dame Press, 1981), pp. 133–136. For further discussion of conflict among incommensurable values in Greek tragedy, see Martha Nussbaum, *The Fragility of Goodness, Luck, and Ethics in Greek Tragedy and Philosophy* (New York: Cambridge University Press, 1986), especially chap. 3.

Page 111: Hump & rough sailors
London, *Sea Wolf*.

Page 112: The solitary hero
Trevanian, *Shibumi* (New York: Crown, 1979).

Page 116: Jesus on the widow's mite
Mark 12:41–44 and Luke 21:1–4

Page 117: The positive golden rule
Rolston, "Golden Rule."

Page 118: Assessing value of goals
This topic was discussed earlier in "Action, Excellence, and Achievement," *Inquiry* 19 (1976):277 and in "Are Luddites Confused?" *Inquiry* 22 (1979):381. Material used here with permission.

Page 121: Br'er Rabbit
Joel Chandler Harris, *Br'er Rabbit* (London: Pelham Books, 1977), pp. 16–17.

Page 128: Doing the thing right vs. doing the right thing
Ephraim R. McLean, "Assessing Returns from the Data Processing Environment," in *Effective Versus Efficient Computing*, ed. Fred Gruenberger (Englewood Cliffs, NJ: Prentice-Hall, 1973), p. 12.

Page 129: Odysseus insulted
Homer, *Odyssey*, tr. Samuel Butler, ed. Louise R. Loomis (New York: Walter J. Black, 1944), book 8, p. 92.

Page 129: Odysseus's response
Ibid.

Page 129: Plato on unathletic traders
Plato, *Republic*, tr. Paul Shorey, in *The Collected Dialogues of Plato*, eds. Edith Hamilton and Huntington Cairns (New York: Random House, 1966), book 8, 555a.

Page 130: Socrates on ranking powers
Plato, *Gorgias*, tr. W. D. Woodhead. See, for example, 448e, 451d–452d.

Page 134: The Talbot heroes
Shakespeare, *Henry VI, Part 1*, act 4, sc. 5–7.

Page 137: Falstaff
Henry IV, Part 1, act 5, sc. 4.

Page 139: Cyrano as playwright
Edmond Rostand, *Cyrano de Bergerac*, tr. N. Wolfe (Mount Vernon, NY: Peter Pauper Press, 1941), pp. 54–55.

Page 139: Coriolanus
Shakespeare, *Coriolanus*, act 2, sc. 1.

Page 140: Richard III
Shakespeare, *Henry VI, Part 3*, act 5, sc. 6.

Page 140: Priam's plea to Hector
Homer, *Iliad*, tr. Samuel Butler, ed. Louise R. Loomis (New York: Walter J. Black, 1942), book 22, p. 338.

Page 141: Hector's desperate resolve
Ibid., p. 343.

Page 141: Hector's grim foresight
Ibid., p. 98.

Page 141: Shakespeare's version of the war debate
Shakespeare, *Troilus and Cressida*, act 2, sc. 2.

Page 141: Odysseus's honor rhetoric
Homer, *Iliad*, book 2, pp. 28–29.

Page 142: Papageno shrugs at glory
W. A. Mozart, *Die Zauberflöte* (New York: University Books, 1971), act 2, sc. 22.

Page 142: Brutus's family tradition
Shakespeare, *Julius Caesar*, act 2, sc. 1.

Page 142: Oedipus's inflated self-image
Sophocles, *Oedipus the King*, pp. 63–64.

Page 142: Overaspiring males
Laurence J. Peter and Raymond Hull, *The Peter Principle* (New York: William Morrow, 1969).

Page 143: Aufidius turns ugly
Shakespeare, *Coriolanus*, act 1, sc. 10.

Page 144: Brazen Henry IV
Shakespeare, *Henry IV, Part 1*, act 5, sc. 1.

Page 144: The shameless peasant
Graham Greene, *The Power and the Glory* (New York: Viking, 1982), p. 164.

Page 146: Helena puts success above honor
Shakespeare, *All's Well That Ends Well*, act 4, sc. 4.

Page 146: Macbeth's comeback
Shakespeare, *Macbeth*, act 1, sc. 7.

Page 147: The American's queasiness
Henry James, *The American* (London: John Lehmann, 1949).

Page 148: Revenge in Montenegro
Milovan Djilas, *Land Without Justice* (New York: Harcourt, Brace, 1958).

Page 149: Telemachos on Orestes
Homer, *Odyssey*, book 3, p. 30.

Page 149: Hamlet's complaint
Shakespeare, *Hamlet*, act 1, sc. 4.

Page 149: Troilus's move
Shakespeare, *Troilus and Cressida*, act 2, sc. 2.

Page 149: Hamlet's acceptance of revenge duty
Shakespeare, *Hamlet*, act 4, sc. 4.

Page 150: Claudius to Laertes
Ibid., sc. 7.

Page 150: Laertes's response
Ibid., sc. 5.

Page 150: Machiavelli
Niccolo Machiavelli, *The Prince*, tr. L. Ricci, revised by E.R.P. Vincent (New York: New American Library, 1952), chap. 17, p. 90.

Page 154: Tradition in Japan
Ivan Morris, *The Nobility of Failure: Tragic Heroes in the History of Japan* (New York: New American Library, 1976).

Page 154: Jesus on not aiming too high
Luke 14:28.

Page 156: Brutus's beneficent assassination
Shakespeare, *Julius Caesar*, act 2, sc. 1.
Page 156: Brutus's love of Caesar
Ibid., act 3, sc. 1.
Page 156: Andromache's plea
Homer, *Iliad*, book 6, p. 97.
Page 156: Priam's plea
Ibid., book 22, p. 338.
Page 156: Hector's hopelessness
Ibid., book 6, p. 98.
Page 157: Faust's passion for achievement
Johann Wolfgang von Goethe, *Faust, Part 1*, eds. R-M. S. Heffner, Helmut Rehder, and W. F. Twaddell (Boston: D. C. Heath, 1954), Studierzimmer.
Page 158: Atomic scientist: beneficence vs. decency:
R. Wilson, "The Conscience of a Physicist," *Bulletin of the Atomic Scientists* 26 (June 1970), p. 31.
Page 158: Henry V's pep talk
Shakespeare, *Henry V*, act 4, sc. 3.
Page 158: Williams on war vs. decency
Ibid., sc. 1.
Page 159: Henry V on king's dilemma
Ibid., sc. 1.
Page 160: Humiliation from spectacles
Joseph Heller, *Good as Gold* (New York: Simon & Schuster, 1979), p. 316.
Page 162: Socrates on good dancer vs. good man
Plato, *Lesser Hippias*, 373a–376b.
Page 165: Fromm
Eric Fromm, *The Art of Loving* (New York: Harper & Row, 1956).
Page 166: Plato on beautiful as useful
Plato, *Republic*, book 5, 452d and 457b.
Page 162: Socrates on escape
Plato, *Crito*, tr. Hugh Tredennick.
Page 166: Iago scorns honest servant
Shakespeare, *Othello*, act 1, sc. 1.
Page 168: Lady Macbeth
Shakespeare, *Macbeth*, act 1, sc. 5.
Page 169: Lady Macbeth on not failing
Ibid., sc. 7.
Page 171: Splendid villain
An earlier version of some of these ideas appeared in "The Spectre of the Splendid Villain," *International Journal of Moral and Social Studies* 4 (Spring 1989:4). Used here with permission.

Notes

Page 171: Milton's Satan
John Milton, *Paradise Lost* (New York: Walter J. Black, 1943), book 1, p. 95.
Page 171: Devil as prince of this world
John 12:31, 14:30, and 16:11.
Page 172: Goethe's Mephistopheles
Goethe, *Faust*, Studierzimmer.
Page 175: The foreigner
Larry Shue, *The Foreigner: A Play* (New York: Dramatists Play Service, 1983).
Page 176: The Psalmist
Psalm 73.
Page 177: Amelia's lack of knowledge
William Thackeray, *Vanity Fair* (New York: Random House, 1950).
Page 183: Thomas More
Robert Bolt, *A Man for All Seasons* (New York: Random House, 1960), p. 158.
Page 185: Richard III (This quotation is slightly paraphrased.)
Shakespeare, *Richard III*, act 5, sc. 3.
Page 185: Kindergarten
Robert Fulghum, *All I Really Need to Know I Learned in Kindergarten* (New York: Ivy Books, 1988). See pp. 4–5. The material quoted comes from a flyer called "Parenting News," circulated locally in Denver by Auraria Child Care Center, April 1987.
Page 186: Psychologists on boys vs. girls maturing
Helen Block Lewis, *Psychic War in Men and Women* (New York: New York University Press, 1976).
Page 187: Plato on successful villain
Plato, *Republic*, book 2, 359d–360b.
Page 191: Macbeth's despair
Shakespeare, *Macbeth*, act 5, sc. 4.
Page 192: Achilles to Priam
Homer, *Iliad*, book 24, p. 388.
Page 193: Doing trivial things obscenely well
This insight came from a conversation with Peter H. Lee.
Page 193: Apollo on shame
Homer, *Iliad*, tr. Robert Fitzgerald (New York: Oxford University Press, 1974), book 24, p. 630. Note: Butler uses "conscience" in his translation; Fitzgerald uses the word "shame," which is more accurate in the context.
Page 194: Plato on admiring and imitating
Plato, *Republic*, book 8, 551a.

Key Terms

Achievement: Doing better things better.

Aesthetic norms: Standards for judging the beautiful and the ugly.

Aesthetic norms of conduct: Standards for warranting pride or shame over splendid or pathetic conduct.

Audience: The onlookers (real or imagined) seen as admiring or despising.

Base conduct: Weak or ugly conduct that warrants humiliation.

Beneficence: Actually improving the lot of others.

Benevolence: Wishing others well.

Code: Specific set of standards accepted in a given community.

Downrank: To lower the rank order of people or of activities.

Glory: Warranted satisfaction and admiration for achievement.

Goal norms: Standards mandating the desirable promoting of certain situations.

Guilt (being guilty): The state of deserving to suffer for having wronged others.

Guilt (feeling guilty): The feeling (warranted or not) that you are guilty.

Honor: Warranted self-esteem at avoiding base conduct.

Humiliation: The feeling that your conduct is ugly or displays weakness, appropriately hidden.

Limit norms: Definite rules specifying certain types of conduct to avoid or to perform.

Logical scarcity: (vs. merely physical scarcity): When positions at or near the top of a ranking order can be held only by one or a few. For example, nothing can count as first prize for everyone.

Moral norms: Standards for warranting guilt.

Norm: Standard for judgment (a rule or an ideal).

Norm type: A family of norms with similar logical structure. (Achievement, beneficence, honor, and decency are norm types.)

Normative: Relating to standards for judgment (vs. fact).

Philosophy: That set of questions which cannot be answered patly and yet cannot be ignored (includes questions about "really" valid norms).

Sanction: The good or bad feeling that serves as an enforcer for social norms.

Self-esteem: Ranking of the self as more or less worthy.

Self-interest: Concern for meeting basic needs along with long life, health, wealth, and comfort.

Self-regard: Concern for one's status or merit (under aesthetic norms) as splendid or pathetic.

Self-respect: Judging the self as meeting standards.

Shame (being shamed): The state of being ugly or displaying weakness in conduct.

Shame (feeling ashamed): The feeling (warranted or not) that you are ugly or that your conduct has displayed weakness.

Shameless: The state of not feeling shame when you should.

Splendid villain: The person who voluntarily violates moral standards while displaying admirable power.

Standard: Criterion for judging.

Utilitarian: (1) A person who adheres to the moral theory that the principle of utility (act to prevent harm and promote benefit) is ultimately authoritative. (2) An act or instrument that supports the utilitarian ideal.

Warranted: State of a standard thoughtfully enough considered to justify feelings of pride, guilt, humiliation, or moral self-respect as appropriate.

Bibliography

Main Works

Andersen, Hans Christian. *The Complete Fairy Tales and Stories*. Translated by Erik C. Haugaard. Garden City, NY: Anchor Press, 1974.

Aristotle. *The Basic Works of Aristotle*. Edited by Richard McKeon. New York: Random House, 1941.

Augustine. *Confessions*. Translated by Edward Bouverie Pusey. New York: Oxford University Press, 1982.

Austen, Jane. *Pride and Prejudice*. New York: Dell, 1959.

Benedict, Ruth. *Chrysanthemum and the Sword: Patterns of Japanese Culture*. Boston: Houghton, Mifflin, 1946.

Benson, Jann. "A Legacy of Ethical Atomism," *Canadian Journal of Philosophy* 13 (June 1983): 193.

Benson, Jann, and Freeman, Marion. "Los ideales y el honor en *Querer la propia desdicha* de Lope de Vega," *Káñina, Revista Artes y Letras* 12 (1988): 91.

Bolt, Robert. *A Man for All Seasons*. New York: Random House, 1960.

Carlisle, Henry. *The Jonah Man*. New York: Alfred A. Knopf, 1964.

Djilas, Milovan. *Land Without Justice*. New York: Harcourt, Brace, 1958.

Erikson, Erik. *Childhood and Society*. 2d edition. New York: Norton, 1963.

Fromm, Eric. *The Art of Loving*. New York: Harper & Row, 1956.

Fulghum, Robert. *All I Really Need to Know I Learned in Kindergarten*. New York: Ivy Books, 1988.

Goethe, Johann Wolfgang von. *Faust, Part 1*. Edited by R-M. S. Heffner, Helmut Rehder, and W. F. Twaddell. Boston: D. C. Heath, 1954.

Greenberg, Joanne. *Rites of Passage*. New York: Holt, Rinehart & Winston, 1972.

Greene, Graham. *The Power and the Glory*. New York: Viking, 1982.

Gregory, Dick, with Lipsyte, Robert. *Nigger*. New York: Dutton, 1964.

Hare, R. M. *Freedom and Reason*. Oxford: Clarendon Press, 1963.

Harris, Joel Chandler. *Br'er Rabbit*. London: Pelham Books, 1977.

Heller, Joseph. *Good as Gold.* New York: Simon & Schuster, 1979.

The Holy Bible. Authorized or King James version. Philadelphia: Universal Book and Bible House, n. d.

Homer. *Iliad.* Translated by Samuel Butler. Edited by Louise R. Loomis. New York: Walter J. Black, 1942.

———. *Odyssey.* Translated by Samuel Butler. Edited by Louise R. Loomis. New York: Walter J. Black, 1944.

Honig, Edwin. *Calderón and the Seizures of Honor.* Cambridge, MA: Harvard University Press, 1972.

James, Henry. *The American.* London: John Lehmann, 1949.

Kaufman, Gershen. *Shame: The Power of Caring.* Cambridge, MA: Shenkman, 1980.

Kjetsaa, Geir. *Fyodor Dostoyevsky: A Writer's Life.* Translated by Siri Hustvedt and David McDuff. New York: Viking, 1987.

Lewis, Helen Block. *Psychic War in Men and Women.* New York: New York University Press, 1976.

———. *Shame and Guilt in Neurosis.* New York: International Universities Press, 1971.

London, Jack. *The Sea Wolf.* New York: Bantam Pathfinder edition, 1960.

Lope de Vega. *Five Plays.* Translated by Jill Booty. Edited by R.D.F. Pring-Mill. New York: Hill and Wang, 1961.

Lynd, Helen Merrell. *Shame and the Search for Identity.* New York: Science Editions, 1966.

Lyons, Dan. "The High Honor of Big Lily Bart" (mimeograph, 1987).

———. "The Spectre of the Splendid Villain," *International Journal of Moral and Social Studies* 4 (Spring 1989): 4.

Machiavelli, Niccolo. *The Prince.* Translated by L. Ricci. Revised by E.R.P. Vincent. New York: New American Library, 1952.

MacIntyre, Alasdair. *After Virtue: A Study in Moral Theory.* Notre Dame, IN: University of Notre Dame Press, 1981.

Maugham, Somerset. *Of Human Bondage.* Garden City, NY: Doubleday, 1936.

McLean, Ephraim R. "Assessing Returns from the Data Processing Environment," in *Effective Versus Efficient Computing,* edited by Fred Gruenberger. Englewood Cliffs, NJ: Prentice-Hall, 1973.

Melden, A. I. *Human Rights.* Belmont, CA: Wadsworth, 1970.

Miller, Arthur. *Death of a Salesman.* New York: Viking, 1949.

Milton, John. *Paradise Lost.* New York: Walter J. Black, 1943.

Morris, Ivan. *The Nobility of Failure: Tragic Heroes in the History of Japan.* New York: New American Library, 1976.

Morris, Jan, ed. *The Oxford Book of Oxford.* New York: Oxford University Press, 1978.

Morrison, Tony. *Beloved.* New York: New American Library, 1988.

Mozart, W. A. *Die Zauberflöte.* New York: University Books, 1971.

Nussbaum, Martha. *The Fragility of Goodness, Luck, and Ethics in Greek Tragedy and Philosophy.* New York: Cambridge University Press, 1986.

Paz, Octavio. *Labyrinthe of Solitude.* New York: Grove Press, 1985.

Péristiany, J. G., ed. *Honour and Shame: The Values of Mediterranean Society.* London: Weidenfeld and Nicolson, 1965.

Peter, Laurence J., and Hull, Raymond. *The Peter Principle.* New York: William Morrow, 1969.

Plato. *The Collected Dialogues of Plato.* Edited by Edith Hamilton and Huntington Cairns. New York: Random House, 1966.

Robinson, C. A., Jr., trans. and ed. *An Anthology of Greek Drama.* New York: Rinehart, 1951.

Rostand, Edmond. *Cyrano de Bergerac.* Translated by N. Wolfe. Mount Vernon, NY: Peter Pauper Press, 1941.

Sartre, Jean-Paul. *Being and Nothingness.* Translated by Hazel Barnes. New York: Philosophical Library, 1956.

Shaffer, Peter. *Equus.* New York: Avon Books, 1974.

Shakespeare, William. *The Complete Works of William Shakespeare.* Edited by William Aldis Wright. Garden City, NY: Doubleday, 1936.

Sharp, Cecil J., ed. *One Hundred English Folksongs.* New York: Dover, 1975.

Shue, Larry. *The Foreigner: A Play.* New York: Dramatists Play Service (Acting Edition), 1983.

Thackery, William. *Vanity Fair.* New York: Random House, 1950.

Thucydides. *The Peloponnesian War.* Translated by John H. Finley. New York: Modern Library, 1951.

Trevanian. *Shibumi.* New York: Crown, 1979.

Viorst, Judith. "... So My Husband and I Decided to Take a Car Trip Through New England," in *New York Times,* February 15, 1989.

Wharton, Edith. *The House of Mirth.* New York: University Press, 1977.

Wilson, R. "The Conscience of a Physicist," *Bulletin of the Atomic Scientists* 26 (June 1970).

Wolfe, Tom. *The Right Stuff.* New York: Bantam Books, 1980.

Suggested Readings

Adkins, Arthur W. H. *From the Many to the One: A Study of Personality and Views of Human Nature in the Context of Ancient Greek Society, Values and Beliefs.* Ithaca, NY: Cornell University Press, 1970.

———. *Merit and Responsibility: A Study in Greek Values.* Oxford: Clarendon Press, 1960.

Becker, Ernest. *The Denial of Death.* New York: Free Press, 1973.

Berger, Peter. "On the Obsolescence of the Concept of Honor," *Archives européennes de sociologie* 11 (1970): 339.

Bradshaw, John. *Bradshaw on: Healing the Shame That Binds You.* Deerfield Beach, FL: Health Communications, 1988.

Braudy, George. *The Frenzy of Renown: Brandy Fame and Its History.* New York: Oxford University Press, 1986.

Castiglione, Baldassare. *The Book of the Courtier.* Translated in 1561 by Thomas Hoby, with an introduction by Walter Raleigh. New York: AMS Press, 1967.

Cervantes Saauedra, Miguel de. *The History of the Ingenious Gentleman Don Quixote of La Mancha.* Translated by P. A. Motteux. Edinburgh: Grant, 1908.

Council, Norman. *When Honour's at the Stake: Ideas of Honour in Shakespeare's Plays.* London: Allen & Unwin, 1973.

Duby, Georges. *The Chivalrous Society.* Translated by Cynthia Postan. Berkeley and Los Angeles: University of California Press, 1977.

Epstein, Joseph. *Ambition, the Secret Passion.* New York: E. P. Dutton, 1980.

Ferguson, Arthur B. *The Indian Summer of English Chivalry: Studies in the Decline and Transformation of Chivalric Idealism.* Durham, NC: Duke University Press, 1960.

Froissart's Chronicles. Edited and translated by John Folliffe. London: Harvill Press, 1967.

Gardner, John W. *Excellence: Can We Be Equal and Excellent Too?* Revised edition. New York: Norton, 1984.

Gide, André. *Lafcadio's Adventures.* Translated by Dorothy Bussy. New York: Vintage Books, 1953.

Goffman, Erving. *The Presentation of Self in Everyday Life.* Woodstock, NY: Overlook Press, 1973.

———. *Stigma: Notes on the Management of Spoiled Identity.* Englewood Cliffs, NJ: Prentice-Hall, 1973.

Goode, William J. *The Celebration of Heroes: Prestige as a Social Control System.* Berkeley: University of California Press, 1978.

Hamilton, George Rostreuor. *Hero or Fool? A Study of Milton's Satan*. Folcroft, PA: Folcroft Press, 1969.

Heller, Joseph. *Something Happened*. New York: Alfred Knopf, 1974.

Hobbes, Thomas. *De Cive, or The Citizen*. Edited by S. P. Lamprecht. New York: Appleton-Century-Crofts, 1949.

Isenberg, Arnold. "Natural Pride and Natural Shame," *Philosophy and Phenomenological Research* 10 (September 1949): 1.

Jacoby, Susan. *Wild Justice: The Evolution of Revenge*. New York: Harper & Row, 1983.

Larson, Donald R. *The Honor Plays of Lope de Vega*. Cambridge, MA: Harvard University Press, 1977.

Lyons, Dan. "Action, Excellence, and Achievement," *Inquiry* 19 (1976): 277.

———. "Are Luddites Confused?" *Inquiry* 22 (1979): 381.

———. "Unobvious Excuses in the Criminal Law," *Wayne Law Review* 19 (March 1973): 925.

Massey, Stephen J. "Is Self-Respect a Moral or a Psychological Concept?" *Ethics* 93 (January 1983): 246.

Montaigne, Michel de. *The Essays of Montaigne*. Translated by John Florio. New York: Modern Library, 1933.

Morris, Herbert. *Guilt and Shame*. Belmont, CA: Wadsworth, 1971.

———. *On Guilt and Innocence: Essays in Legal Philosophy and Moral Psychology*. Berkeley: University of California Press, 1976.

Nagy, Gregory. *The Best of the Achaeans: Concepts of the Hero in Archaic Greek Poetry*. Baltimore: Johns Hopkins University Press, 1979.

O'Brien, Michael J., ed. *Twentieth-Century Interpretations of "Oedipus Rex": A Collection of Critical Essays*. Englewood Cliffs, NJ: Prentice-Hall, 1968.

Payne, Robert. *Hybris: A Study of Pride*. New York: Harper & Row, 1960.

Pearson, Carol, and Pope, Katherine. *The Female Hero in American and British Literature*. New York: Bowker, 1981.

Pieper, Josef. *Leisure, the Basis of Culture*. Translated by Alexander Dru, with an introduction by T. S. Eliot. New York: Pantheon Books, 1964.

Prosser, Eleanor. *Hamlet and Revenge*. Stanford, CA: Stanford University Press, 1971.

Radin, Paul. *Primitive Man as Philosopher*. New York: Dover, 1957.

Riezler, Kurt. "Comment on the Social Psychology of Shame," *American Journal of Sociology* 48 (January 1943): 457.

Rumrich, John Peter. "Milton and the Meaning of Glory," *Milton Studies* 20 (1984): 75.

Sabini, J., and Silver, M. "Character: The Moral and The Aesthetic," *International Journal of Moral and Social Studies* 2 (Autumn 1987): 189.

Sartre, Jean-Paul. *No Exit and The Flies*. English versions by Stuart Gilbert. New York: Alfred A. Knopf, 1965.

Schneider, Carl D. *Shame, Exposure and Privacy*. Boston: Beacon Press, 1977.

Seneca, L. A. *Seneca's "Hercules Furens": A Critical Text*. Introduction and commentary by John G. Fitch. Ithaca, NY: Cornell University Press, 1987.

Shalvi, Alice. *The Relationship of Renaissance Concepts of Honour to Shakespeare's Problem Plays*. Salzburg: Institut für englische Sprache und Literatur, Universität Salzburg, 1972.

Shaw, George Bernard. *Arms and the Man*. Baltimore: Penguin Books, 1952.

Silver, Maury, et al. "Humiliation: Feeling, Social Control and the Construction of Identity," *Journal for the Theory of Social Behavior* 16 (October 1986): 269.

Skulsky, Harold. *Spirits Finely Touched: The Testing of Value and Integrity in Four Shakespearean Plays*. Athens: University of Georgia Press, 1976.

Slater, Philip E. *The Glory of Hera: Greek Mythology and the Greek Family*. Boston: Beacon Press, 1968.

Slote, Michael. *Goods and Virtues*. Oxford: Clarendon Press, 1983.

Sophocles. *Philoktetes*. Translated by Gregory McNamee. Port Townsend, WA: Copper Canyon Press, 1986.

Strauss, Leo. *The Political Philosophy of Hobbes: Its Basis and Its Genesis*. Translated by Elsa M. Sinclair. Chicago: University of Chicago Press, 1952.

Strawson, P. F. "Social Morality and Individual Ideal," *Philosophy, the Journal of the Royal Institute of Philosophy* 36 (January 1961): 1.

Taylor, Gabriele. *Pride, Shame, and Guilt*. Oxford: Clarendon Press, 1985.

Walzer, Michael. "Political Action: The Problem of Dirty Hands," *Philosophy & Public Affairs* 2 (Winter 1973): 160.

Watson, C. B. *Shakespeare and the Renaissance Concept of Honor*. Princeton, NJ: Princeton University Press, 1960.

Wattles, Jeffrey. "Levels of Meaning in the Golden Rule," *Journal of Religious Ethics* 15 (1987): 107.

Webster, John. *The Duchess of Malfi*. Edited by J. R. Brown. Cambridge, MA: Harvard University Press, 1964.

Wyatt-Brown, Bertram. *Southern Honor: Ethics and Behavior in the Old South*. New York: Oxford University Press, 1982.

Index

abandonment, 89, 104–6; fear of, 161

achievement, 49–50, 52, 53, 61, 78, 85–86, 115, 122–37, 155, 159, 160–61, 173, 189–91; beneficence and, 123, 157–58; cheating for, 181–82; contexts for, vii, 21, 123–25; decency and, 185; dishonorable, 176, 183; giving up, 144–45, 193–94; goals of, 116, 126–27, 177–78; honor and, 128–30, 132–35, 139–41, 146–47, 153–54, 186–87, 193; moral norms and, 157–59; open-endedness of, 125–26, 128; relative, 124–25; repression of, 23–25; revenge and, 148; risks of, 140–47; self-image and, 142–43; shame and, 143; timeless, 124–25; women and, 147. See also nonachievement

action: concreteness of, 14, 16; norms and, 7–13

admiration: courage and, 61; harmful, 194

aesthetic norms, 52, 67, 115, 122, 130, 135, 159, 173, 189–90; definition of, 51; humiliation and, 190; influence of, 193; moral norms and, 155–59; responding to, 192; women's liberation and, 146–47

Alda, Alan: male liberation and, 83

ambition, 78, 157, 167–69; fulfilling, 139–40; misdirected, 193

anger: humiliation and, 2; moderation of, 66; relief through, 1–2

apology, guilt and, 106

Aristotle, 82, 84; on achievement, 124–25, 128; on honor, 69, 70, 130; optimistic view of, 105; on reputation, 76–77; on shame, 38; on virtue, 65–67

audience, norms and, 95–96

Austen, Jane: on reputation, 99–101

beauty, abstractness of, 17

Benedict, Ruth: on reputation, 75

beneficence, 49–53, 61, 67, 86, 115, 117–22, 173, 185, 191, 193; achievement and, 123, 157–58; decency and, 119–20, 122, 130, 135, 158; goal norms of, 116; guilt and, 116; honor and, 155–57, 166; humiliation and, 156–57; intentions and, 120–21; love of, 21; means for, 158; moral credit for, 156; relative, 117–18; timeless, 117–18; utilitarians and, 121–22; value of, 118–19

glory, 53, 73, 104, 123–25, 132,
140, 187, 190, 191; decency
and, 158–59; diminished, 177–
79, 181–82; honor and, 120,
130–31; morality and, 159; results of, 117; shame and, 116,
176. *See also* achievement
goal norms, 52–53, 113, 120, 136–
37, 173; culture and, 116; definition of, 51, 115, 117
goals: cheating for, 181–82; choosing, 128–29; living up to, 48,
127–28; means for, 135–37;
seeking, 179–81
Goethe: on achievement, 157;
splendid villain and, 172
Golden Rule, 54, 58, 186; negative, 55, 59–60, 117–18; positive, 117–19
good, 50; aesthetic uses of, 162–64
Greene, Grahame: on shamelessness, 144
Gregory, Dick: on shame, 30–31,
39
guilt, vii, 8, 25, 161, 164, 172, 189,
191; avoiding, viii, 48, 117; beneficence and, 116; cross-cultural, 32–33, 54; excuses for,
39–41; expunging, 106; fear of,
15, 45, 190; feeling, 4, 27, 37;
handling, 36, 43, 105–6, 158–
59; humiliation and, 35–37,
174, 187; reactions to, 36; self-
image and, 49, 160; shame and,
viii, 27, 29, 34–43, 49, 105–6,
155, 159–60, 173, 183. *See also*
humiliation

happiness, open-endedness of, 119
hate, 75–76

heroism, 154
Homer, 192; on achievement, 129,
140–41, 155; on revenge, 149
honesty, 7, 10, 69, 78, 115
honor, 19–21, 26–27, 29–30, 48–
49, 53, 85–86, 115, 123, 160–
61, 173, 185, 187, 190–91;
abstractness of, 17; achievement and, 128–30, 132–35,
139–41, 146, 147, 153–54, 186,
193; American, 46–48; beneficence and, 155–57, 166; burden
of, 144; changes in, 91–95;
chauvinism and, 80–84; community and, 88–90; cross-cultural,
32–33; decency and, 22–23, 25,
80, 153, 169, 174, 183, 186; elements of, 22–23, 52, 70; forgetting, 90; function of, 109–10;
genuine, 177; glory and, 120,
130–31; ideals of, 70; insult
and, 74; limits on, 18–19, 37,
45–48, 72, 73, 117, 124; living
up to, 109–10; moderation of,
66; morality and, 25–26, 159;
preserving, 31, 89, 104, 144,
166; racism in, 83–84; rank and,
71–73, 78; repressing, 21–26,
75, 148; reputation and, 73–75,
79; revenge and, 147–48; role
of, vii, 21; self-esteem and, 76–
78; shame and, 26, 46, 70, 78–
80, 167; social norms and,
17–18; structure of, 70–80; symbolism in, 82; timeless, 177; violation of, 134, 159, 166, 190;
virtue and, 70; warrants for, 95–
96; women's, ix, 79–83, 146–47.
See also dishonor
hubris, 103